Discover Your Destiny

"Eye hath not seen, nor ear heard,
neither have entered into the heart of man,
the things which God hath prepared
for them that love him."
—1 Corinthians 2:9

Cary Schmidt

Striving Together Publications
4020 E. Lancaster Blvd.
Lancaster, CA 93535
800.201.7748

ISBN 978-1-59894-049-7

Printed in the United States of America

Dedication

This book is dedicated first to my children—Lance, Larry, and Haylee. They are a wonderful part of my destiny! They truly are three "best friends" whose destinies I am helping to discover. If for no one else, this book is for them. My life's prayer is that they would embrace the truths preserved in these pages.

This book is also dedicated to my wife—Dana. To this day, I'm more in love than ever and so unspeakably thankful that God allowed our destinies to include each other! What an awesome God! Dana, thank you for wrapping your whole life into mine and for sharing the dreams that God has placed into my heart! I love you more than words can say.

Finally, this book is dedicated to my brother-in-law—Michael Evans. Michael, thank you for your good influence upon my children. As you enter into your own "young adult" journey, keep your soft heart for God and your hunger for God's best! God is going to bless your life greatly as you seek Him!

Special Thanks to

Pastor Paul Chappell—a great pastor, mentor, and example in every area of life. Thank you for allowing me to serve in such a wonderful ministry.

LBC Student Ministries Graduates and Families—I am exceedingly thankful for the years that God has allowed us to share. You truly are my "joy and crown of rejoicing"!

The Early Proofreading Team—There is a small army of young adults who read early copies of these chapters. Their initial thoughts and encouragement was a real blessing to me. Thank you for giving your time in reading and sharing your thoughts.

Melinda Cazis and Lisa Stoner—For taking a personal interest in the final proofing and correcting of this manuscript. In the midst of a busy ministry, I know you didn't have time to help with this. Thank you so very much!

A Personal Word from the Author

Dear Reader,

As this book goes to print, a big part of my heart goes with it—a really big part. I can't explain how God has placed you (the reader) on my heart. I can't describe the burden for the next generation that He has placed upon my heart. I truly hope the words of this book and the biblical truths discussed will serve as guideposts along your journey into God's perfect will.

A few weeks ago, I sat down with my wife and read her the final chapter of this book. I couldn't get through it without getting choked up. In that moment, I felt as though I had completed one of the most important projects of my entire life. I sincerely hope reading this material will impact you as much as writing it has impacted me.

The truths we will uncover together will far outlive us. It is my prayer that you will read with an open and responsive heart and that you will quickly act upon the truth in your personal life. To the extent that I apply biblical principles—please submit to God's Word in your life. You will never regret giving Him total control of your future. This is what you were made to do! It's your destiny!

May God mightily bless your life…and the lives of those you will influence! Thank you so very much for reading!

Sincerely,
Cary Schmidt

Contents

Preface from Dr. Don Sisk

I am grateful that Brother Schmidt asked me to read the manuscript of *Discover Your Destiny*. I was thrilled as I read page after page. It is very readable; young people will love it! Parents, youth directors, pastors, and educators will find it a great asset as they minister to young people.

This book comes from a heart full of the love of God—a heart that is burdened for young people. Brother Schmidt manifests a great love for God, his church, his family, and for a lost world. I predict a great distribution for *Discover Your Destiny*.

Dr. Don Sisk
President/General Director Emeritus
Baptist International Missions Inc.

Preface from Dr. Paul Chappell

Cary Schmidt is one of the leading authorities on youth ministry in America today. I am confident that, as you read this book, your heart will be thrilled, challenged, and encouraged through each chapter. It is unusual to find a man who, not only has successfully developed the lives of hundreds of teenagers through proven biblical principles, but who also can articulate those principles from a scriptural and entertaining perspective.

This book has been an encouragement to my heart for several reasons. First, because I know Cary Schmidt. It has been my joy to know him since his teen years and to see his life develop as one of the pastoral staff here at Lancaster Baptist Church. He is a man of integrity who loves his family and truly loves the teenagers under his influence.

Second, this book is written from a proven perspective. Many Christian authors today are not actively involved in local church ministry. I would much rather learn from someone who is actually in the trenches, working with young adults in today's society. Cary Schmidt is personally involved in "people-ministry." He visits, prays with, counsels and helps young adults on a daily basis. Although he is an instructor at West Coast Baptist College, he is not simply sharing good ideas from other places. He actually works with young people in the context of the local church, day in and day out.

Additionally, I appreciate the fact that this book is replete with scriptural principles. Often, Christian books are filled with secular philosophy, but this book will give every reader biblical principles by which to live.

On a personal note, I appreciate Cary Schmidt because of the impact he has had on my family and our ministry. I have four children who are preparing to serve the Lord Jesus with their lives. While my wife and I have done our best to instill God's Word in their hearts, we also attribute the direction of our children to the leadership of Cary Schmidt. He has been a joyful model before them and, while other youth pastors have quit the youth ministry or have left in disgrace, Brother Schmidt has walked faithfully before our children. As a parent, my heart is full of gratitude to him and his wife for their investment.

As a pastor, my heart is equally grateful. Last year, 27 out of 31 seniors who graduated from our youth group, found their way to a Christian college. Those who did not attend Christian college are equally loved and encouraged by our church and Brother Schmidt. Yet, we are thrilled with the hunger for serving God that exists in the lives of our teenagers. This hunger has not been developed through pressure tactics or force, nor has it been accomplished through extreme devices or promotions. (I am amazed at how our fundamental churches loathe the world's philosophy of music in the Sunday morning worship services, yet we copy the extremes of today's youth in Christian youth rallies.) Thankfully, Brother Schmidt has found a balance in having fun and keeping God's Word at the center of student ministry.

I would encourage every Christian young adult in America to read this book. I would encourage every parent and youth worker to read this book. It will provide you with godly insight for helping young adults make right decisions. Thank you, Brother Schmidt, for a job well done and may God bless the readers as they discover Jesus Christ's destiny for their lives.

Dr. Paul Chappell
Pastor, Lancaster Baptist Church
President, West Coast Baptist College
Spring 2003

introduction

Introduction
Before We Get Started
What About Eternity?

Everything you are about to read in this book is based upon the assumption that you have a personal relationship with Jesus Christ and that you believe the Bible to be God's perfect Word to mankind. In these pages we're going to explore your life and your future. Yet, there's a bigger concept that you may need to explore first—eternity. The single most important question that you will ever answer is this—"If I were to die today, would I spend eternity in Heaven with God?"

The Bible tells us in 1 John 5:13, "These things have I written unto you that believe on the name of the Son of God; that ye may know that ye have eternal life…." The simple truth is God wants you to know where you're going! So, let me give it to you in a nutshell:

First, you must understand your need for a personal Saviour. The Bible is very clear that we all have a huge problem called sin. Romans 3:23 says it this way, "For all have sinned, and come short of the glory of God." This verse simply means that none of us are perfect. Are you willing to admit that?

The problem is this—sin has a high price tag. Romans 6:23a says, "the wages of sin is death." In other words, the price for sin is eternal death apart from God in a place called Hell—not a good thing! Because of our sin, none of us can make it into Heaven alone.

Here's the good news—God sent help! The rest of Romans 6:23 says, "but the gift of God is eternal life through Jesus Christ our Lord." Again in Romans 5:8 God says, "But God commendeth his love toward us, in that, while we were yet sinners, Christ died for us"! This leads us to the second step:

You must believe that Jesus Christ wants to be your Saviour! Jesus Christ came to Earth as God in the flesh, lived a perfect life, and then voluntarily died on a cross because He loves you. On that cross He literally paid for all of your sins. He took your blame! He punished Himself for your wrong doings. What a great gift!

John 3:16 says, "For God so loved the world, that he gave his only begotten Son, that whosoever believeth in him should not perish, but have everlasting life." God, in His awesome love, came to Earth to make a way for you to be forgiven of your sins and given eternal life!

Finally, you must place your full trust in Jesus Christ as your personal Saviour. Romans 10:13 says, "For whosoever shall call upon the name of the Lord shall be saved." In verse ten of that same chapter God says, "For with the heart man believeth unto righteousness; and with the mouth confession is made unto salvation." He says it's as simple as believing and receiving! It's as simple as asking!

If you've never asked Jesus Christ to be your personal Saviour, I encourage you to do that before you read any further! With Him in your heart, this book will make a lot more sense. You could stop right now and sincerely pray something like this:

Lord Jesus, I believe that you are God, that you died for my sin, and that you rose again from the dead. I know that I am a sinner, and I ask you now to be my personal Saviour. I'm placing my full trust in you alone, and I now accept your gift of eternal life. Thank you for keeping your promise! Amen.

You'll never regret that decision! Let's move on...

one

Chapter One
It's Not Easy Being Dysfunctional
Starting the Journey from a Point of Need

It happens to us quite often really. My wife and I will find ourselves in some crowd of people, maybe an after-church fellowship or a family get-together, you know, the kind of thing where adults sit around and talk about things like the economy or "teenagers." Important stuff. Problem stuff. They're having a great time, sipping coffee, chatting about life, and generally enjoying fellowship. Over the years we've learned to adapt to this environment. (Except for the coffee thing. I still can't handle that. Give me an ice-cold coke in the morning, and I'm happy.)

We've done an okay job at adapting to the course of conversation—keeping up with the economy, world issues, or weather. Yet, it's never very long before we're both looking for "our people!" It's like some tribal instinct or something. After a few minutes of this "grown-up" conversation, we're looking around for the teens or the young adults in the crowd—someone we can identify with. I guess you could call it some sort of social dysfunction.

Before I was a teenager, my parents were youth workers, which meant I went to almost every youth function every week for years. When I was a teenager I was very involved in the youth group and sports, and for the last ten years I've been a youth pastor of a growing youth ministry. So, in short, the vast majority of my life has been spent in the presence of people between the ages of 13 and 25. Even now, if you gave me the choice of sitting at a Chinese buffet with a group of teens tossing stupid jokes around the table or sitting at the same buffet with grown men talking about some tech-industry merger (though I could enjoy both), I would usually have a better time with the teens. It's not easy being dysfunctional.

Congratulations, you're great at being a kid!

Chances are, you picked up this book because you are between the ages of 15 and 25, which means—you too are dysfunctional. Unless you're just way ahead of your time, you probably still enjoy a good Scooby-Doo cartoon and a pop tart just like I do. Hey, maybe we're normal, and everyone else is dysfunctional! Seriously, as a young adult, you know just enough about life to be dangerous! Now, don't get upset at me—just hang in there, because it's true. Everybody wants to feel like they've arrived when they turn eighteen. You can vote; you can drive; you can stay out late. The world says, "You are now grown up!"

Just don't get too hooked on that line yet. Reality is, you're just now getting really good at being a kid! Think about it! What do you really know about buying a home, rearing children, getting a good interest rate on a new car, developing a career, or even keeping a marriage together? Honestly, probably very little. You probably know just enough about these things to get yourself into trouble, but this is the stuff of adult life. This is the stuff you're going to be doing sooner than later—and NOW is the time to get ready.

Now, being a kid on the other hand…you're probably pretty good at that. You could whip out a quick one-page book report in no time flat. If some fourth-grader needed help in math, you're "the man"! You've got all kinds of answers for things like: "How to Clean Your Room So Mom Will Never Know" or "How to Cope with an Insane Substitute Teacher" or "How to Use Pain to Dominate a Younger Sibling" or even "How to Pass Geometry." This stuff is easy for you. You've been there and done that.

The problem comes when somehow we reason that all of this has made us ready for adult life. Somehow we assume that we've passed the tests, we've gained the credentials, and we're ready to sail. We think having been successful kids makes us ready to be successful adults, but nothing could be farther from the truth!

Think about that for a minute. That's like thinking that being good at kickball makes you ready for the World Cup. Just because you got a hit in tee-ball doesn't mean you're ready for the World Series, and just because you passed your driver's test doesn't mean you're ready for the Daytona 500.

People who think this way are not right in the head! They're not all there! Are you one of them? Are you tired of being a kid? Are you sick of people treating you like a child? Have you been feeling like the years of your teen life are dragging by and will never come to an end? Do you crave respect and freedom? Are you ready for people to see you as the adult that you have become?

On top of that you're probably excited about the future. You've got ideas. You've got plans and dreams. You know where you want to go, what you want to become, and how your life will be lived. You are "the man" (or woman)! You're ready to charge into adult life, and you probably even get irritated when people try to give you advice for which you did not ask. High school or college has prepared you for the land of adulthood, and you are convinced that your destiny awaits—you're ready to seize the moment!

You are delusional. It doesn't work that way. Passing the tests of childhood doesn't mean you're ready for the major leagues. In fact, being so self-confident is one of the surest ways to fall flat on your face. (We'll talk about that later.) Truth is, the world is full of people who are great at being kids, but they make terrible adults. They are immature, insecure, and they make decisions that ruin lives. They look happy on the outside, but they are miserable on the inside, and their future will get worse.

The fact of the matter is you have come a long way, and you didn't get here by being totally stupid. Sure you've done a good job up to this point. You've passed some grades, figured out how to please your parents, turned in a few science projects, and if you're really good, maybe you've even flipped a few burgers and assembled a few Happy Meals. (Hey, maybe you're that person who never gives my kid his sauce with his McNuggets!) Honestly, if you were completely "out to lunch" you wouldn't even be holding this book. So, we'll give you some credit from the start, but probably not as much as you would give yourself. It took a lot to get where you are, but it's going to take a lot more to get to your destiny.

> *We're all facing life with horrific spiritual deficiencies, which makes us all dependent upon God, His grace, and His awesome leading in our lives.*

I know, it's a harsh reality, but just stop for a moment and say it softly—it's easier to take. "I'm dysfunctional." There now, that's not so bad is it? Say it again, "I'm dysfunctional." Ah, much easier. A few more times, and it will even start to sound pretty cool. Now, go find a parent or someone you trust and share your newly discovered reality. "Mom, Dad…I'm dysfunctional!" Chances are, you won't find anyone who disagrees with you, which will prove my point. They'll probably say things like "We know Honey, but we've always loved you like you're normal," or "That's okay, Sweetheart, you can still have a good life."

I looked up the word *dysfunctional*. One of the definitions is "unable to function normally as a result of disease or impairment." The disease is sin—specifically pride—and the impairment is immaturity, and we all have it. (So don't think I'm only picking on you.) We're all facing life with horrific spiritual deficiencies, which makes us all dependent upon God, His grace, and His awesome leading in our lives.

The difference between you and someone forty years older than you is that #1—you haven't ruined your life yet! (You may think you have, but believe me, you haven't—there's hope.) And #2—you haven't lived long enough to learn life's biggest lessons the hard way. Most people spend the better part of several decades realizing how little they really know about life—and most of them NEVER realize how much they need God. As you read the pages of this book, hopefully you will avoid those mistakes. There's no reason to forfeit your future "learning the hard way"!

It will be a wonderful day in your life when you accept the fact that you are not ready for the adult life you are about to enter. The decisions you must make are bigger than you. You haven't been down this road before. Why is it so hard for young adults to see and admit that? You will finally be on the road to true success when you can admit to yourself and others that you do not have the wisdom and the knowledge to survive alone. For only then can you truly become the recipient of all God wants to give you.

God's best for your future starts at a point of need, not a point of strength. If you view yourself in a position of strength, if you have the "I'm my own man" disease, you are in for some serious disappointment. People with this disease spend a large portion of their lives figuring out that they are not really as great as they think.

If, on the other hand, you view yourself in a position of need, if you see the decisions you face through the eyes of humility and sincerity, then you will be driven to read on. More importantly, you will be driven to the Lord, to His Word, and to His guidance through godly adults that you trust. If you are approaching your future with an uncertain mixture of excitement, hesitation, fear, and anticipation, then you are certainly approaching a position of blessing. If you know that you need God, then He will be found, and His blessings will follow. God tells us that He "resisteth the proud, but giveth grace unto the humble" (James 4:6). Also, He promises in Proverbs 8:17, "I love them that love me; and those that seek me early shall find me."

Lest you think I'm picking on you—I'm in the same boat! Though I'm a little farther down the road than you are, I still face an uncertain future every day! I still find myself totally and utterly dependent upon God's leading day by day so that I may continue discovering my own destiny. This is how it will be the rest of my life!

This book flows from a mixture of life lessons and ministry lessons that God has taught me from His Word over the past twenty years. It's the product of my own journey of decision-making as well as the journey of hundreds of other young adults that I have known and shared ministry with over the past decade. I share these thoughts with you simply because I'm passionate about helping you to experience God's absolute best for your future.

I've seen too many friends and too many students graduate from high school and ruin their lives with bad decisions. I'm convinced that there's a better way, and in these pages I hope to kick-start you into the wonderful journey of discovering God's best for your future. I hope to burn into your own heart a passion to settle for nothing less than God's best!

Playing life by God's rules

Simply put, there is no other true life. There are substitutes. There are second-hand copies. But you have only one destiny designed by God and only one life with which to discover it. You can't rewind. You can't start over. You'll never pass "go." One chance is all you get. Who ever heard of a game where you only get one turn? Welcome to real life. These are God's rules. You go around one time, then you stand before Him to give an account. You cannot see the future; you cannot cheat. You cannot really be sure of anything but Him. You and only you will give account for you. You cannot blame anyone or anything else for mistakes or failures. You will be given full and unrestricted access to God, but only by faith. You cannot see Him or audibly hear Him. You will be given His Word and His promises. You will be subject to His laws, yet given the free will to rebel against a select number of them. In the end, you will face eternity. You will answer only to God, and you will live somewhere forever. There are no time-outs, and you never know for sure when the game will end. As you are learning the game, it has already started, and it could end at any moment. You'll know that the game is over when you are flat on your face before Jesus Christ. Your turn will be first. You are the only player in your "race," and it's always your turn. On your mark; get set; go!

Life is awesome! It really is great to be an adult and experience God's gifts day by day, but there are many risks. There are many ways to miss God's awesome plans for your future. In these pages, we will journey through a process of spiritual growth and decision-making that will help you step by step through the decisions ahead.

They work! I can prove it. First, they've worked for me personally. To His glory, I can honestly say that I'm living the destiny that God prepared before I was born. But that's only by His grace. I've made my share of wrong decisions, but each one was by my own choice. Every time I've followed God, He has proven that His Word and His plan are always best!

But don't take my word for it. These principles work because they are from the Bible. The principles that I will share with you come directly from God's Word—the Bible. The Bible is a supernatural Book with a supernatural message from God. It is His guidebook for your life. It is absolutely true. Thousands have tried to disprove it, but failed.

...choose to trust God and discover His good plan one day at a time as He unveils it to you.

There are dozens of proofs that I could share with you to prove that the Bible is true and trustworthy. If you're not "there" in your heart, I would challenge you to start studying the issue and settle it soon. You will fail in life if you live without the guidance of God's Word; however, if you will apply the principles that we will discover, you'll be guaranteed, with God's help, that every major decision in your future will be made correctly.

Hundreds of times in the past decade I've sat down at a McDonalds or a Chinese buffet with a teenager and talked about the future. I never get tired of it. Dozens of times I've taught these principles to my eleventh and twelfth grade Sunday school class. I never get tired of that either. I view this book in the same way I do those moments. This is perhaps my only chance to sit down with you and share some things that you must know about your future. So, relax. Open up your heart and decide that you want to learn as much as you can about the journey ahead.

I wish I could tell you how awesome it's going to be. I can't see your future any more than you can. The rules don't allow that. You just have to choose to trust God and discover His good plan one day at a time as He unveils it to you.

I'm going to write these principles the same way I would share them if we were talking in person, so bear with me. I like to laugh— so, sometimes I'll get a little bit ridiculous. I also like to compare things to other things so they make sense. Sometimes that gets ridiculous too, but it's effective in making a case. Sometimes my best way of making a point will be to share a personal experience. I hope you won't see this as a "self-trip." This is just what I know from God's hand at work in my own life.

Our "talks" will be my best effort to help you understand that you belong to God (or should), and that your only hope for true happiness and godly success will be found as you follow Him with complete and seemingly reckless abandon. Let me warn you now, this is heavy stuff! It's HUGE! This stuff affects generations, and I refuse to go easy on you. I'm going to "tell it like it is"—like it or not. I'm sure, at some points of this book, you won't like what I'm saying, but I promise you that I'll only share truths that are supported from God's Word. So, your argument is with Him not me. If you could see the end from the beginning, there would be no argument. Yet, through God's Word and through the help of those who have "been there before" in a vague sort of way, we *can* see the end from the beginning.

You probably have a lot of questions about your future. Questions like "What is God's will?" "How can I find it?" "How will I know for sure?" "What does it mean to be called into ministry?" "How do I know if I'm called?" "When will I know?" On and on the list could go. I hope you're hungry for answers, because that's a great start. You're going to love the journey!

William Jennings Bryan said, "Destiny is not a matter of chance; it is a matter of choice. It is not a thing to be waited for; it is a thing to be achieved." There is no substitute for aggressively seizing your destiny in God's will and experiencing the life that God planned for you before you were ever born.

So, now that you've admitted that you're dysfunctional, and you know that I am too, turn the TV off and grab a pop tart—let's start discovering your destiny!

"...he is a rewarder of them that diligently seek him."
—Hebrews 11:6

two

Chapter Two
Welcome to the "Mistake Zone"
The Ten Most Dangerous Years of Everyone's Life

One of the dearest friends I've ever had was in his late seventies when we met. His name was Don, and I met him the first Sunday he visited our church. Don was a kind, tender-hearted man that loved the Lord with all of his heart.

One of the most memorable events of my life took place with Don about five years ago as I was on my way back to the church from lunch. I happened to be driving by the corner where Don worked as a crossing guard. He had been on my heart for a few days, and I thought, "Why not drop by and see him for a few moments?"

Sure enough, there he stood, waiting for school to get out. I quickly parked the car, and we exchanged greetings, glad to see each other. After a few moments of small talk, I was just about to get back into my car when Don got a look like he had something else to say. Sensing a seriousness in his face, I paused for a minute and asked him if everything was okay. He was silent for a second, and then he started to cry. As I put my hand on his shoulder, my mind raced wondering what could possibly be wrong. I had seen Don cry at church, but this was different. He was burdened about something.

He struggled for a second to regain his composure, but then the tears started flowing again. By this time I was really getting worried, and I think he could tell. He put his hand in the air as if to say "Just wait; I'm okay." So I just waited.

The mistake zone is a period of time between childhood and sanity where most people do stupid things.

A second later he pulled out his wallet and said through tears, "I want to show you something." He had more things in his wallet than my wife has in her purse—and that's a lot! It was amazing how many old photos and business cards he began to sort through until he came upon what he was looking for. It was a small, white, laminated card. From my place I couldn't quite read what it said. He stared at it for a moment, and then handed it to me as he dried his eyes with a handkerchief.

I was beside myself wondering what in the world was going on, until I looked at what he handed me. I held in my hand a miniature "ordination certificate." It was dated prior to 1947, and it was formally worded pronouncing that Don had surrendered his life to the gospel ministry of Jesus Christ. It was signed by the ordaining council of a Baptist church in Long Beach, California. In an instant I felt as though I were in a time warp. I was looking at a 50-year-old ordination certificate for a man who, to my knowledge, had never been in the ministry. I didn't know what to say. We both stood there speechless for a minute when Don finally began to tell the story.

"You know how you sing 'I Surrender All' at church sometimes?" he asked.

I acknowledged him.

"Well, I don't ever sing that one." The tears started again as he continued, "because, I never did."

I tried to interrupt to say something of comfort, but he stopped me and continued, "God called me. I'm sure of it. But just a short time after that ordination certificate was signed, I decided to join the military instead of going into the ministry. Not long after, I met a girl and married her and then served in World War II. After the war, I got a job and started a family. I never really got around to serving the Lord in ministry. My first marriage didn't work out; my kids grew up; I got remarried, and now here I am." Again the tears flowed.

I tried to interject that there was still time for God to use him, but Don stopped me again.

"No. My chance has passed. I look at Pastor and you and the other men on staff, and I know that God wanted me to do that, but my chance has passed."

I didn't know what to say. I knew for sure that God was there in that moment and had placed a divine lesson before me. The world around us had faded away, and it was as if we were the only two people on the planet. I stared at the ordination card again in disbelief. Again I looked into Don's eyes. Before me stood a man who was, admittedly, coming to the end of his earthly race, with no option for starting again.

Then he said these words, which I will never forget.

"Cary, once you know…once you know that you're supposed to serve God, and you decide not to…you'll never be happy doing anything else. You can get by. Life happens, and you get by…but nothing, the rest of your life, will ever really make you happy." Once again, he fought the tears, and so did I.

I have never felt so helpless in all my life. I tried to tell Don that he could give God the years he had left, but that brought little hope. Then I realized, he didn't share this with me because he wanted hope. He shared it with me to warn me of the consequences of disobeying God's call. He was raising a red flag in a young man's mind to say, "Don't ever quit. Don't ever live life your way. Don't ever leave God."

I'll never forget those few minutes with Don on that street corner. What began as a seeming whim to stop and say "hi" became one of the most valuable life lessons I have ever learned. Those moments are burned into my heart as though with a hot iron. I felt as though time stood still, and God gave me a taste of what life would be like "outside" of His perfect will.

Everyone must travel through the mistake zone, but not everyone has to make life-altering bad decisions.

Some could argue, as I have in my own mind, that Don was a good Christian man who loved the Lord. He was in church every week and even served as an usher. He was successful in his work and was happily married to a wonderful woman. He was a good grandfather and a faithful man. All this is true. He was *all* of this, yet inside he lived with the continual knowledge that his life should have happened differently. He lived knowing that he never experienced his destiny as God had planned it. This was a painful hurt in his heart that apparently never went away—I could see it in his eyes as we spoke.

You are there, where Don was prior to 1947. You're at the dawning of adulthood with nothing but promise on the horizon and a world of choices staring you in the face.

You are now in "the mistake zone."
Look around and see the casualties.

Introducing the Mistake Zone

Have you ever seen that show from the fifties "The Twilight Zone"? It's one of my favorites. No matter what the plot, there's always some poor, unsuspecting soul who has to suffer through some bizarre nightmare of a story line. It always started with Rod Serling warning you that this unlucky person was about to enter "the twilight zone," and it always ended with his matter-of-fact wrap—something like "and so it goes in…the twilight zone."

So get this picture: I'm your narrator, and you are about to enter a dimension of time and space. It's a dimension where people do things on their own with little regard for the consequences, a dimension where people think they know everything, and rarely admit that they don't. It's a dimension where decisions are made that determine the outcome of the rest of your life and where generations are impacted by the choices you will make. You are about to enter "the mistake zone."

The mistake zone is a period of time between childhood and sanity where most people do stupid things. The mistake zone can be roughly estimated to be between the ages of 17 and 27, give or take a few years either way depending on your individual life. It's the time of life when almost all of your biggest decisions will be made, yet it's the time of life when you are the very least equipped to make those decisions. Scary? You bet. Can you avoid it? Absolutely not.

If you are seventeen years or older, you're there now! So stop! Before you make another major decision, take a look at the landscape of people who have been through the mistake zone. You'll find casualties no matter where you look. You'll find unwanted pregnancies, abortions, and sexually-transmitted diseases. You'll find alcoholism, drug abuse, and chain-smokers. You'll find divorce, custody battles, and broken lives. You'll find relational abuse, substance abuse, and sexual abuse. You'll find bad credit, lost jobs, and bad investments. You'll find school drop-outs, down-and-outers, and even up-and-outers. You'll find casualties on skid row and at the Ritz Carlton. No one is exempt from the pain and scars of the mistake zone. Not even you.

You're not exempt from any of these things, and neither am I. The mistake zone is no respecter of persons. Your background or pedigree won't buy you an advantage. Everyone must travel through the mistake zone, but not everyone has to make life-altering bad decisions. Sure, we all make mistakes; no one is perfect, but you can make it through the mistake zone without ruining your life. You don't have to be a casualty.

One more thought, making it through the mistake zone doesn't mean you're exempt from future mistakes. I'm not off the hook, and neither are your parents. It just means that you made it through a potential mine field of bad decisions. There will be plenty of chances to blow it beyond twenty-seven, but for those who do make hugely bad decisions, most of them are made in "the mistake zone."

So let's think about it. Here's a list of decisions that you will probably make between the ages of 17 and 27.

- ◆ College
- ◆ Dating
- ◆ First Job
- ◆ First Car
- ◆ Friends
- ◆ Career Field
- ◆ Marriage
- ◆ Career Location
- ◆ Living Quarters
- ◆ Children and Family
- ◆ Church
- ◆ Personal Walk with Christ
- ◆ Life's Purpose and Mission
- ◆ Financial Values

That's a pretty long list. Take a look at it again and remind yourself that most of these decisions will be made over the next ten years in your life. These things are *gigantic*! These are mammoth decisions that must be made, and you're just now starting adulthood with no way of really knowing for sure which way is right for your future. Seems unfair doesn't it? Seems somehow out of whack! God intentionally places these huge, beefy decisions on your plate, and you've just barely started "teething"! He knows you're not ready, but He's put you here anyway. Makes you wonder what kind of strange sense of humor He really has doesn't it?

That's not it at all. He's put you here so that you will feel very small in the face of such overwhelming circumstances. He wants you to feel that the odds are terribly against you so that you will know without any doubt how desperately you need Him. "Strange" would be if God put you there with no access to Himself or His guidance. No, this is just a faith-based relationship. We'll get to that later.

Seems crazy that so many people trudge right on through with no thought of God at all. You know why? They've been taught that life is some sort of cosmic mistake, and that they are nothing more than a genetic, evolutionary freak of nature—which means nothing matters anyway. Friend, that's not the case, and we'll talk about that later as well.

For now, let's look more closely at these decisions. You're not quite "freaked out" enough yet for my liking, but you soon will be.

"Remember now thy Creator
in the days of thy youth, while the evil days
come not, nor the years draw nigh, when
thou shalt say, I have no pleasure in them;"
—Ecclesiastes 12:1

three

Chapter Three
In the Heart of the "Mistake Zone"
Understanding the Risk

Most people are resigned to the fact that you just have to go through this "mistake zone," and you'll learn the hard way. Of course, most young adults "box themselves in" by refusing to hear any advice from those who care. So, they are condemned to "learn the hard way."

Honestly, adult life is a big enough adjustment, and there's no sense in carrying baggage that you don't have to carry. So, let's examine each of the major decisions you'll face in the upcoming years and try to grasp just what you're up against.

College—If you're in high school this is probably your first major decision to conquer. Which one? What kind? Where? The college you choose will most likely lead to the person you marry, the career field you pursue, and the friends you keep. This will determine where you live, what you will do with the rest of your life, who you become like, and whose children you have. This will determine who your grandkids will be and who their kids will be...

and so on. Whoa…big stuff. This is definitely a major decision that you want to get right!

Dating—What kind of person will you date? If "looks" are your primary criteria, you're headed for a world of misery. (Although, I wouldn't go so far as to tell you to marry someone ugly.) Believe me, when you meet God's match for you, you'll think this is the best looking person on the planet. That's an easy one for God.

What guidelines will you follow in your dating life? Who will you give an account to? How will you keep from ruining your testimony? Will your dating life reflect Christ and help you become a better Christian? These questions will formulate the basis for choosing a spouse, a life's mate. This is huge!

Will you date a non-Christian? Other than the fact that it's clear in the Bible, it's just common sense. If God is real and your faith is real, then your family must be founded upon eternal values. God's Word is the blueprint for the family and the glue that holds it together. If you don't at least have true faith in common, you're headed for sure disaster. God says in Amos 3:3, "Can two walk together, except they be agreed?" and 2 Corinthians 6:14 says, "Be ye not unequally yoked together with unbelievers: for what fellowship hath righteousness with unrighteousness? and what communion hath light with darkness?" By the way, don't fall for the trap that you can date this person and win him to Christ. Win him to Christ, see him discipled to faithfulness—*then* date him. Very few people succeed with dating as an outreach. It's never right to do wrong to do right.

Job—Where will you work through young adulthood? Most people get some small job in high school that causes them to face a lot of life-shaping questions. Will you work on Sundays? So many young adults get so infatuated with getting their first few paychecks that they will kiss Sunday church goodbye for the first minimum wage offer that comes along. They love the sound of being able to say "I have to work." There's something very adult-ish about that.

Now, don't get me wrong. I know plenty of faithful Christian adults with families and responsibilities that are occasionally required to work on Sundays and do everything they can to avoid it. I'm not talking about that. I'm talking about a young adult who just needs a few bucks for some clothes or a youth activity who will stop attending church altogether for $6.50 an hour. Really now, how much is God worth to you? You'll find out when you get your first job. I've seen dozens of teens set God aside for a few bucks with seemingly no thought of it. I've seen hundreds of others take their stand for God, and God always meets their needs—always— usually with better jobs! In the process, their faith grows, and a solid foundation of faith for future decisions begins to form.

So, as a side note, choose now, before you get your job, to stay in church regardless. Starter jobs are easy to find. Good workers are hard to find, and God will provide better for you than you will for yourself. Keep Him first, and watch Him work it out. If you have a job now that requires you to miss Sunday church, talk to your manager, get your parent's and pastor's advice, and even consider putting in your notice if you have to. Put God to the test, and let Him prove Himself to you. Stepping out in faith is easier now than it will ever be, and you'll need the valuable foundation of faith for bigger decisions in your future. In other words,

...how much is God worth to you? You'll find out when you get your first job.

learn to trust God with $6.50 an hour, and it will be easier to trust Him with $80,000 a year, when your kids will be watching you.

People who refuse to trust God when they are young never develop the foundation of faith that they need when bigger storms and harder tests come their way. Remember David and Goliath? David trusted God with the bear and the lion, which made it easier for him to trust God with Goliath. The same principle will work for you.

Plus, you've got to realize that you need church! It's God's ordained institution for meeting your spiritual needs. You cannot be right with Him if you are not faithful to a Bible-believing church. It's simple, and it's in the Bible. Hebrews 10:25 says, "Not forsaking the assembling of ourselves together, as the manner of some is; but exhorting one another: and so much the more, as ye see the day approaching." What happens at church is what will keep you spiritually healthy and growing. You need church as much as you need your next meal—and a lot more than you need a paycheck.

On your job, will you stand for right? Will you laugh at dirty jokes and accept invitations to wild parties? Will you be a credible testimony for Christ, or will you quietly hide your Christianity for the myth of acceptance? What will you do for money? What will you do with your money? These values and more start coming into focus with the starting of your first job and will determine a wide variety of details about your adult life.

First Car—Will you have a car soon? Will God provide for you to buy one? What kind? How much should you pay? What interest rate will you get, and how will you know if you got a good deal? How much money will you need to keep it running? Can you pay insurance? How will you treat it? How will you drive it? …on and on the list goes.

The world is quietly awaiting your answer. By it they will determine what kind of person you are. If you drive recklessly, people will rightly judge you as immature and unprepared for real responsibility. People will tell their kids they can't hang out with you. You'll be a statistic in someone's message or an illustration in some parental lecture of "who not to be like." Is that what you want? Really? Do you want people to look at you and say, "Stay away from that kid"? Is that worth a few "donuts" in the church parking lot or a "drag race" on the edge of town? No. But, it happens all the time in the mistake zone.

Friends—Who will you hang around and spend time with? Who will you be like and be associated with? What kind of person do you want to become? Who will you decide you want acceptance from and why even care about acceptance? These issues are very significant. People will mentally judge you based upon the people you spend time with. "Not fair," you might think. Wrong. It's completely fair, and you do the same thing. You're human, and God makes it clear that man looks at the outward appearance (1 Samuel 16:7).

"Yeah, but God looks at the heart," you argue.

Yeah, but man looks at the outward appearance. People only have what you give them to formulate their opinion of you. If it's a bad opinion, it's probably your fault. Don't go blaming everyone else for misjudging you. Take a look in the mirror and study what you're giving them to work with. Start with a good look at your friends.

The fact is people are right in judging you this way because you will become like the people you spend time with. So rather than looking for who's cool, who's "in," or who's acceptable, start looking for who you want to be like and be associated with and make them your friends. This decision determines who you will be like which again has profound effects on everything else—who will marry you, who will hire you, who will help you in time of trial…on and on.

> People only have what you give them to formulate their opinion of you. If it's a bad opinion, it's probably your fault.

Career Field—What will you spend your life doing? There are many noble things to do with your life. Ministry is good. Faithful Christians in secular fields are vital also. The question is not "what do you want to do?" As we'll see later, that can be a dangerous way to think. The question is—what is your destiny? What were you made to do? What fulfills your eternal purpose for being on this planet? When you answer that question, you will be truly happy.

Chances are you know what you want. Scary thing is you may or may not be right. I mean, what you think you want may be absolutely wrong for your destiny. In which case, you won't know it until a few years down the road—probably after you exit the mistake zone. So, you will have to make a choice, but you have no real way of knowing that what you want is what God wants. Sounds too bizarre for reality, but it's true. The world is full of elderly people who never really found their purpose for being alive. You don't have to become one of them.

Marriage—Who will you marry? What kind of person will you marry—I mean, beyond "pretty" or "handsome"? Come on, go a little deeper than that. How will you know this person is emotionally stable? How will you be guaranteed you won't end up deserted, cheated on, or left hanging out to dry? Thousands of couples every year, who once stood at a wedding altar madly in love, stand in a living room beating each other's brains out or stand in a courtroom fighting over cars and kids. People who once dreamed of living in love for the rest of their lives now live in hate. How can that happen? What makes you exempt? No one thinks it will happen to them.

Your marriage will not be perfect. At best it will be a solid relationship that forges through trials to become a refined lifetime love. That's at best. No marriage is easy, and no marriage just falls into perfect place. Happy marriages and lifetime loves are discovered through years of commitment and personal change. But happy marriages are worth fighting for. They are always happier after the forging process than they were before it. The whole relationship gets better over time, but how will you know for sure that you've got someone committed to loving that intensely?

How will this person treat your children? How will they respond when you do something stupid? How will they spend money or keep the house? What will it take to really make them "ticked off." Just what does this person do when he or she is "ticked off"? What will he or she want to do with the rest of your life?

All of these questions are huge, and most of them cannot be answered for certain until after you're married! Isn't that great news! You'll fall in love and get married, and then you'll start to really get to know the person you married. About ten years later, if you are one of the few that make it, you'll feel like you're starting to get to know your spouse, and you'll thank God you followed Him—or you'll wish you had.

> *How will you be guaranteed you won't end up deserted, cheated on, or left hanging out to dry?*

Now don't freak out and say something stupid like "I'm never getting married." If that's God's plan, then fine, but in reality, marriage is awesome. It's just not what pop-culture would lead you to believe. It's something much different and actually much better.

The great part is God has a plan for making sure you get the right person! We'll talk about that later. So for now, don't sweat it.

Career Location—Where will you live? What company or organization will you work for? Will the job be solid? Will the ministry "stay afloat"? Where will your family grow up? Who will your kids be friends with? What church will you attend? What community will you live in? Who will babysit your kids and influence your family? What school will you send your kids to? These questions have enormous implications on many parts of your future and family. You must get it right. You must believe there is a God-ordained purpose and plan for all that must be discovered.

Living Quarters—What kind of place will you put your family in? How much will you have to pay? When will you purchase a home, if ever? How? What does it take to get into an apartment? How do you know what is best when you've never traveled this road before?

Children and Family—When should you become a parent? How do you prepare for parenthood? How many children will you have? What will you teach them, and where will you take them to have fun? How will you discipline them? How will you express love to them? How will you help them avoid the mistakes you made? Can you even count the generations of people to come from your family that will know Christ or not know Him based on your decisions? Will you pray with them and read God's Word to them? Will they know God because you know Him, or will they forsake Him because you never really knew Him?

Mind-blowing isn't it? I mean, by now you're probably choking on your pop tart and considering never watching another Scooby-Doo cartoon. But wait, let's not go to unnecessary extremes. Thanks to kids, there will hopefully always be a "Scooby-Doo" in your future, no matter how intense these decisions get. Keep reading. There's just a few more.

Church—Will you go to church since your parents won't be making you? What kind? Will you serve faithfully? Will you be what God wants you to be in your church family? Will you help to bring others to Christ in that church? Will you find a solid Bible-believing church home or will you choose a compromising, middle-of-the-road, never-leave-your-comfort-zone type of place?

Personal Walk with Christ—Will you know Christ personally and stay faithful to Him in your heart? Will your children follow your faith or leave it? Will God be a small part of your big picture, or will He be your big picture? Will God be that part of your life that you run to only when you're in trouble?

These decisions will have much to do with your own personal sanity as well as the spiritual health of your family for generations to come.

Life's Purpose and Mission—What will be your motivation for getting out of bed every morning? Why endure the daily grind of paying the bills, feeding the family, fixing the car, and mowing the lawn? Why get up, go to work, come home, and go to bed just to do it all over again every day? Will you live for money? Money makes a terrible god. Will you live for ego? No telling what you'll do then. Will you live for pleasure or fun? You'll spend your life running from one thing to the next never to be full of joy and always ending up empty and wishing you were someone else.

Will you live your life for things? That's no good—they can't love you back. Things break. Things rot. Things get stolen. Things don't last very long. Things can't go with you when you die. Things make terrible gods. Don't live for things. Use things and be thankful for them when God gives them to you. Remember that it's God that gives you richly all "things" to enjoy. But don't worship them.

What will you die with? What will be the ultimate goal of your life and reason for living? What would you like people to say about you after you're dead?

"Nobody could play basketball like that guy!"—naaa.

"Man, did she make a beautiful homecoming queen!" wrong.

"He made a mean Big Mac when he worked at McD's"—I don't think so.

"He had the coolest boat in town!"—probably not.

"He never saw his family! What a workaholic!"—hope not.

"Who gets all his money?"—now we're in trouble.

You have to live for something. You will have a mission, whether you realize it or not. So, what will it be? Let me give you a couple of clues. It should be something that lasts forever, and it should be something that God designed you to do. We'll come back to this.

Financial Values—How much will God be able to trust you with? Will you place Him first in your life and prove it by your tithes and offerings? Will you fight with your spouse over money? What values will your kids learn about money? Will you invest money you cannot keep into an eternity that you cannot lose?

There are other decisions that we didn't look at, and since everybody is different you'll probably face some questions that are unique to your life and destiny. Each of these questions will be answered in the few years ahead and will follow you throughout your life for better or for worse. You'll be forever linked to the outcome of the decisions you make. Inseparable, they will follow you the entire course of your life and will be irreversible.

Remember that it's God that gives you richly all "things" to enjoy. But don't worship them.

So, now are you sufficiently freaked out? Well, take a breather if you have to. Put a paper bag over your head if need be. Watch Scooby-Doo for a few minutes if that will make you feel better, but generally speaking, get used to it.

Aside from any serious trials, about the biggest concern of your life has probably been how to get rid of a really embarrassing pimple. Now you're in the mistake zone. The stakes are high, and the decisions are imminent. (That means you have to make them soon!) Don't panic. Don't wimp out. Hang in there. You'll get through, but if you're shaking in your boots a little bit, good. You should be. Your kids will be very happy that you are serious about entering this time with great caution and care. Your grandkids will come up to you in Heaven someday just to say thank you. Most importantly, on your death-bed, you'll look back with no serious regrets. You'll face God knowing with deep joy and satisfaction that you lived your destiny.

About Don, one thing I didn't mention. His life unfolded outside of God's perfect plan for one reason. He made a wrong decision back in 1947—smack in the middle of his own "mistake zone." Did he live a full life with good memories and much personal honor? Yes. Did he love God and know His blessings? Yes. Did he experience his destiny? No. That's what hurt. That's what brought tears to his 78-year-old eyes. That's what brought the sting of regret and remorse. He made one wrong decision that led to a series of wrong decisions that led to a destiny of his own making with no second chance.

He will forever have my love and respect for many reasons, but one in particular. He took a young man aside for a moment, a young man in his own mistake zone, and showed him a glimpse of what a heart feels like sixty years after one bad decision. That took some serious humility and honesty. It took courage and faith.

We need more men like him who will pull aside people like you and me to warn us of the tragedy of doing life our own way. Perhaps in some way, God will allow Don's story to help you avoid similar mistakes, and in so doing, will make even a bad decision have eternally good consequences—good for Don, good for you, good for future generations. That's the beauty of God's cosmic economy (more on that in another chapter).

Think of the mistake zone like a minefield, and only God knows where the mines are. He's ready to guide you through. You can run headlong through, alone if you choose. But, if you trust Him, follow Him, and seek Him, you won't get blown up. While people all around you are making wrong decisions, you can defy the odds. You don't have to be a victim of the mistake zone. It's real, and it's NOW, and it's here for a while. Walk softly, stranger.

God's promise to you, if you will let Him guide you through the "minefield" of decisions, is found in Psalm 91:7–9, "A thousand shall fall at thy side, and ten thousand at thy right hand; but it shall not come nigh thee. Only with thine eyes shalt thou behold and see the reward of the wicked. Because thou hast made the LORD, which is my refuge, even the most High, thy habitation."

So, this is your host speaking. The characters of tonight's tale of fate have been handed a sudden dose of reality. What they do

Think of the mistake zone like a minefield, and only God knows where the mines are. He's ready to guide you through.

with it, by God's grace, will truly determine their destiny…in the mistake zone. Good night.

> "Behold, God is my salvation; I will trust,
> and not be afraid: for the LORD JEHOVAH is my
> strength and my song; he also is become my salvation."
> —Isaiah 12:2

four

Destiny—My Place in the Cosmic Cookie Mix

Understanding Time, Eternity, and Destiny

So by now you're probably going, "Great, I'm dysfunctional; I'm in the mistake zone, and I'm in way over my head. Can it get any worse?" Hang in there, this is where the good news starts! I've been pretty eager to get to this part.

The way it didn't happen—dispelling the lie of evolution

If you attended a public school, you've probably been sitting in a science class at some point when your teacher began talking about the origin of life. It all sounds so scientific. It goes something like this: first there was just space and gas and stuff. What kind of stuff, we're just not sure. Where the stuff came from? Well, we're just not sure about that either. We'll avoid those questions for now (how convenient, especially when the Bible doesn't avoid any of them). So there was gas and stuff. By the way, this was billions and billions of years ago (maybe kazillions—who knows). Well, like some kind of cosmic cookie mix, this gas and stuff sort of drifted together. How or why we don't know. Then, suddenly, it all got so close together that it exploded! KABOOM!

We're talking some kind of serious explosion here. It's called the "big bang" but it should really be called "the really, really, really big bang" because out of this bang came all sorts of gigantic stuff. All of a sudden there were planets, stars, meteors, black holes, and galaxies. As if that's not amazing enough, out of all of this galactic gumbo came an amazing little planet that somebody named "Earth." This planet became the perfect place for the spontaneous formation of some pretty important things—like water and oxygen. How or why, there's no way of knowing. Due to the presence of these important, life-sustaining elements, life decided to spontaneously start! WOW! That's like saying that your deodorant decided to spontaneously apply itself or your pop tart spontaneously toasted itself!

WOW! That's like saying that your deodorant decided to spontaneously apply itself or your pop tart spontaneously toasted itself!

Oops, but I forgot to mention—these were pretty primitive life forms. They were single-cell life forms, which are almost as dumb as telephone poles or bowling balls. So, for billions and billions of years these single-cell life forms just floated around in water. Where the water came from we can't really explain, and why it took so long for them to find each other? That's a mystery too! I guess "billions of years" just sounds so scientific that it makes us stop thinking logically. If I can't comprehend a billion years, how could I ever comprehend how this galactic gumbo eventually gave birth to me? Basically, we're expected to just accept it and move on.

So, one day, after billions of years, these single-cell life forms bumped into each other on the micro-organism superhighway, and what do you know? They "hit it off"! They liked each other so much that they decided to stick together, and then they starting splitting into pieces and making more single-cell life forms. These things were worse than rabbits. Before they could celebrate another 10 billion birthdays, there were millions of them floating around in this giant terrestrial soup bowl. It was a big, beautiful world of single-cell families treading water and singing "We Are the World."

Well, a few million years passed before somebody finally decided to break ranks and do something really "out of the box"— like grow a tail or sprout fins. Suddenly, like the fall of some great regime, single-cell life was "out"! Nobody was happy being a single-cell-life-form anymore. Evolving was the "in" thing to do. If you weren't blinking, breathing, swimming, or slurping, before too long, you were *nobody*! The world of microbiology was suddenly mass chaos! No fear. No rules. No order. The motto of the day was "just mutate"! If you didn't grow a limb or sprout an appendage, you were nothing more than a "building block" of life!

Eventually the rage settled down as life hit another barrier of development. Everything was "oceanic." Water was it! Life was pretty simple, really. Wake up, swim, eat something smaller than you, swim some more, hope something bigger than you didn't come along, sleep, do it all again. Day after day, year after year this went on. It only took a few million years for this to get old, until somebody else started thinking "out of the water"! This was the Chuck Yeager of the evolutionary process—the first one to break the land barrier! (And you thought it was the little mermaid.)

One day this thing (no one knows what to call it really) jumped out of the water and landed on the beach like some kind of teenage-mutant-ninja-frog-fish. Don't even try to ask where the beach came from. So now this thing probably went "uh-oh, where'd the water go?" After a few seconds, this brilliant little blob figured out that if he didn't learn to breath air pretty quick, he'd die. (Too bad our peon twenty-first century fish have lost that evolutionary ability.) Now, after millions of years of development, this thing grew lungs in record time! (It's amazing what we can do when we really have to!) After a quick look around, he figured he liked land, but getting around on fins was pretty hard. So, in another "flash" of evolutionary brilliance he sprouted a couple of legs and arms and became our great, great, great, great, great (to the 15th power) grandfather—the father of the frog family.

Another few million years passed as this frog thing gradually and radically reinvented himself to father every life form known on planet earth. He and his descendants invented the most amazing developmental cycle ever conceived. They developed hair, feathers, wings, heads, beaks, teeth, brains, tails, and trunks. Together they formed the circle of life, but even with all this brilliance they lacked one key ability—the ability to reason. But, they had no idea. They were all content just eating and being eaten. Life had hit another developmental wall. Every day was the same again. Wake up, eat something smaller than you, stay away from things bigger than you, walk around (or crawl), sleep, and do it all over again tomorrow.

The monkeys messed everything up this time. They weren't content just being stupid. No. They had to go and evolve again. The process started with walking—on two legs not four. Of course, this took several thousand years of practice, but, wow! was the jungle community alive with wonder! Then they started making new noises, losing hair, cooking food, drawing pictures, and thinking logically. This all happened so fast that it took the other species by surprise. One day

Anyone who buys into that couldn't have come from monkeys! Monkeys are much smarter than that.

there was a tail, the next day, no tail. Other species stopped trying to "keep up with the Jones." It just wasn't worth it anymore. So, before long these monkeys became the dominant species on the planet, renamed themselves "man," and started organizing a civilization. They built mud huts, grew plants, invented things, and started calling the other animals "pets." Except for T-Rex. They called him "sir." Boy, were they glad when "Mother Nature" called in the ice age on him.

Fast forward a few hundred thousand years and you'll find these monkeys writing books, building skyscrapers, driving cars, and even teaching little monkey children how they all got here. They walk, they talk, they think—they have no maker but themselves, no eternity but the grave, no purpose but their own desires, and no authority except "Mother Nature." They are the supreme beings having brutally and tenaciously carved out their own existence from single-cell swimmers to Wall Street stockbrokers in just a few hundred billion years. They've conquered every form of extinction except death and figured out every imaginable question except "why?" Now playing at a theatre near you "The Amazing Multifaceted, Mutant, Monkey-People"!

C'mon! Don't tell me you bought that, even for a second. Anyone who buys into that couldn't have come from monkeys! Monkeys are much smarter than that.

I know. I've over simplified it, but the same tale as told in modern day biology books is no less ridiculous. By the way, lest you think otherwise, this stuff is not science; it's religion. There's nothing scientific about it. Chew on these details for a while:

1. Not one shred of valid evidence exists that evolution ever happened.
2. No evidence exists that evolution continues.
3. A universe is no more likely to spontaneously form than a car.
4. No evidence has ever suggested that animals can cross species and produce fertile offspring.
5. Evolution is not observable which means it's not science; it's speculation.
6. History, true science, and archeology all support the biblical account of creation.
7. Evolution is a religious system of blind faith; the Bible offers a personal relationship of intelligent faith.

The way it really happened and why it matters

I guess evolution and creation do agree about one thing. There was a really, really, really big bang. But when and how? The moment that God said, "Let there be…" the universe came into existence in a moment of creative speech. It all happened instantly, and all it took was a few words from the mouth of God! That's how awesome and powerful your God is! He didn't even have to wave His hand or stomp His feet. Just His words did it all.

If you believe that we were put here by the collective efforts of a gaseous explosion, a single-cell revolution, and the circle of life, go directly to the nearest emergency room; your brain may have stopped functioning. The universe itself shows the intelligent, creative design of Almighty God. You cannot see the wing of a butterfly or the pattern in a snowflake without seeing intelligent design. You cannot study the human nervous system or the growth of a newborn baby without seeing that it all shows the touch of a brilliant Master Designer. It takes willful ignorance to believe evolution. All it takes is common sense and simple faith to see creation and to see that "The heavens declare the glory of God; and the firmament sheweth his handywork" (Psalm 19:1).

> *If evolution is true, then you have no divine origin, no Heavenly Father who loves and cares about you, no definitive purpose for being, and no absolute truth to follow.*

What does all this have to do with you and the decisions that you're going to make? Everything! Your view of these things forms the foundation to the way you think. Your decisions will be made through your value system or "what you value." Your value system is founded upon what you believe about life's origin and purpose.

If you believe evolution, then life is nothing more than an accident. You are nothing more than a cosmic freak of nature. If evolution is true, then you have no divine origin, no Heavenly Father who loves and cares about you, no definitive purpose for being, and no absolute truth to follow. You can be your own god. If you don't like something or someone, you can destroy it. If you want something, you can take it. "Anything goes" in the value system of evolution—survival of the fittest. There is no wrong and right, just whatever gets you ahead on the developmental curve. If evolution is true, there is no plan, no reason, and no hope. If it's true, you have no eternal value. There is no significance to your existence, and you have nothing to look forward to. You are just a building block for the next phase of evolution.

The more that people believe this, the more that anarchy will creep into our society. This thinking leads to a lifestyle with no rules, no restraints, and no happiness. It says, "Do whatever you want, whenever you want, and forget about being responsible for your actions." But, it's a miserable existence because there's nothing happy about being "an accident"!

If you believe that God created all that exists, then you believe that He created you! This changes everything about your value system. If God created you, He must care about you and love you. Since God is eternal and God is good, He must have had an eternally good purpose for making you. Since God knows everything and can do anything, you must be pretty important to Him. He must have something that only you can do in His eternal plan; otherwise, why would He need you? God does nothing without purpose. He wouldn't "make you" just for the fun of it. We're not God's "pets."

Your destiny began in eternity

Second Timothy 1:9 presents it this way, "Who hath saved us, and called *us* with an holy calling, not according to our works, but according to his own purpose and grace, which was given us in Christ Jesus *before the world began.*"

In truth, it goes farther back than the beginning of time. Your destiny started in eternity. Eternity is timeless—not bound by the time/space continuum. It has no minutes, days, or years. Imagine that you are standing in a room with one wall that extends forever in every direction. Forever! There's no end to this wall.

Now imagine that there is a flea or a spec of dust on that wall. For sake of illustration, that tiny spot could represent "time" as you know it, from beginning to end. Yes, time had a definite beginning, and it will have a definite end. Time is far less on the wall of eternity than a flea or a spec would be on the wall of our illustration. But God had a reason for creating "time." He has a vital purpose that will be accomplished.

"Blessed be the God and Father of our Lord Jesus Christ, who hath blessed us with all spiritual blessings in heavenly places in Christ: According as he hath chosen us in him before the foundation of the world, that we should be holy and without blame before him in love: Having predestinated us unto the adoption of children by Jesus Christ to himself, according to the good pleasure of his will, To the praise of the glory of his grace, wherein he hath made us accepted in the beloved. In whom we have redemption through his blood, the forgiveness of sins, according to the riches of his grace; Wherein he hath abounded toward us in all wisdom and prudence; Having made known unto us the mystery of his will, according to his good pleasure which he hath purposed in himself: That in the dispensation of the fulness of times he might gather together in one all things in Christ, both which are in heaven, and which are on earth; even in him: In whom also we have obtained an inheritance, being predestinated according to the purpose of him who worketh all things after the counsel of his own will: That we should be to the praise of his glory, who first trusted in Christ" (Ephesians 1:3–12).

God chose you to be a critical part of His eternal purpose before the foundation of the world. The true extent of our purpose for living will only be fully understood when we get to Heaven—it's that awesome!

Since God can see the end from the begir
everything about you before He made you—inclu
and your sins (even the ones you think no on
Yet, He still made you. He must love you anyway
ever done surprised Him. He's never regretted you.
experiment or His science project.

You are His masterful design—a brilliant part of an eternal plan for the ages. When God was putting together His plan for time and eternity, He came to your birthday and discovered a vacancy. He knew exactly whom He needed to fill that place in the grand matrix of His plan—and He designed you to fit it perfectly. He carefully shaped your likes and dislikes, your gifts and abilities, your desires and dreams to intertwine perfectly with His eternal objective. You have a function, a reason for being, a divine mission assigned to you in eternity past! You have a role in God's drama, significance in God's eyes, a pursuit in God's cause. You have a destiny designed and given to you by God Himself, and you will only be truly happy and fulfilled when you live out that destiny!

"Objection," you might say. "Are you saying that I have one purpose for being, and I can only be happy by fulfilling that one purpose among all the options of life?"

That's exactly what I'm saying. It's called destiny. I didn't invent it; God did. I'm just trying to open your eyes to it before it passes you by.

Look at what God says

"Before I formed thee in the belly I knew thee; and before thou camest forth out of the womb I sanctified thee, and I ordained thee a prophet unto the nations" (Jeremiah 1:5).

"By thee have I been holden up from the womb: thou art he that took me out of my mother's bowels: my praise shall be continually of thee" (Psalm 71:6).

And now, saith the LORD that formed me from the womb to his servant…" (Isaiah 49:5).

"But when it pleased God, who separated me from my mother's womb, and called me by his grace" (Galatians 1:15).

"For whom he did foreknow, he also did predestinate to be conformed to the image of his Son, that he might be the firstborn among many brethren" (Romans 8:29).

God knows you better than you could ever know yourself! He made you. I don't mean He "cookie-cut" you in a mass production assembly line. I mean, He carefully, meticulously hand-crafted you with 100% of His attention. He can do that without losing control of the rest of the universe, because He's God. In fact, there hasn't been one second since the moment of your birth that you haven't had 100% of His attention focused on you!

Just stop and let that blow your mind for a second. Where are you right now? Look around. He's there, looking at you. Are you in trouble? No, this is good news. He loves you. He's interested in you. He died to prove His love and to buy you back into His family. He's anticipating that you might sense Him, speak to Him, respond to Him, and trust Him. So go ahead. Stop reading for a minute and give Him your attention. C'mon, He's not going to hurt you. Just put the book down and talk to Him; tell Him what you're feeling or going through. Tell Him "thank you" for all that He's done for you. Tell Him you love Him. Go ahead…

Okay, now let's get going again. (Did you do it? Don't cheat and keep reading—just do it!)

Okay, how about now? It's great isn't it? Hopefully you just had a "God moment"! That's one of those moments where you just enter into His presence quietly, and you know beyond any doubt that He is there, He is real, and He cares deeply about you (Hebrews 4:16). Without these moments, your Christian walk is all "textbook." Without these moments, you probably won't make it very far. It's these moments that remind you that there truly is a God, an eternity, and a very big purpose for your existence in this "mass of humanity" called earth.

The fact of the matter is you have a destiny—a divine mission from God that He intends for you to fulfill. Now let me help you understand a few things about it.

Your destiny is unique to you.

No one else can be you or be like you. God made you totally unique to His plan, and you fit your place perfectly. No one else can fill your place or carry out your mission in God's plan. You were made to enjoy it, to succeed at it, to understand it, and to truly be happy doing it.

Your destiny is awesome.

God is good. He only invents good things, and He only plans good purposes. God is no threat to your desire for a good life. He created that desire, and He plans to fill it with the good life that He designed.

You will only be truly happy as you fulfill your destiny.

It's a law of life that you cannot escape. It's like Don's story. You might "get by," but it can be a lot better than that. Living your destiny presents an exclusive inner joy and contentment that only God can give. You have to believe that there is a level of joy and satisfaction in life that comes only by fulfilling your God-given purpose. When you are living your destiny, you pillow your head at night with real peace and with a full heart regardless of what the circumstances of life may be throwing at you.

Your destiny will give you a true sense of divine security.

Have you seen how some people deal with tragedy? They go nuts. But have you seen how someone close to God deals with tragedy? They respond completely differently. It's still hard, but there's stability, peace, and an unshakable resolve that guides the life of someone who is living out their destiny. They know that everything is okay. They watch life as if from the grandstand. Nothing can touch them. Eternity is just around the corner, and everything is just fine. They're like the carefree kid on summer vacation in the back seat of the car. "Dad's in the driver's seat, and we'll be there soon enough!" What a great way to live life!

Your destiny represents true success.

So what if you make a lot of money and drive a nice car? So what if you get promoted, and people think you're great? So what if everything falls into place externally, and you appear to be "on top of the world," if you're not fulfilling any eternal purpose! That's a recipe for despair and emptiness. True success is finding and living the mission that God created you for. True success is knowing that you are seeing the script unfold just the way God wrote it in the grand design of His eternal purpose!

Your destiny can be missed.

The concept that God sees the end from the beginning might confuse you. You might ask, "How does this mean that I have a free will?" Yet in God's design, there is no conflict between your free will and His master plan. Somehow, in His brilliance, He will see His eternal purpose to completion while simultaneously allowing you to freely choose whether or not to be a part of it. And don't think it's a "set up." Though He may know what your decisions will be, they are no less your free will. When it comes to your destiny, God gives you the final decision. He gives you the free will of accepting or rejecting it. You can live life His way or your way. It all depends on whom you trust more—God or yourself!

Your destiny is now.

Your destiny is not something that will happen to you someday. It is not a distant possibility; it is a present reality. God has a purpose for you *today*—not just someday! You can live every day knowing that you are experiencing God's perfect will for your life.

In the pages ahead we'll talk a lot about your future, but you need to understand that destiny begins right now. In addition to this, you might be reading these pages several years into the mistake zone. Perhaps you've made some bad decisions, and you fear that you've messed everything up. God has a fantastic solution for this that we'll elaborate on more in a later chapter. Suffice it to say that you haven't missed your chance to experience your destiny. You may have made some bad decisions, and there may be some consequences that you live with—but God specializes in second chances. Rest assured there are a lot of wonderful days ahead for you in God's eternal purpose!

Destiny arrives from God by faith on a "need to know basis."

If you're like me, you'll want to see the whole trip mapped out from start to finish. "God, what am I going to be?" But God reveals His plan only as you need to know. He will make sure you know exactly what you need to know—*when* you need to know it. He will show you very little up front. Don't get frustrated in not knowing. Rest in knowing this: God knows, and you'll be there soon enough—as you follow Him by faith.

Finally, your destiny is a deliberate choice.

Your destiny won't happen by accident! Hebrews 11:6 teaches that God rewards them that *diligently* seek Him. Your destiny in God's will must be pursued and must be selected carefully among all the options that the devil will try to distract you with. It will be no easy thing to select your destiny. You will be required to enter into the process very prayerfully and wisely. It will take serious consideration, study, prayer, and counsel. It will take complete and unconditional surrender. It *will* be worth it all.

So, don't fall for that "cosmic cookie mix" approach to life. It's nothing more than a foolish deception. It's the product of blinded hearts and vain imaginations (Romans 1:19–23) from people who deny God and are unwilling to recognize His existence and His sovereignty. You are not a mistake, a mishap, an accident, or a spontaneous event. You are not an insignificant spot on some evolutionary dot-to-dot puzzle.

You are the product of a meticulous Master Planner. You are the intentional design of an Almighty God who values you and cares infinitely for you. You are the apple of His eye, the focus of His attention, and the key to His plan for this generation and for the ages. You are exactly as He created you, and you have a divine purpose. You have an eternal mission, and you will never be happier than when you find it and fulfill it.

So, let's take the next step in finding it…

> *"Before I formed thee in the belly*
> *I knew thee; and before thou camest forth*
> *out of the womb I sanctified thee…"*
> —Jeremiah 1:5

five

Chapter Five
Destiny Shmestiny...
I Have Plans, Man!
Understanding How Your Plans Mesh with God's Eternal Purpose

Sometimes I look at my kids and wonder how I got here! I don't feel any different than when I was eighteen. I look a little different—less hair, mainly. Every now and then, I time warp back mentally when my kids say "Hey, Dad!" It's almost like, "Hey, kid, who are you callin' Dad?" Then I remember the flash of events that flew by over the last fifteen years, and I return to normal. "Yes, son, what is it?"

Life went very slowly until I turned eighteen and graduated from high school. The next thing I know, I'm in my thirties, celebrating more than a decade of marriage, and watching my kids grow up as fast as they possibly can! (It's like they're obsessed!)

My youngest son, Larry, is famous for coming up with crazy combinations of words or phrases that make the whole family laugh. The other day, while holding his stomach, he said, "Dad, I don't feel so good. I think I'm about to bark!"

How do you show compassion for someone who is sick to their stomach and simultaneously laugh because they're about to "bark"? It's quite a challenge! I forced down my laugh and calmly said, "Well, son, go ahead and bark—WOOF, WOOF!!" The laughter followed.

He smiled innocently, laughed a little, and said "Noooo, Dad, not that kind of 'bark'—the other kind!"

"Oh, the other kind. You mean like the 'throw-up' kind?"

"Yeah, that kind."

Well, he never did "bark" and eventually, later that night, I broke. I couldn't bear the thought of his friends laughing at him for needing to "bark" when he was in high school. So, as I tucked him in and I prayed with him, I quietly said, "Larry, the right word to say isn't *bark* it's *barf…*"

Suddenly he giggled knowingly and said, "Ooooh yeaah, I forgot!"

Innocent ignorance. That's exactly where we are with God sometimes. He is our loving Heavenly Father who knows everything and only has good thoughts for our future, and we are childish in comparison. Our minds don't even have the capacity to imagine the possibilities of what God sees.

The thing that most impressed me about Larry was his willingness to admit he was wrong. He actually laughed! What a great attitude toward life! I'm not talking about laughing when you do wrong—I mean being able to laugh at your own ignorance and accept the truth when you see it. It's a great strength.

One day after kindergarten class, Larry came home and confidently stated, "Mom, Dad, I know what I want to be when I grow up!"

My attention piqued! The moment I had been waiting for! My son had responded to God's call upon his life at the tender young age of five! I looked intently, expecting some profound discourse on how he reached his spiritual decision. I had always heard these amazing stories from parents about the marvelous and heavenly things their children said at some unexpected moment. I knew my time had come, and I was about to hear a great spiritual insight "from the mouths of babes."

"That's great Larry. What do you want to be?"

"An X-MAN!" he said flatly.

I didn't know whether to laugh or cry. Was this the end? My son, who I had dreamed would live faithfully for God, was determined to be a comic book character? I had a flash-forward to his graduation speech when he would publicly thank me for being his father and tell the whole world he was planning to be an X-Man. Was this the moment my parental heart would be broken? Or, was this a five year old being silly? (I hoped.)

Pretty quickly I snapped out of it and looked over at my wife. She was thinking the same thing. I could see it in her eyes. Then we both broke the moment with a hesitant laugh. "That's funny, Larry—people can't really be X-Men." He persisted, and we let it go, hoping it would never return. As of three years later, it hasn't—yet. (Whew!)

I must choose between my plans and God. They cannot both rule.

Here's the picture. You're the child, God is the Father, and you have plans. You may have even announced them to God and everybody else in your life. "I'm going to be a (fill in the blank)." To you these plans are as serious as anything else in your life. They are your dreams. They represent the things you like to do and would hope to do the rest of your life. These plans may be self-centered—make money, be famous, have popularity. Or they may be good pursuits—teach school, be a physical therapist, or help the needy. These may even be ministry pursuits like preaching the Word of God, being a missionary, or being a pastor's wife.

Yet, as of this moment, these dreams are yours. Whether or not they are God's cannot be confirmed yet. The only thing you can conclude with any certainty is that these are your dreams. I'm not saying that they don't have a place, and I'm not saying that they are wrong—so stay with me for a minute. I'm only saying you have no way of knowing for sure at this time whether they fit into God's plan, and you probably don't need to know.

God made you with certain abilities and gifts. He created your personality and your likes and dislikes, and the truth is, they will no doubt play a huge role somewhere in your destiny. The danger is these dreams and desires can easily, quickly, and quietly take the very place of God in your heart. They can become your primary pursuit. They can silently become the hunger of your heart and the thirst of your soul. It's usually not a conscious decision, but rather a gradual progression. You may not even realize that this has happened.

Idolatry is committed any time a person places anything where only God belongs.

Sometimes we convince ourselves that our ambitions are *good*. You might feel pretty good that you're taking life by the horns and making it happen. Actually, this thinking can be a clever cover up for nothing more than self-centered ambitions. I'm not saying that you should be directionless; I'm just saying that your ambitions must not take God's place of preeminence in your heart.

Over the years I've talked to dozens of young adults who, before they were even out of their teen years, had completely written the script of their entire life—for God. So often these scripts even represented noble desires and good things, but they were written by the child and handed to the Father as though the child was doing the Father a favor! Are you there? Have you written the script for God, clearly detailing in your mind exactly the way you think it should happen? Are you expecting that He will read it, sign it, hand it back to you, and bless you for doing something honorable with your future?

I've even seen people take this approach to serving God in ministry. The child of God determines very early what he will do for God and what he will not do for God (i.e. "I will be a pastor."

or "I will be a youth pastor."). And he is sure that God is impressed with such a spiritual decision-making process. But the reality is often this person has entered into a very subtle form of idolatry. When God leads elsewhere, this child will not follow because he is bent on his own will above God's and doesn't even realize it.

Idolatry is committed any time a person places anything where only God belongs. It may or may not include bowing down to a statue or hugging a tree. For Christians, it is much more subtle than that. Any time you pursue a desire or dream in the place of pursuing God, you have dethroned God. Any time you determine what you will do *for God*, you have replaced God with your own desires. The sad part is many times these are God-given desires— good dreams that are never realized the way they should have been, because God was not the object of the pursuit.

Paul warned the people in Corinth, "Wherefore, my dearly beloved, *flee from idolatry*" (1 Corinthians 10:14). Jesus said it this way in Revelation 2:4, "Nevertheless I have somewhat against thee, because thou hast left thy *first love*."

It is entirely possible that you could never fully experience your dreams and desires simply because you were so intent on pursuing them that you left God in the dust! Sounds strange, but it's true—and it happens all the time. Jesus Christ should be your first love, and you should be willing to leave any personal ambition behind to follow Him and to fulfill your purpose in His plan!

You must understand that God will ultimately fulfill every one of the good desires He's put into your heart, but He probably has a less direct route to getting there than you would hope for. Your script for life would probably make a beeline to your biggest dreams, but God's may take a few detours that will make you ready to fully experience His richest blessings.

So, here's what we can conclude about your dreams— your plans.

1. Only God can confirm if they are right for your destiny.
Remember that His wisdom is infinite, and He sees the end from

the beginning. Also, He knows you intricately. Just because you *want* to do something doesn't make it right. You may get what you want only to find out later that you really don't want it. That's a common discovery in the mistake zone. You're wise to approach your personal desires with some measure of hesitance. You're wise to guard yourself from totally giving your heart to your desires. See them as a potentially good thing, but also a potential distraction from the best thing!

2. If you pursue personal ambition in the place of God, you will never find your destiny. You'll be detoured on the "grandfather of all rabbit trails"! Your Creator designed you to pursue Him, not to pursue ambition. Life gets messed up when this gets out of order.

3. You could be wrong. You must be willing to take a neutral position on your plans. No matter how much you want something, always remind yourself that you've been wrong before and you could be now. This is true no matter how *right* your desires feel.

4. God could change your desires. We'll expound on this later, but what a great concept. God could snap His fingers, and *POOF*— you would want something else! That's how powerful He is. You'd never even know what hit you. You probably know someone who is doing something for God that they said they would *never* do when they were your age. What happened? They challenged God, and He took them up on it. He changed their desires. Now, they love doing what they thought they would hate. Personal plans or desires are flexible with God. He's more concerned with your heart for Him. He's not nervous that you don't want to do something. That's an easy fix for Him.

5. God could give you better dreams. This is perhaps one of the best reasons for holding your own plans with a loose grip. Think of it this way. Compared to God's, you have a very small imagination. What if you have imagined far less than He has? What if His plan is enormously better than yours? What if you get to Heaven, and you find out that God would have been considerably more generous with you than you were with yourself? Now that would be seriously depressing. That would be like listening to the Super Bowl on a cheap AM radio only to find out later that you had a free VIP pass to sit on your team's bench!

6. **Even good desires can become idols.** Watch out. Deciding to do something *for God* is vastly different than deciding to do *whatever God leads*. The first is idolatry. The second is surrender. Make God your first love. Give Him the throne of your heart. He died to pay for it. He deserves that place. He has nothing but good in mind for your future. He sees the future clearly. It's the only sane and safe position to be in. I'm not saying that you should completely drop all of your desires. I'm just saying that they have to be kept in check. Make your plans subservient to God's will.

7. **Gifts and abilities should be developed but not pursued.** Those interests and abilities that God created you with will probably fit perfectly into His plan down the road. You should develop them and learn everything about using them, but you should not selfishly pursue them. For example, if you can sing, you should learn how to sing to your full potential. Develop your gift. But the day you set God aside so you can be a singer or the day you decide for God that you *will* sing for Him, whether He wants you to or not—you've crossed the line into idolatry.

My will or God's will—what will it be?

This really boils down to a matter of your will and God's will. The devil will do everything he can to cause them to clash and to cause you to follow your own will. Jesus said in the garden of Gethsemene, "…not my will, but thine…" (Luke 22:42). In that moment He was battling the greatest spiritual battle of the ages. Thankfully, He set His own will aside for the perfect will of God. Because of His decision, you can know that you're going to Heaven along with millions of other people through the ages.

The human will can be a deceptive thing, even when we think we have good desires. We must not allow even good desires to sidetrack us from God's best desires. It's possible for a person to want something so intensely that he is blinded by it. We can convince ourselves that something is God's will, never really giving God a chance to prove us right or wrong.

If you truly want to find out if your plan matches up with God's, then let it go. If God brings it back to you in His time, then you'll know it's the right thing, and you will enjoy greater fruit in it. If that plan never returns, you can be sure it wasn't God's will, and you can fully expect Him to replace it with a better plan.

The truest test of your first love is this question: if you found out that none of your personal plans were to be fulfilled in God's perfect will, would you still want to follow God? If your answer is "no" then there are two primary problems. First, you've elevated your own intelligence above God's. (You are your own god!) Second, you've failed to truly understand who God is and what His perfect will is really like.

In a nutshell, your own plans may or may not have a place in your future. Don't let that bum you out. If that's the case, believe me, you won't miss them. Either way, you cannot trust your plans; you must trust God. You cannot pursue your dreams; you must pursue God. You cannot allow your desires to distract you from your destiny. One of the most miserable ways to live life is to get exactly what you want, yet never fulfill your divine purpose!

> *We must not allow even good desires to sidetrack us from God's best desires.*

Don't let your

Letting go of my plans only to find they were God's

Let me personalize it for a moment. When I was your age, (don't you hate it when adults say that—I did too—now I *am* one, and I'm doing it! Agghh, what's wrong with me?) I had two primary interests—sports and music. I played every sport I possibly could in high school—just for fun. If I wasn't at school or sports practice, I was generally either reading or playing the piano. I used to imagine what it would be like to conduct an orchestra or have a song published. Music could have become my first love, and that thought scared me. I knew it would be a bad mistake if that happened. So, I literally made a conscious decision to put music into the "hobby" classification of my life so that God would stay in His rightful place.

God put that decision to the test. He let me prove that music was not my god. For several years of college, I had almost no involvement in music other than occasionally in private time. When I entered ministry I almost completely set it aside. I even reached a point where I stopped writing music. God gave me other priorities that were clearly His will and calling, and I was truly content and happy in God's perfect will. I had completely relinquished my desires to His control, and He had shaped and molded them to match His plan at every turn.

To my surprise, through a strange course of events, suddenly God brought it all back like a tidal wave, all at once! I couldn't have predicted it, and I could never have manipulated it in my own strength. I can't even say that I was "hoping it would happen." I really had let these things go.

Within a few short years after that time, I found myself conducting an orchestra and seeing songs published. Talk about weird! I didn't do this! I didn't arrange for it to happen. If I had tried, it wouldn't have happened. I can look back and truly say that God did it. It was His design, His purpose, His grace, and it's to His glory.

It's really hard to take credit for something that you know you had nothing to do with. I'm amazed at how God took me from my dreams and then brought me right back to them seven years later, when I had finally decided they didn't really matter when compared to Him!

Now think for a moment. Good Christian music is a good thing and would have been a godly pursuit. I could have very easily convinced myself and everyone else that it was God's will for me to pursue music. Everyone would have been supportive of me. Yet, in my heart I would've had to set God down and lift music up. In doing so, I may have ultimately achieved my personal dream, but I would have missed my destiny, and I would be empty today because of it.

You'll never regret keeping God first and letting Him determine the usefulness of your abilities and desires in His own time.

There are thousands of blessings I would have missed out on if I had pursued my own plans rather than God's, and I may never have really experienced the fulfillment of my dreams.

That's just my story. Talk to others, and you'll find similar experiences. You must keep your personal ambitions in the "optional" category. Have a "take it or leave it" approach to the things you like. You'll never regret keeping God first and letting Him determine the usefulness of your abilities and desires in His own time.

Finally, be like Larry. Be willing to laugh at yourself. Be willing to admit that the way you see things may not be right. Be careful about marching up to God and saying, "I'm gonna be an X-Man!" In that very statement you might be putting a big red "X" right through the best life that you could ever live. Being an X-Man or being "your own man" can never come close to being "God's man."

Determine first and foremost that you will belong to Him, and in time, He will prove to you that all He has is yours!

> *"He will fulfil the desire of them that fear him:*
> *he also will hear their cry, and will save them."*
> —Psalm 145:19

SIX

(handwritten notes) Foundation – Dysfunctional mistake Zone important to God / You are important / Plans? be neutral / Tools –

Chapter Six
It's Time to Get Serious
Tool #1 for Right Decision-Making—A Serious Mind

Let's review for a minute. First, we're all dysfunctional! (Isn't that a blessing?) Simply put, that just means we're incapable of doing life right on our own. Second, if you're between 17 and 27 years of age, you're in the mistake zone—the most decision-intense time of your life, and the time when most bad decisions are made. Third, you'll be forced to make decisions in the mistake zone that will determine the course of your life and many lives after you. Fourth, you were created by God to fulfill a specific eternal purpose; you have a destiny. Finally, you have personal desires, your own will, and specific strengths and abilities that could either work for you or against you in helping to find your destiny.

That's a lot to swallow, but now we're going to get into what you need in your "tool belt" in the years ahead. There are several tools that everyone uses to make decisions. For those decisions to be right, you need the right tools. The first tool we'll talk about is "a serious mind."

About the time I turned seventeen, my dad made what I thought was a profoundly great statement. I can't remember the circumstances. We must have been talking about life and the future or something. As the "capstone" of the conversation he said, "Cary, life is what happens to you while you're making other plans." *Where's God*

Whoa! Vapor lock! I stopped. I stared. I tried to comprehend this profound bit of wisdom and the greatness of the mind from which it came. To say the least, I was impressed. Wow, was he smart! I knew he was wise—very wise—but I had no idea. I rehearsed it in my mind. "Life is what happens to you while you're making other plans." It took a while to sink in, but as you can tell it has stayed with me all these years. I've thought of it often. I've repeated it to others. I've often reminisced on the moment when those great words fell from my wise father's lips.

> I know plenty of young adults who let their destiny slip by while they were busy making plans.

About four years ago, I was sharing that great bit of wisdom with a friend. He paused. He looked at me wonderingly. Then he smiled. "Your dad didn't say that."

How dare he! I was shocked! I was in dismay! I had heard it with my own ears. Of course my father said that! It's been framed and hung in the "quote hall of fame" of my heart for many years with his name right under it! "Of course he said it."

"No he didn't. That's a line from some old song!"

My "quote hall of fame" came crumbling down right before my very eyes, then I just laughed! My dad had done it again! Not long after, I told my dad about that event and thoroughly *chastised* him for allowing me to think he had made that statement up.

"Hey, I never said I made it up." he said, excusing himself.

What's worse is that I've been using some line from a song as advice for young adults for years! I felt betrayed. I still bear the emotional scars.

I can't say that I know the song that the line came from, but I can say that I know plenty of young adults who let their destiny slip by while they were busy making plans. They were too busy having a good time. They had their friends, their fun, their things, and they were living for the "here and now"! They did whatever felt good, and they rarely gave the next day, or the next year, or the next decade a second thought.

Two summers ago, our family was looking forward to vacation. It had been a difficult but a blessed year for us. My wife, Dana, had been in the hospital and on bed rest for many months through a very uncertain pregnancy. When finally our little Haylee arrived, she was five weeks premature and had to be in the NICU for two weeks. After that, she had a very weak immune system, which meant she was sick a lot. As a result, for a period of many months we didn't go out much—no Chuck E. Cheese, no date nights, no miniature golf, and very little family fun outside the four walls of our home (though there was plenty inside!). So, we were really looking forward to vacation!

Finally, the day arrived—the day we had talked about for months with Lance and Larry. It was time to go on vacation. We had spent days packing, getting ready, and talking up all the fun we were going to have. We were pretty pumped!

We have a family tradition for vacation. We always play the song "You've Got a Friend in Me" from *Toy Story* as we pull out of town. We've done that for about five years in a row. So, as another year of "You've Got a Friend in Me" came to an exciting conclusion, I put on my fatherly voice and commanded the attention of the entire family.

"Everybody! Lance, Larry, Haylee, Mom—we're ON VACATION!!!"

Lance cheered. Haylee slept. Mom agreed with a smile. Larry frowned.

"Nuh, uhhhh," he said in denial.

I didn't understand his problem. "Yes, we are, Buddy! We're ON VACATION!" This time I said it with a big smile and a lot of excitement expecting him to jump on the happiness train with the rest of us.

"This is vacation? I thought we were going some place fun for vacation!" He folded his arms and sat back with a pouting frown.

Then I realized—to Larry, vacation was a destination. To me, vacation was a state of existence—a condition of the mind—pressure release, relaxation, unwind, kick back, knock around, do nothing but spend time together. Larry and I were once again in gridlock on the communication traffic grid.

I spent the next fifteen minutes trying to figure out how to help a five-year-old mind understand the concept of "vacation." You wouldn't believe how hard that was. He finally got it, and you wouldn't believe how much fun we had on vacation!

I know young adults that are like Larry. They think adulthood is some magical destination. They are expecting some momentous arrival date when the things of childhood will pass, and suddenly the things of adulthood will come clearly into view. For now they are content with PlayStation, sports, Twinkies, and TV. They're having a lot of fun! Mom still does their laundry, Dad still pays the bills, and life is good. The refrigerator is full; there's still money in birthday cards; there will be multiple gifts under the Christmas tree (maybe even a stocking of candy); Easter still has a basket of goodies; and summer is still about "being out of school"!

People like this don't see that adulthood is upon them. It's now! While they are waiting for some tribal ceremony when they will shake off the trappings of childhood and accept the mantle of adulthood, life has already started to pass them by. To this kind of person life is still about "playing"!

Paul said in 1 Corinthians 13:11, "When I was a child, I spake as a child, I understood as a child, I thought as a child: but when I became a man, I put away childish things."

Being a kid was great! I know there are plenty of kids today with serious trials and loss, but generally speaking a kid's life is carefree. Most American kids wake up with two things on their mind—candy and playing! It's like some kind of obsessive mission that they are on from the moment they wake up to the moment they fall asleep at night. "I must find candy! I must play!"

Do you remember being a kid? During the school day you couldn't wait for recess. You couldn't wait to get home and play. And you knew that God was smiling down on you if you were fortunate enough to get *two* recesses in the same school day! Playing was the theme of life. No matter where you were or what time it was, you were always interested in playing. You could play in church, in the grocery store, and even in the backseat of the car—and you have the scars to prove it!

You knew that God was smiling down on you if you were fortunate enough to get TWO recesses in the same school day!

Then there was the candy thing! If some kid was fortunate enough to have a pack of gum at school or some leftover Halloween candy in his lunch box, he was the "King of the hill." Everybody was his friend. I can still remember as a child thinking of the day that I would be a "dad." My first thought was, "I'm going to take my kids to 7–11 and buy them candy." In my mind that was the definition of good parenting!

Adults seem to have lined up on two entirely different sides of this candy mission. The first team was made up of grandparents, storeowners, Sunday school teachers, and sugar merchandisers. They couldn't give you enough candy! When you were with these people, they didn't care how much you bought or ate. If you were good, they gave it to you for free. If you were bad, they bribed you with it. It was a win-win situation. You just couldn't lose. It was heaven.

The second team was made up of parents, dentists, teachers, and mean people. Their goal was to keep candy from you! They invented all kinds of tales: "You'll spoil your appetite." "We're about to have dinner." "You'll rot your teeth." "You can't chew gum in class." "It's not good for you." and on and on. If they caught you eating it they would ask you things like: "Where did you get that?" "Who told you that you could have that?" "Did you ask?" and more. They were the self-appointed "candy sheriffs"—almost as if there were some deep unresolved candy-deprivation in their own past, and they were taking their anger out on you. It's still a problem today. Sad, really.

My kids have a completely different problem, an anomaly that few children ever have to face—a mother who eats it all before they can get to it. Though I tend to lean toward the "candy-sheriff" team from my own unresolved anger, my wife is a completely different story. She could eat candy for three meals a day the rest of her life and still not have enough. If you hide candy, she finds it. If you wait to eat it, she beats you to it. Her motto is "search and destroy"! If she saved all the candy wrappers she went through in a given year, they would stretch completely around the earth three times. Candy makers love her. She never goes anywhere without a secret stash. She will make a fantastic grandmother!

Candy and playing—the essence of childhood.

Yes, childhood was wonderful. Though parts of it can live on forever (my wife being a good example), you also have to come to terms with the fact that it's time to shoulder additional responsibilities. The fun doesn't completely go away; it just has to share equal time with serious decisions and duties.

Being serious doesn't come naturally.

The Bible says in Titus 2:3–7, "The aged women likewise, that they be in behaviour as becometh holiness, not false accusers, not given to much wine, teachers of good things; That they may teach the young women to be sober, to love their husbands, to love their children, To be discreet, chaste, keepers at home, good, obedient to their own husbands, that the word of God be not blasphemed. Young men likewise exhort to be sober minded. In all things shewing thyself a pattern of good works: in doctrine shewing uncorruptness, gravity, sincerity."

These verses say that young men and women must be taught to be "sober." The word *sober* literally means "to be brought to your senses and challenged to be disciplined and serious about life." The implication is that someone needs to grab you by the shoulders and tell you how serious life has suddenly become! Apparently being sober doesn't come naturally for young adults, or God would not have placed that command in the Bible.

Gird up the loins of your mind.

Again it says in 1 Peter 1:13, "Wherefore gird up the loins of your mind, be sober, and hope to the end for the grace that is to be brought unto you at the revelation of Jesus Christ."

"Gird up the loins of your mind" is a reference to what a runner would do prior to starting his trek. In Bible times, before a man could run, he would have to fold up the long clothing that he wore so that his legs could move with speed and agility. If he tried to run without "girding up his loins" he would be severely hindered and would probably stumble and fall.

In this verse God is commanding you to "gird up the loins of your mind." The command is that you would get serious. Take that part of your mind that still wants to spend life playing and eating candy and "gird it up"—wrap it up tightly in control so that you don't stumble and fall. Bring it into discipline so that you can run speedily and respond quickly to God's leading in your life.

A sober mind knows when to be serious and when to have fun. A sober mind understands the stakes and focuses itself on issues that are really important. You could choose to start being serious, or you could wait for your bad decisions to "smack" you into being serious. It's your choice.

For instance, think about this question. How do you act in English class? There are two types of people in the world—those who don't like English class, and those who HATE it. I'm not asking if you like it; I'm asking how you treat it. The fact is, even though it's not all that enjoyable, it's incredibly important.

If your primary language is English, then you will probably be using English to communicate for the rest of your life. If you know the language, then you can communicate well—which means a better job, fewer fights with your spouse, and maybe being able to kindly talk your way out of a traffic ticket. There are all kinds of wonderful uses for the English language. The less you know about English, the harder time you'll have communicating. Young adults with serious minds know how to take English seriously. That's just one example among thousands.

"Girding up the loins of your mind" means you must be able to focus your mind, develop it, think seriously with it, and use it effectively. It also means you must guard it from the trash and philosophies of the world.

Let me ask you another question. Do you know what you believe and why? Most young adults cannot give an intelligent answer for why the Bible is trustworthy, why Jesus Christ is God, or why evolution couldn't have happened. If you gird up the loins of your mind, you'll be compelled to discover these answers for yourself. If you are the type of person that just accepts what you're told, your faith and your future will be unstable because it rests on men rather than on truth.

The Christian faith makes sense! It's supported by evidence. Do you know what that evidence is?

God has given you a mind, and He has provided a fact-based faith, an intelligent faith. The Christian faith makes sense! It's supported by evidence. Do you know what that evidence is? If not, then find out. Then, when your faith comes into question, it won't crumble. It will stand the tests of ridicule or criticism because you have "girded up the loins of your mind."

Be aware of your enemy.

God says in 1 Peter 5:8, "Be sober, be vigilant; because your adversary the devil, as a roaring lion, walketh about, seeking whom he may devour."

This time God brings life to another level of seriousness. He says that you are the target of an assassin. He says that you have an enemy, the devil, who wants to absolutely destroy and devour you. Stop for a minute and make sure you're comprehending this!

You are a target! Someone is out to get you. Life is not a sandbox. You won't always have Mom and Dad looking out for you. Up to this point everybody else has been sober for you. Now it's time to be sober for yourself! You have an enemy that people, all your life, have tried to shield and protect you from. As you launch out on your own, you're going to get eaten if you don't start watching your back. It's time to get sober! If you head into adulthood with nothing more than bubble gum, baseball cards, your iPod, and your basketball—you'll be knocked down pretty quickly.

On the one hand, you have a good and loving Heavenly Father who wants to bless and care for you. On the other, you have the father of lies, a roaring lion, waiting to devour and devastate you. In the middle, you have a decision to make. It's the first decision I'm going to challenge you to make right now.

Get serious about life.

Determine that there will be many moments in the coming days when you will seriously seek God, study His Word, and contemplate His direction for your future. That sounds basic, but many young adults head down the wrong path at just this point. They never realize how serious it all is.

I challenge you to focus your heart, discipline your mind, and set your affection on the things of God. Ask God to help you understand what's at stake and what the risks are. Ask Him to help you "gird up the loins of your mind" so that you can run freely and effectively for Him. Ask Him to mature you and make you ready for the responsibilities He will give you. Ask Him to help you be SOBER.

First Thessalonians 5:6 says, "Therefore let us not sleep, as do others; but let us watch and be sober."

My friend, you live in a world of sleeping people. No doubt you have friends that are asleep spiritually. People don't see the spiritual battle for their souls, and they enter into decisions with little advance thought. They make decisions out of sheer whim! They are completely apathetic about the spiritual implications of their actions. It's one thing to buy a new car on a whim (though I wouldn't suggest it). It's another thing to get married, lose your purity, change churches, or have children on a whim. But people do these things all the time!

I dare you to be different. Purpose in your heart to be vigilant and alert. Ask God to bring you to your spiritual senses. Ask Him to mature you. Maturity is not a destination or a tribal ceremony. Maturity is the acceptance of responsibility. Every young adult wants to be thought of as mature, but few choose to seriously shoulder the weighty responsibilities of adulthood. Some are scared. Some are ignorant or simple minded. Some are rebellious. Some are courageous. Which one are you?

> *Maturity is the acceptance of responsibility. Every young adult wants to be thought of as mature, but few choose to seriously shoulder the weighty responsibilities of adulthood.*

I hate to be the one to break it to you, but you're not on your childhood summer vacation anymore. Life is now much more than candy and summer break, and people will quickly bestow the title of "mature" upon you if you will accept responsibility. Life will happen whether you want it to or not. It's happening even now. Are you making other plans? Are you too busy having fun to stop and be serious?

The road ahead will be an odd mixture of growth experiences. It will include plenty of the great things you experienced in your childhood—vacation, toys, the Jetsons, and "Fun Dips." It will also include some heavy responsibility. You'll need the ability to be vigilant and sober.

Soon enough, you'll not only be sober for yourself. You'll need to be sober for your kids—who will spend all of their time obsessing over playing and eating candy. For their sake, learn it now. They need you to be vigilant for them! Their future depends on it.

Oh, by the way, there's one other decision you need to make. Choose your team on the candy issue—help the children.

"But while men slept, his enemy came..."
—Matthew 13:25

seven

If You Are Among the Very "Pure" In Heart
Tool #2 for Right Decision-Making—A Pure Heart

Have you ever heard that song "Young at Heart"? You remember—"Fairytales can come true; it can happen to you, if you're young at heart…." That sounds great, but I would rather you know this principle, "Your *destiny* can come true; it can happen to you, if you're *pure* in heart!" A pure heart is the second tool that you must have in your decision-making toolbox.

I think the point of that song was that you should always enjoy the simple treasures of life—like the moon. My baby girl has just recently discovered it. She looks for it every night; she giggles when she finds it; she even talks to it! She loves the moon, and when she can't find it, she just settles for a streetlight.

She also loves her blankey, her binky, and her babies. I call her the "binky billionaire" because she has so many. The other day I looked at her, and she had two of them in her mouth, one of them on her shirt, and another one in her hand. She looked back and said "bee-bee!" in a muffled tone. I guess it hasn't occurred to her that they don't serve much purpose if you only have one mouth.

I'm okay with you staying young at heart, so long as that doesn't mean you stay ignorant at heart. Yet, there's something much more important about your heart. Your heart is a tool that you will use to make decisions for the rest of your life! You probably never thought of your heart as a tool, but that's exactly what it is.

When I was growing up, there was one thing that repeatedly drove my dad insane. We had a family of boys, and we always needed tools for something. My dad traveled some for work, so it wasn't always convenient to ask him where the tools were or which ones we could use. And, when you're busy tearing something up, building a tree fort in the woods, fixing a friend's bike, or killing garden spiders, you need the right tools. Our dad had them. He had a pretty good collection of tools, and if we couldn't find just what we needed, usually we could make something work. Generally, the tools were all neatly organized down in the basement, unless we boys had been through an unusually busy season of need.

Your heart is a tool that you will use to make decisions for the rest of your life!

And needs were coming up *all* the time. Sometimes we just needed to strip all the bark off of some unlucky tree from the ground up. Other times we needed to dig up the grass to find worms for fishing. One time we needed to build a go-cart track in the backyard—all the grass had to go. (That was quite a job, and we got a pretty good start on it before my dad killed the project—and almost killed us.)

Yep, we were pretty quick to help ourselves to Dad's tools, and they were almost never used for what they were actually intended for. To this day, I'm sure he doesn't know some of the outlandish things a ratchet set can be used for. Remember George Washington Carver—the guy who invented all the uses for the peanut? Well, my brothers and I—we were the G. W. Carvers of Dad's toolbox.

All this led up to those rare moments when Dad was actually going to use his tools for something. Mom's list had gotten long enough, and her repeated requests for help had gotten loud enough, that it was time to get the tools and get to work. It was never anything interesting or adventurous—usually just a leaky faucet, a broken toilet, or a minor home improvement. This is usually when we would try to get out of the house and go play, because we knew it was only a matter of time.

"Cary, Matt, Mark…where's my crescent wrench?"

It usually took a few minutes, but eventually one of us would 'fess up, meekly, blaming one of the others. "Uh…I think Matt was using it at the tree fort to hit Mark with and hammer nails. He also took your big electric saw."

The tools were never where he wanted them when *he* needed them, but they were always there when *we* needed them. Dad was great about keeping them so organized for us. It was beautiful. If we lost them, we would just shrug our shoulders like no one on the planet had seen what he needed. Eventually he would replace it. I'm sure the woods around that house to this day are like a "graveyard for abused and forgotten tools." It's mostly my brothers' faults.

The fact is there are few things more frustrating than needing a tool for something and not having it. I'm notorious for going to the store and getting something for the house without giving any thought to the tools needed for the job. On top of that, I have the world's worst tool collection. I guess I'm reaping what I sowed. I've spent my fair share of time *beating* on some pipe because I didn't have a pipe wrench. My way of fixing a leaky faucet or toilet is to turn the water valve off and stop using it. I don't get along so well with tools.

What is your heart?

Your heart is a tool made by God for a specific purpose. It allows you to feel life's emotions, discern life's desires, and decide life's direction. It is a tool of discernment and the source of inner motives. Unless you're dead, this is how your spiritual heart functions.

Literally said, your heart is your mind, your will, and your emotions. Your heart is "what you feel," "what you want," and "what you think." It is the sum total of your innermost being. It represents a part of you that few people see, and it guides and directs you twenty-four hours a day. It never stops functioning, and you are constantly turning to it for feedback on how to feel, what to think, and what to want.

The Bible says it this way in Proverbs 4:23, "Keep thy heart with all diligence; for out of it are the issues of life."

The way you think and feel in your adult life will be determined by your heart. Every time you make a decision, you turn to your heart for advice. It constantly gives you feedback about every experience. Even now, as you read, your heart is the silent commentator in the background, helping you sift through the information, discerning whether it's right or wrong, deciding whether you will accept it or reject it. (Hopefully it's dialed in and concentrating rather than reminding you of your boyfriend or girlfriend right now.) Your heart is the seat of your conscience and the unseen influencer in every choice you make.

In order to make right decisions in the days ahead, you must understand your heart and how it functions. You must understand the dangers of your heart and how to keep your heart. If it functions properly it will guide you into God's will; if not, it will guide you away from His will.

Your heart is what God sees and cares about the most.

First Samuel 16:7 says, "But the Lord said unto Samuel, Look not on his countenance, or on the height of his stature; because I have refused him: for the Lord seeth not as man seeth; for man looketh on the outward appearance, but the Lord looketh on the heart."

There seems to be two extremes in this particular verse. The first extreme causes me to focus only on my heart and reason that the outward appearance doesn't matter. Quite often this verse is used as an excuse for bad behavior. We reason "Hey, God looks on the heart, so it doesn't matter what I look like, what I wear, or how people perceive me." That's not an accurate application of this verse. The fact that God sees my heart is not a license to live wrong outwardly; it's a reason to make sure that my right living is genuinely from the heart. The Bible teaches clearly that God wants me to care about my outward appearance before men, but not to the neglect of the inward man. If my outward performance doesn't flow from a pure heart of love for God, then it's nothing more than show, which makes me a "man-pleaser" not a "God-pleaser."

The other extreme is that some people focus only on the external appearance and performance as the standard for spiritual growth and nearness to God. If I wear the right clothes, walk the right way, wear my hair right, attend the right functions, and speak the right lingo, people will think I'm spiritual! I can be far from God in my heart

Your heart is "what you feel," "what you want," and "what you think." It is the sum total of your innermost being.

but appear outwardly to be very spiritual. The Christian life then becomes a carefully strategized system of outward conformity.

In this way of thinking, I conform so that people will accept me. I play the part outwardly because people believe me, and I never really develop the inward heart of my spiritual relationship with God. This is a very frustrating way to live the Christian life, and it usually doesn't last very long. I will ultimately work harder at covering my bases and keeping up my act than I would at just being genuine with God and others. Plus I'm cheating myself out of a truckload of blessings that come from walking with God personally.

The balance of these two extremes is a commitment to both the heart and the outward fruit of a personal relationship with Christ. You should determine that your outward walk before men will be blameless. Proverbs 22:1 says, "A good name is rather to be chosen than great riches, and loving favour rather than silver and gold." God wants you to "walk worthy of the calling," and He wants the world to see you and your good works and glorify Him because of them (Matthew 5:16). Yet, you should also determine that this life would genuinely flow from an inward walk with Christ. Don't conform; be transformed from the inside (Romans 12:1–2)!

Matthew 15:8 says, "This people draweth nigh unto me with their mouth, and honoureth me with their lips; but their heart is far from me." Don't let anyone tell you that God doesn't care *why* you do what you do! He certainly does. He cares as much or more about *why* you do things as He does *that* you do them. God looks at your heart first, and He knows exactly where you are spiritually even at this moment. He knows what you want, what you feel, and what you think, and more than anything else, He wants you to have a heart for Him.

Your heart can guide you away from God's will.

Your heart can actually be a negative influence in your life. The Bible is filled with stories and examples of men and women who were led astray by their hearts. Time does not permit us to delve into an exhaustive study of all the various negative conditions that the human heart can experience, but here are a few. The Bible says the heart can be:

+ Evil—Genesis 6:5
+ Obstinate—Deuteronomy 2:30
+ Discouraged—Numbers 32:7
+ Double—1 Chronicles 12:33
+ Sorrowful—Nehemiah 2:2
+ Froward—Psalm 101:4
+ Proud—Psalm 101:5
+ Perverse—Proverbs 12:8
+ Deceitful—Proverbs 12:20; Jeremiah 17:9

- Wicked—Jeremiah 17:9
- Foolish—Proverbs 22:15
- Wrongly Trusted—Proverbs 28:26

Did you see that list? It looks like a character description off of *America's Most Wanted*! Take a look at it again. That's really a pretty scary list. Realize, those words are not referring to what *someone else's* heart can be. This is what *your* heart and what *my* heart are capable of! This is not just the *worst* of humanity. This is humanity *in general*.

The sad part is many young adults make decisions from a heart that is corrupted by one of the above. If there's a time you don't want to make a decision of any kind, it's when your heart is proud, deceitful, wicked, or obstinate (or any other one of the above words). Doing so would guarantee you to be wrong.

Think of it this way—your heart is the lens, or the glasses, through which you will look to make decisions. If your heart is any of the above, you'll be looking through a dirty or tainted lens. You won't be able to clearly see reality, and you won't be able to make a right decision. It will look right from your perspective, but your perspective will be skewed by the condition of your heart. You cannot afford to make life-changing decisions through the lens of a deceitful or an obstinate heart!

For instance, I know dozens of young adults who come from broken homes. Perhaps you have. That break-up represents a painful experience resulting in perhaps a long period of pain and questions. I've seen many young adults defy the odds, seek God's help, and allow His grace to move them from that pain into His perfect will. I've seen many others who refused to deal with it. They harbored it. They became bitter and angry. They grew up and faced major decisions with a bitter heart. The bitterness and anger became the lens through which they chose the future of their lives. In every case these decisions are wrong.

Quite often these same young adults became friends with others who had the same issues of bitterness and anger. How do they find each other? It's easy. When any two people are looking through the same impure lens of bitterness and anger, the world looks the same, and they quickly find each other. In the lives of these young adults, every experience takes on the "color" of the bitter and angry perspective through which they view the world. It's all about the impurities in their hearts.

I've seen young adults marry someone their parents didn't approve of just to spite them. I've seen teen girls give away their purity because their heart was hurt by a father who left them. I've seen young men run off into their own devices just to make their parents suffer. These hearts, in corrupted conditions, drove their "humans" to do things that hurt themselves, and every time the pain was made worse by the decision. These people always hurt themselves more than anyone else. The saddest part is that these decisions can never be "unmade." Their price tag is high, their reward is painful, and their damage lingers for a lifetime.

Your heart can guide you into God's will.

Matthew 5:8 says, "Blessed are the pure in heart: for they shall see God." I must have read that verse a thousand times before it sank in. This doesn't just mean that those whose sins are forgiven will see God in Heaven. I believe there is a deeper application that applies to you right now.

You cannot afford to make life-changing decisions through the lens of a deceitful or an obstinate heart!

As you head into adulthood, more than anything else, you need to be able to see and discern God at work in your life. You need to be able to recognize His hand. In the face of a million options and opportunities, you need to be able to see which one has God's thumbprint on it. You need to see God, and this verse makes it clear that a pure heart is the only lens through which you can do so.

On the flip side of our last list, the Bible gives another list of words that apply to the human heart. Your heart can be:

- Wise—Exodus 35:35; Job 9:4
- Stirred for the Lord—Exodus 35:21
- Willing—Exodus 35:5
- Glad—Deuteronomy 28:47
- Perceptive—Deuteronomy 29:4
- Inclined toward God—Joshua 24:23
- Rejoicing—1 Samuel 2:1
- Changed—1 Samuel 10:9
- Perfect with God—1 Kings 8:61
- Tender—2 Kings 22:19
- Set to Seek God—1 Chronicles 22:19
- Prepared to Seek God—2 Chronicles 12:14
- Clean—Psalm 51:10
- Established—Psalm 112:8
- Wholly for God—Psalm 119:10
- Searched and Known—Psalm 139:23
- Kept with Diligence—Proverbs 4:23

These are all positive conditions of the heart. When functioning properly, your heart will interact with God, with His Word, and with His Spirit within to lead and direct you into paths of righteousness. My pastor has said many times from the pulpit, "When the heart is pure, the vision is clear!"

When it comes to spiritual danger, God will use a pure heart as an early warning system in your life. Your heart will be able to discern danger, sense a mistake, and respond quickly to God's leading. What a great gift God has given us in this tool of "the heart."

Several years ago, some friends came out to visit us from the East Coast. It was their first trip west, and we were really looking forward to showing them some of the sights of southern California.

There's a lot to see and do in southern California, though not all good, and we had planned a full day to give them a tour. Now, I'm not a big fan of Hollywood, and I especially don't spend much time there; but on occasion, we drive through to show people the famous sites. It's nice to say you've been there once—that's about it.

Well, on this occasion we actually got out of the car at Grauman's Chinese Theatre where all the footprints and handprints of famous people are. It's kind of silly really, people walking around putting their hands and feet into concrete, trying to see whose shoes they could've worn. (I was almost sure I saw a lady putting her foot on Mr. Ed's hoof print—I think it was a fit!) Anyway, we had to park a good distance off the street in the dark, and it wasn't a very secure feeling. Being aware of the regular news stories of southern California, I was on "high alert"! Man, I was tense—ready for action, ready to defend my humble wife by pushing my friends into a would-be attacker's way, so we would have time to run! I was poised and alert—every nerve attuned to the darkness. My friend on the other hand was totally oblivious to any danger (probably due to the fact that he's about 6'5" and nicknamed "Moose"!)

When it comes to spiritual danger, God will use a pure heart as an early warning system in your life.

As we were on our way back to the car, in the dark, looking like "easy-prey tourists from Alabama" I noticed something move in the shadows to the side of us (my friend, still oblivious). I looked more earnestly and sure enough, it was a darkly clothed figure, seemingly watching us, responding to our approach and waiting to slip in behind us. Suddenly, I was totally tuned out to what my friend was saying, and I was jolted into self-defense mode! Just as I suspected, this dark figure slipped in behind us on the sidewalk and was following us into the darkest part of our walk. Just ahead a few feet was a row of trees that hung over the sidewalk creating a darkened area out of view from the streetlights. I panicked! I looked around. There was nobody—no police, no Marines, no Air National Guard, no Red-Cross workers, not even any other tourists—nobody but me, Moose (who was still talking, oblivious), and our weakling wives. *We were going to die—I could feel it.* Twelve more steps to the trees; the guy was getting closer—eight more steps to the trees, still closer.

"Ugh-um," I cleared my throat and interrupted conversation with a hushed tone. "Uh, I hate to mention this, but we better get out into the street right now," I said as I nudged Moose and gently pulled my wife's arm.

They didn't understand. Six more steps…

This time I spoke with a little more urgency, still hushed, "Guys, there's a serial killer following us, and we'd better get out into the street lights—or we're going to die!"

This time we all moved quickly directly into the middle of the street, just to the side of the dark grove of trees and directly under a bright street lamp. You'll never believe what happened next. That dark shadowy figure stopped in his tracks, watched us for a moment, and turned back around to where he was originally waiting.

"Whoa, that was weird," someone said.

"Yeah, I keep forgetting where we are," Moose added (no longer oblivious).

Now my heart was really going. I felt as though we had just narrowly missed a very bad thing. I thought, "I saw that guy way back there, kept watching him in the corner of my eye, and just had a really bad feeling that he was up to something."

To this day, I believe God helped us avoid something bad that night. I still haven't been back to that area and haven't missed it.

Simply because I was familiar with the crime of that area, my senses were heightened to an awareness that no one else in the group had. While everyone else felt fine, I felt quite alarmed. When others were enjoying conversation, I was wondering what songs they would sing at my funeral. While dinner was a good memory for the rest of the group, mine was about to return. What was the difference? My sense of fear and danger had put my whole body on alert and had acted as an early warning system.

When functioning properly, that's how your heart will work. God's Holy Spirit will be your early warning system and will work through your heart to alert you to spiritual danger. God wants to use your heart to help you see things that others won't and understand things that others miss. People with impure hearts move forward into spiritual danger, never seeing it. People with pure hearts see God's warning and see the spiritual danger before it comes. More importantly, people with pure hearts see God's hand at work in every situation and every decision.

Your heart must be regularly purified.

Do you wear eyeglasses or know someone that does? What must you do to eyeglasses on a regular basis? Clean them. Glasses get stuff on them. People sneeze; people eat greasy foods; the world is just a dusty, grimy place—so glasses must be cleaned on a regular basis. When you wear them for a short time they get smudged, dirty, and blurry. If you go for a long time without a cleaning, it can become quite difficult to see the real world through a dirty pair of lenses. When the glasses are dirty, the whole world looks dirty, and nothing looks right.

Even so, your heart is subject to a myriad of influences through the course of life and must regularly be purified and cleansed. Now, truly, if you've trusted Christ as Saviour, your sins were completely cleansed by the blood of His cross. I'm talking about your day-to-day relationship with God. Your clarity of spiritual vision can easily become tainted and cloudy. Your heart can become smudged with the world's philosophies and filthiness. This world truly is a dirty place spiritually, even when you're committed to fighting the filth.

Perhaps you have become involved in some deliberate sin or habit that is continually wreaking havoc on your spiritual condition. Perhaps through music, internet, video games, magazines, books, movies, friends, or TV you've been literally bathing your heart in the mud of this world. While your salvation may not come into question by these actions, your spiritual health and vision certainly does. What kind of spiritual vision do you think these sins create? These behaviors do the same thing to your heart that a mud puddle would do to your eyeglasses. They blind you. They coat your heart with impurity so that you can't see God; you don't recognize His call; and you cannot respond quickly and accurately to His prompting.

Please let this sink in. For years you may have wondered why people have been on your case. Your parents won't let you watch certain TV shows. Your youth pastor has tried to warn you about wrong music. Your pastor has preached against hanging out with the wrong crowd

Your clarity of spiritual vision can easily become tainted and cloudy. Your heart can become smudged with the world's philosophies and filthiness.

and going places you shouldn't go. Why? Because they want you to be miserable, and they want to take all your "fun" away? No! Because they realize how harmful these things are to *you*. They want you to have clear, spiritual vision. They want your decisions to be right from a pure heart with wisdom and discernment. They want you to see the danger for yourself before it's too late!

I urge you to make these things right for your own sake. The media of this world provides much more than entertainment. It provides a lot of spiritual pollution. Taking it all in with no caution and care would be like wrapping your lips around the tale pipe of a Fed Ex truck and breathing deeply for a couple of hours. You'd be dead, and I know plenty of young adults who have lost all ability to see God; they've lost all sensitivity to spiritual danger. They are like walking dead people spiritually, because their hearts have been caked with the filth of the world.

If you will make right decisions in the days ahead, they will flow from a pure heart. Thanks to the Lord Jesus Christ and His death on the cross, you don't have to pay for your sins; you just need to acknowledge them before God. He is ready and willing to forgive you. First John 1:9 says, "If we confess our sins, he is faithful and just to forgive us our sins, and to cleanse us from all unrighteousness."

How to have a pure heart

So how? How can you, right now, have a clean heart? It's possible, and it's not hard. God already did the hard part, and He's ready and waiting for you to come to Him.

Psalm 119:9 says, "Wherewithal shall a young man cleanse his way? by taking heed thereto according to thy word."

When David sinned before God, he wrote these words in Psalm 51:"Have mercy upon me, O God, according to thy loving-kindness: according unto the multitude of thy tender mercies blot out my transgressions. Wash me throughly from mine iniquity, and cleanse me from my sin. For I acknowledge my transgressions: and my sin is ever before me. Against thee, thee only, have I sinned, and done this evil in thy sight: that thou mightest be justified when thou speakest, and be clear when thou judgest. Behold, I was shapen in iniquity; and in sin did my mother conceive me. Behold, thou desirest truth in the inward parts: and in the hidden part thou shalt make me to know wisdom. Purge me with hyssop, and I shall be clean: wash me, and I shall be whiter than snow. Make me to hear joy and gladness; that the bones which thou hast broken may rejoice. Hide thy face from my sins, and blot out all mine iniquities. Create in me a clean heart, O God; and renew a right spirit within me. Cast me not away from thy presence; and take not thy holy spirit from me. Restore unto me the joy of thy salvation; and uphold me with thy free spirit."

While sin always has its consequences, you can come right now to God and be cleansed thoroughly from its presence and power in your life. The devil wants you to run from God when you're out of fellowship with Him. He paints the picture in your mind like God is angry and ready to squash you. The reality is God is waiting like the father of the prodigal, with open arms ready to welcome you back home. He will not only accept you, He will cleanse you and make you new. He will restore you to fellowship, and He will give you a pure heart and clear vision.

Over the years, I've seen dozens of sin-hardened young adults sit in church with their arms folded and their hearts cold toward God. Then God does something to break through the coldness, and that young adult responds. It may be at a teen camp or a revival, but at some point that person confesses his ways and seeks God's cleansing. At that precise moment, this person receives an entirely different perspective on the spiritual universe. It's as though the layers of dirt and grime have been scoured from the surface of his heart, and he is seeing God's reality for the first time. His entire outlook changes. People whom he once viewed as enemies are suddenly friends. Bible truths he once resisted, he now embraces. The sweet smile that was long buried by misery has suddenly returned with deep joy.

While sin always has its consequences, you can come right now to God and be cleansed thoroughly from its presence and power in your life.

This is God's process of cleansing the heart, and it could happen to you right now. If you feel God's tugging as you read these words, I urge you to find a quiet place of prayer, open Psalm 51, and completely open your heart to God's cleansing touch. Confess to Him, ask Him to cleanse you, and return to your reading a changed person. More importantly, you will see your life through the pure lens of God's wisdom. Your whole perspective will change.

If you feel sure that you are right with God this moment, then make it your habit to regularly return to God through prayer and through His Word to keep your heart clean. It will become tainted without you even knowing it. Your vision will be skewed just from your mere existence in this dirty world. We all must maintain that purity of heart if we are truly to see God in our daily lives.

Your heart can be changed.

One final thought before we move on. A heart that's right with God is a pliable thing in God's hands. God says it this way:

"But now, O LORD, thou art our father; we are the clay, and thou our potter; and we all are the work of thy hand" (Isaiah 64:8).

"O house of Israel, cannot I do with you as this potter? saith the LORD. Behold, as the clay is in the potter's hand, so are ye in mine hand, O house of Israel" (Jeremiah 18:6).

"A new heart also will I give you, and a new spirit will I put within you: and I will take away the stony heart out of your flesh, and I will give you an heart of flesh" (Ezekiel 36:26).

When your heart is right with your Creator, some amazing things are possible. Since your heart represents your feelings, your desires, and your thoughts, God can change the way you feel, think, and desire something. It's an awesome process!

> A heart that's right with God is a pliable thing in God's hands.

Think of it this way. God made my taste buds, right? He made them like the taste of Big Macs. But, if He wanted to, He could make them hate Big Macs and like the taste of drywall screws. (Ridiculous, I know, but work with me here.) He could. He could change my craving for Big Macs into a craving for carpet fibers if it served His eternal purpose.

That's how your heart is in His hands. It's soft and moldable. If you want something He doesn't want you to have, He can change your desire. If you like someone your parents don't approve of, He can change those feelings. If you don't want to be a missionary and eat raw fish, He could give you the strong desire to do nothing but missions and eat nothing but raw fish. If the music you like is wrong, He can give you the taste for the right kind! Suddenly your heart is completely flexible to see and follow God's purpose no matter what. Now we're getting somewhere.

If you've made it this far, you should be very excited! You're most certainly on the right course to making some of the greatest decisions of your entire life. There are still some key things to know and discover, but you've already made it over some of the biggest hurdles.

Your heart is an amazing gift from God. It's a tool to be used for a vital purpose. If you keep it clean, it will serve you well. You'll not only enjoy the childish things of life like "the moon" and "Bazooka bubble gum," but you'll see God, and you'll sense His hand at work in every situation.

This is the best part. You'll have a head start—if you are among the very "pure" in heart.

See you in the next chapter.

"Blessed are the pure in heart: for they shall see God."
—Matthew 5:8

eight

I Don't Want to Grow Up—
I'm a Toys R Us Kid!
Tool #3 for Right Decision-Making—A Courageous Spirit

The transition from childhood to adulthood brings many changes and many "paradigm shifts"! (This is another way of saying "a total change in your perspective.") In fact, it can be downright "shock therapy" for your perspective sometimes. Some of these transitions are great—like being able to drive—but others of them are about as much fun as a root canal!

College was a big one for me. The Lord led me to a Bible college that was 2,000 miles away from home, which meant for the first time in my life, I was leaving my family. We were pretty close, and to this day, it was one of the hardest things I have ever done. I'll never forget standing in the San Jose airport as my final high school summer was screeching to a halt. My Mom had spent the entire summer packing trunks and boxes of things I might need. You would have thought I was going on some kind of safari or survival expedition where there were no Wal-marts or grocery stores.

Suddenly the summer came crashing closed, and my last day at home was over! That day was great. We had a cook-out, goofed around with some friends, and stayed up late packing and talking. I couldn't sleep. I even got sick that night (nerves). Then we got up early and headed for the airport.

After postponing boarding the plane for as long as I could, I finally heard the last boarding call. This was the "do or die" moment. I hugged my brothers—no big deal saying goodbye to a brother. I hugged my dad—you know dads hardly ever cry. *Then* I hugged my mom.

Now, I'm not really an easily emotional person, especially when friends are watching. But at that moment, something inside me snapped. Somebody flipped a switch in my heart, and I started to cry—I mean really cry. I was crying like I don't think I ever have.

This is the time when others make a judgment call about what kind of adult you will be.

It wasn't hesitation—I knew I was doing the right thing. It wasn't sorrow—I was glad to be following God's will. It was just the sheer emotion of such a momentous "break" from family. I buried my head in my mom's shoulder so that I didn't embarrass myself, but it was too late. Everybody was laughing. They actually thought I was joking! That's how ridiculous I sounded. But, believe me, it was no joke. I think it was one of the two hardest moments of my life. For I sensed that I was saying goodbye to life as I knew it, and it would never really return. Everything would be different now. I was in uncharted waters. That was a difficult feeling.

Everything in me wanted to unpack my cool stuff, move back into my great bedroom, and maintain that status quo of a wonderful childhood. Yet, there was a higher calling—the calling of adulthood and the calling of God to serve Him. That's the only thing that compelled me to take that long walk down the jet-way onto that airplane that day. I took my seat, read a card from my parents, and cried again. It was misery, excitement, pain, and anticipation all at once. It was an emotional roller coaster from moment to moment.

I knew I would never be a kid again. Yet, I wasn't fully an adult either. It was like being in "no-man's land." People didn't look at me as a child, but they didn't see me as an adult either. They expected me to act like an adult, but they didn't trust me with heavy adult responsibility. For instance, I couldn't have qualified for credit to buy a car; I couldn't have held a high paying job; and I couldn't have held a political office.

This time of life is very much a proving time. It's a time for you to reckon in your own heart who you will be and how your life will unfold. It's also a time to prove yourself to others—how you will handle college with no parents "on your case"—how you will perform on your first real job—etc., etc. This is the time when others make a judgment call about what kind of adult you will be. Most of all, it's a time for you to either "step up to the plate" in courage or "run for the clubhouse" in fear. In the coming years, you will either move forward in life, or you will try to stay where you are. To move forward, you'll need another critical tool in your "decision tool box"—a courageous spirit.

Choose to move forward in life.

Remember that "Toys R Us" campaign that sang "I don't wanna grow up; I'm a Toys R Us kid…there's a million toys at Toys R Us that I can play with"? There's a part of most young adults that secretly sings that song for about four years. Hey, your life has been bikes and trains and video games—why would you want to leave that all behind for bills and canes and insurance claims? For many young adults it goes beyond singing the song or secretly wishing that this easy life didn't have to get harder. They actually try to preserve their childhood. They do everything they can to "not leave home." They stay local. They work local. Local is comfortable. If staying local is God's plan, go for it, but for many it's simply "escapism." They just don't want to grow up.

So, they become 22, 24, 28-year-old kids. They still live at home, still have their model airplanes and Hardy Boys books, and still let Mom do their laundry. They over-stay their welcome in the land of childhood. Some people do this well into marriage by spending large amounts of time at Mom and Dad's—doing laundry, eating dinner, watching TV—rather than building their own family life. This is not only terrible for a young marriage, it's unnatural in the course of human existence. God commands us to "leave" father and mother and "cleave" to each other (Genesis 2:24).

In Exodus 14:15, God commands Moses to speak to the children of Israel and to tell them to "go forward." They had finally left Egypt and were standing at the Red Sea. Breathing down their backs was the entire Egyptian army. Impassible water was on one side, sure death on the other—but God commanded movement in the direction of the water. Here we have the first amphibious nation! I think if I was Moses I would have asked God if He was thinking clearly. Forward? You've got to be kidding! What? Are we gonna swim this thing?

You know the story. Moses had a choice. Go forward and trust God, or stay put and die. Apparently there was nothing worse than "staying put," so he did just as God commanded him. In response to his faith, God opened the entire Red Sea for the Israelites to pass through on dry ground and then drowned the Egyptian army in the same process. What a great God! What a great story! Uh-oh—there's a practical application.

Here you are with the choice of "staying put" or moving forward in life. The child in you wants security—wants to stay in your comfort zone. The adult in you is calling for forward motion. God is calling for forward motion. If you stay put, you'll not only be disobeying God, but you'll bring a slow and painful death to childhood as you know it. If you go forward, there are blessings to be had, victories to be won, life to be experienced, and even some childhood to be preserved. You now have to make a choice. Are you willing to say goodbye to the security of childhood in order to become the adult that God wants you to be? It's a tough, emotional, and trying decision, but one that must be made.

I've seen some young adults deal with this time of life by deciding *not* to decide. Somewhere along the line, they just blew a fuse trying to comprehend it all, and they decided not to face the future. The present and the past were comfortable, so they decided to stay there. They chose to avoid the major issues of life.

This kind of person usually gets a decent starter job locally—something slightly better than flipping burgers—and then they just vegetate! Day by day, they just let life happen to them. They exist while the world moves forward around them. They never think about their destiny, their eternal purpose, or their mission in life. They have no motivation, no vision, no desire, and no passion for life. Their goal is to maintain the status quo of their comfort zone. Can I give you some good advice? *Don't do this.*

> Be like Moses; speak to your heart and tell it to go forward!

If you earnestly seek and follow God's will, and He leads you to work locally, stay in your home church, and start your life right where you are, then obey Him. I'm not talking about you. You have no reason to feel insecure about staying close to home if God leads you that way.

I'm referring to someone who doesn't seek God, doesn't pray, doesn't have any desire to become anything—someone who just defaults in life doing and being whatever they can to get by. This is a lazy approach to life that takes advantage of parents and others. This kind of person builds his life upon *in*decision not *good* decisions.

You cannot avoid the decision-making process, even though a part of all of us would really like to. In trying to do so, you will make bad decisions; it's inevitable. It's a natural law of life that you cannot escape. Trying to avoid facing your decisions would be like trying to escape gravity or trying to keep the sun from rising. You just can't do it.

Be like Moses; speak to your heart and tell it to go forward! Determine with yourself that you will move ahead no matter how painful or uncomfortable the transition. Don't be a "Toys R Us Kid" the rest of your life. For the present, this will put you on a little tougher road, but there will come a day in the near future when you will truly be glad you made this decision.

Be strong and of good courage.

Though few transitions are as difficult as leaving home, there are many others between childhood and adulthood. In some ways each transition is a little bit like getting a bucket of cold water thrown on you in the shower. I'm in my thirties now, and I'm still having these experiences from time to time.

For instance, what does "summer" mean to you? When I was a kid, summer meant freedom. From morning to evening, we played—no school, no homework, no teachers, no books—just blue skies, bike jumps, and bubble gum! It was awesome. To some extent, you probably still have that perspective of "summer." Well, enjoy it; it's quickly coming to an end. In a short time summer will mean nothing more than regular workdays for you, only hotter.

That's the stuff of adult life. That's the "cold water" of transition. The good news is soon you'll have kids who will play all summer long—on your dime! Isn't that cool? You spent eighteen years playing on your parent's dime and now it's payback time.

Another example—What does a theme park mean to you? It probably means having fun with friends, riding great roller coasters, and being tall enough to ride everything. Well, that's about to change too. It did for me.

I loved Six Flags. I grew up going to Six Flags. I went for the thrills, for the fun, for me. It was especially fun to go to a theme park when I was dating my wife, Dana. There was something quite romantic about cotton candy, funnel cakes, and bumper cars. This was my total perspective on theme parks for all of my young twenty-two years—then we had kids.

Just a few short years after my college graduation, our two boys were old enough to take to Six Flags. My first thought was, "This will be a blast. These guys are gonna love the roller coasters!" I wasn't thinking clearly, and my wife made that abundantly clear.

The next thing I know, I'm stuck for an entire day at Six Flags in "Bugs Bunny Land" because my five-year-old Lance and two-year-old Larry aren't tall enough to ride anything interesting (though I did attempt to sneak them on a few death-defying roller coasters to no avail).

We spent the entire day in a part of the park I had never even seen and wished I hadn't. I was aching to ride anything taller than my waist. I even tried to bribe my wife to let me go ride something and meet her later (not a good idea). Other dads my age were there—trapped. We just waved at each other or exchanged a prayerful glance.

Trying to avoid facing your decisions would be like trying to escape gravity or trying to keep the sun from rising. You just can't do it.

Suddenly theme parks were not about *me*; they were about *them*—the kids! I was just their driver and financier!

Fast-forward five more years! Lance and Larry are now tall enough to ride the *cool* rides, but my body has been out of practice for so long, they are no longer fun! Not long ago I distinctly recall being on a roller coaster with Lance and Larry—my brains getting beat out by my safety restraint—and thinking, "Was there really a time in my life when this was fun?" Suddenly I find myself saying "Ooo, I don't feel so good" after riding the Merry-Go-Round! (Agghh, help; I'm trapped in the body of a dead-beat!)

I'm being facetious, but my point is it's a comical transition. If you want to know the truth, there's nothing so priceless as the face of your toddler while riding the race cars in "Bugs Bunny Land"! Until adulthood, life is so self-centered. Once you're an adult, you spend your life for others—your wife, your kids, your husband—and it's a lot better that way. Embrace it!

In no time flat you'll be pushing a stroller—video camera dangling from your neck, diaper bag over your shoulder—and waving to your precious offspring on his first kiddie-train ride. The look in his eyes will hold you spellbound as you watch him wonder at these first experiences. Then, when the ride is over, he'll come running back to you with a smile the size of Texas, arms waving, and eyes wide with wonder. You'll scoop him up, throw him in the air, and that's when it will hit you. You're the parent now—and it's so cool, you'll never look back! You won't even miss the roller coasters—that's how cool it is!

My first trip to Six Flags with my kids was actually my best trip. It was the first time that I spent the entire day watching someone else have fun. My kids couldn't stop hugging me, saying thank you, telling me how much they loved me. I was a *hero*! I had never been a hero before, and honestly, it was a lot better than being "cool" with my high school friends! *So what* if I push a stroller? *So what* if I drive a mini-van? *So what* if I spend money on binkys and diapers? I get to be a *hero*! I get to be loved by the three coolest little people on the planet! That's priceless. See, growing up does have its rewards!

> Your greatest temptation will be to shrink away in fear—fear of the unknown, fear of responsibility, fear of failure. Your decision will impact generations.

In Joshua chapter one, the children of Israel are once again standing in front of an impassible body of water. After forty years of wandering in the wilderness, they were almost ready to cross over the Jordan River into the Promised Land. They had one major problem, other than the river. Their leader had just died. Moses was gone, and God was planning to put Joshua in his place. It was a critical point for the entire nation, but especially for Joshua. Destiny was knocking on Joshua's door! God himself was telling Joshua that he was the next in line, and from reading the chapter, you get the idea that he was a little bit afraid of the responsibility.

God was calling Joshua to a huge leadership role, which also represented a major shift in his life. He was going from the "comfort zone" to the "pressure zone"! He was being told to lead millions of people into a land of unknown battles. He would be responsible for major decisions with unforeseen outcomes. He was one nervous dude. I'm sure there was a part of him that wanted to run into the wilderness and spend the rest of his life tending sheep. (I think there's a part of that in every leader.) The risks were great; the questions were many; and Joshua had a decision to make for the future of an entire nation.

God's command to Joshua is found first in Joshua 1:6, "Be strong and of a good courage...." This same command appears four times in this chapter! It's the very last thing told to Joshua in verse 18, "...only be strong and of a good courage." Why would God go to such lengths to emphasize this? Apparently the temptation was to "be weak and fearful." In the light of such huge responsibilities, Joshua would have felt small, incapable, and intimidated. His fear could have paralyzed him from doing God's will, and thus the fate of a nation would be decided.

Joshua chose to rely on God's promises and to shoulder the heavy responsibilities. He chose to believe that God would be with him. He chose to be courageous in the face of intimidation! He chose to face his fear in God's power. Because he left his comfort zone and stepped up to the Jordan River, the Promised Land was claimed, and the story of a nation was written.

You face the same decision that Joshua faced. There you stand—at your own Jordan River. On one side you have the familiarity of childhood—on the other, the uncharted territory of adulthood. God is calling you to be strong and very courageous. He is promising that He will be with you and that He will give you "good success" if you follow His Word. The task will seem too big for you. The calling will require personal sacrifice and uncomfortable transitions. Your greatest temptation will be to shrink away in fear—fear of the unknown, fear of responsibility, fear of failure. Your decision will impact generations.

I challenge you now to step up to that Jordan River by faith and "go for it"! Choose to have a courageous spirit by God's grace. Know that whatever He asks of you and wherever He leads you, He will be with you. He promises to strengthen you, to guide you, to give you rest, and to bless you. Though you don't see the future, He does! In His strength, you have nothing to fear.

God gave Joshua five statements that reveal five enemies of godly success. These are the things that will keep you from discovering your destiny, and they all revolve around God's command to be "strong and of a good courage."

Five Enemies of Your Future from Joshua 1

Apathy (vs. 6—*Be strong*)—The word *strong* implies that you should be "up to the task" and ready to move on it. It's like someone just kicked you and said, "Get a move on!" Don't be content *not caring about your future. Get on with it.*

Fear (vs. 6—*Be courageous*)—There will be plenty of things to be afraid of. Don't be. If God leads you, go forward and refuse to fear.

Ignorance (vs. 8—*Know God's Word*)—God says you need to know His Word. If you don't know it, you can't follow it, and you'll be spiritually ignorant in life—one of the very worst ways to live.

Rebellion (vs. 8—*Do God's Word*)—Refusing to obey God's Word puts you in a very dangerous category. Saul rebelled, and God said that his rebellion was "as the sin of witchcraft" (1 Samuel 15:23). Rebellion does the same thing to the spiritual mind that drugs and alcohol do to the physical mind. Rebellion causes a person to lose all perspective on reality and do things that just don't make sense.

Distraction (vs. 9—*Be not dismayed*)—This word implies that Joshua could have been distracted from God's will. Determine that you will not be "broken down" or "torn away" from following God courageously. You will certainly have opportunities to do things outside of God's will, and you must be determined not to be moved.

Bottom line…it takes courage. It took courage for me to hug my family, say good-bye to life as I knew it, and board an airplane to the future. It will take courage in your life to face the transitions that God will lead you through. It will require a conscious decision to step up to the banks of your Jordan River with a "no fear" attitude to seize God's blessings for your future.

Here is what God says to you in 2 Timothy 1:7, "For God hath not given us the spirit of fear; but of power, and of love, and of a sound mind." Let that verse sink in and let it change your perspective on the unknowns of the future. Enter the coming decade with a spirit "of power, and of love, and of a sound mind." Remind yourself of this verse when a spirit of fear starts to choke out your courage.

The devil will do anything he can to make you afraid, hesitant, and doubtful of the future. He wants you to shrink away in fear rather than step up in faith. He doesn't want you to cross your "Jordan." Yet, you must. Many people are depending upon you—people whom you haven't met yet, but people whom you will one day love more than yourself!

I echo the words to you: "Be strong and of a good courage." Trust your God to be with you and launch into adulthood with courage! He will never fail you.

So He will be with me

During the eighteen years that I lived under my parent's roof, there was one small symbol of stability that was always there. It was a symbol of authority and provision, a symbol of education and wisdom. It was a symbol of spiritual growth, encouragement, and care. To this day that symbol still holds its place in my dad's shirt pocket—a gold Cross pen. As far back as I can remember, my dad always had a gold Cross pen. He took it everywhere and used it constantly. He used it while working hard on the job to care for his family. He used it to study the Word of God. He used it to pay bills that I helped to create. He used it to write me notes of encouragement at critical times in my life. He used it to pay school bills and to provide for the needs of his own. To this day, when I visit my dad, he still uses his gold Cross pen. The significance of that pen never really hit me. I took it for granted. Though it followed me throughout my entire upbringing, I never really gave it much thought...until a few weeks ago.

Something happened that brought these memories flooding back into my consciousness. I was reminded once again of my father's choice as a young man to face adulthood with a spirit of courage. I considered his character even in the face of mistakes. I was reminded of his steadfast commitment to his own family through the years and of his faithfulness to his Heavenly Father. I considered how his decisions very much impacted my destiny. I suddenly felt as though the baton had been handed to me. Now I'm the father, the husband, the spiritual leader. Now I'm the one that someone else depends upon.

All of this seemed to instantly fill my heart with strength and courage from the Lord. It was as though God was reminding me to continue to go forward in faith with a courageous spirit. I thought of His promise to Joshua, "as I was with Moses, so I will be with thee." I applied that promise personally—as He was with my father, so He will be with me! God used a small gesture to bring this Heavenly reminder to my heart—a gift from some friends. I opened it; I looked at it; I smiled with remembrance. Then with a courageous determination to be the man God wants me to be, I proudly slipped it into my shirt pocket—a beautiful new gold Cross pen.

It's time for you to make the same choice. It's time to shoulder the mantle of adult life with a godly courage and confidence. Claim

His promises and trust His Word. As He was with Moses and Joshua, so He will be with you!

"Finally, my brethren, be strong in the Lord,
and in the power of his might."
—Ephesians 6:10

nine

Hey, Buddy, You've Got Boardwalk!!

Tool #4 for Right Decision-Making—God's Wisdom

So, are you feeling any heavier? Has the decision-making process and all it represents become a little more serious to you over the first eight chapters? If you're like I was, by now, you're scared to death to make a decision! That's a good thing if that *fear* is in truth a fear of God and if it drives you to your knees in seeking Him. It's a bad thing if it drives you to *paranoia*. Don't get psyched out about it all, just get determined.

Up to this point we've discovered some key things that you need to remember: 1) You're incapable of doing this yourself. 2) You're in the mistake zone of life. 3) You have an eternal purpose for God—your destiny. 4) You have desires and abilities that could help or hinder your destiny. 5) Tool #1—You must have a serious mind. 6) Tool #2—You must have a pure heart. 7) Tool #3—You must have a courageous spirit.

Tool #4—The Wisdom of God

There is yet another tool that you must possess in order to make right decisions—the wisdom of God. Wisdom is spiritual understanding, the ability to see and understand things the way that God sees them. Wisdom causes you to see through a situation to understand what's really going on. It looks "beneath the surface" and discerns things that most people completely miss. Wisdom is the ability to understand spiritual truth—God's reality—and to respond properly.

When your grandparents were kids, and TV was still a new idea, one of the first TV shows to be produced was "Superman." When I was a kid, they were still running Superman re-runs after school in the afternoons, and I liked to watch them, even though the special effects left somewhat to be desired (like the way they never showed Superman's feet when he was flying…guess they didn't want you to see that diving board he was strapped to).

There was one really cool thing that Superman could do that always interested me! For some reason the bad guys were always hiding in caves, but that was never a problem for Superman. He had the ability to see straight through rock walls and see exactly where the bad guys were and what they were doing. It's called x-ray vision. (How he always found the right cave?—that's another issue completely.) It seemed that in almost every episode Superman was looking through mountains to find the bad guys making their plans.

> *Wisdom is spiritual understanding, the ability to see and understand things the way that God sees them.*

Wisdom is a lot like spiritual x-ray vision. When God gives you wisdom, He gives you the understanding to see through the rock walls of an issue. He gives you the perception to see the spiritual implications of a decision. He helps you to think through a situation with real discernment, rather than rush in, oblivious to danger.

If the concept of "your destiny in God's eternal purpose" is easy for you to accept, this is probably because you have gained a measure of spiritual understanding and wisdom from God's Word over the years. If this concept is new, unfamiliar, or strange to you, then you are probably new to a walk with Christ, and you're simply lacking some spiritual understanding that makes it clear. If you understand the danger of doing things your own way, it's because God has given you the wisdom to see things His way.

God says it this way in Isaiah 55:8–9, "For my thoughts are not your thoughts, neither are your ways my ways, saith the Lord. For as the heavens are higher than the earth, so are my ways higher than your ways, and my thoughts than your thoughts." Again He says in Romans 11:33, "O the depth of the riches both of the wisdom and knowledge of God! how unsearchable are his judgments, and his ways past finding out!" God sees things as they truly are, not only as they appear. Those who see things His way always come out ahead spiritually. It's that simple.

God is literally saying in this passage, "The way I see things is different from the way you see things—and I'm right!"

Have you ever been on a high mountaintop where you could see for miles? My favorite mountaintop experience is in Yosemite National Park. As a senior-higher, one of my favorite things to do was to pack up my camping gear and go backpacking in Yosemite. After one trip to Yosemite Valley as a tourist, I knew I just had to see more of this amazing place! I literally fell in love with God's handiwork in that awesome national park.

On my first trip, and then on two other trips, my favorite experience was to climb the backside of "Halfdome"—a large rock mountain shaped like half of a dome. At first sight, this mountain looks like something only a crazy person would climb, but in actuality there is a trail that goes up the back side of the mountain that's relatively easy (except for the last few hundred feet—but even that's worth the risk).

After about six hours of climbing and a few hundred final feet of cables, you arrive at the vast and breathtaking granite peak of Halfdome—one of the world's most famous sites. It's awesome! It's about the size of three football fields, and it features one edge that drops a sheer two thousand feet to the floor of Yosemite Valley (where all the non-hikers ride in open-air trams and gawk up with video cameras and Styrofoam cups of coffee).

At the top, there are no tourists trams, petting zoos, or snack shops. At the top, there's just fresh air, windy gusts, tough people, and the world's greatest view! It seems as though you can see the entire world from the top of this magnificent monument, and you could sit for hours studying God's grand design of Yosemite National Park. It's captivating and miraculous.

When it comes to our lives, our view is about like the person in the open-air tram; it's really limited. We can't see around trees or through mountains. We can't see over peaks or above waterfalls. We can really only see what's directly around us. It's actually a pretty crumby view.

But from God's vantage point, it's a whole different story. When looking at your life, it's as though He's on top of the world. He sees the beginning and the end. He knows every bend in the road, every turn, every detail. He sees it all and wants to guide you with His wisdom. When He gives you wisdom, He gives you the ability to see a part of your life from His vantage point, and no amount of human wisdom could ever compare to His view!

I've been continually amazed at how great a difference there is between someone with spiritual wisdom and someone without it. These two types of people can look at the exact same situation and come up with two completely different conclusions and response plans. What seems to be common sense to one seems absolutely foreign to the other. This applies to keeping a marriage together, finding a job, managing your finances, raising your children, and a million other decisions you'll face.

There are two types of people on this planet. There are those who see things the way they really are and respond properly, and there are those who see things the way they think they are, and it takes them a lifetime to figure out they were wrong. The first group learns by seeking godly wisdom. The second group learns by making mistakes.

As a youth pastor, I've taken my fair share of teenagers to McDonalds over the years. In fact, if there were a Guinness world record for this, I'm sure I would hold it. About every other year or so, McDonalds re-invents their prize game "Monopoly" and starts handing out little game pieces on large cokes, large fries, and other products. About the most I've ever won was a free breakfast sandwich. The game goes like this—you get a paper Monopoly game board FREE from the front counter, and then you buy food—lots and lots of food, and you collect game pieces off of the food containers (whether or not you actually eat the food is irrelevant).

As you collect the game pieces, you will occasionally receive an "instant winner" which means you get a free coke or something—yet another way to bring you back to the restaurant so you can buy more food. These "instant winners" bring great cause for rejoicing, and after you stop jumping up and down clapping your hands, you'll look to see what other game pieces you received.

Then you begin matching the game pieces to the free paper game board. Over time (and lots of Big Macs), if you collect any three or four pieces of the same color, you will be the lucky recipient of some great prize—a Sea Doo, an iPod, a computer, a cool car, or even possibly "a million bucks"!! (That's dollars, not deer.) The prizes are always cool enough to get you to buy one more thing, and chances are, in the end, you'll end up with 42 "Park Places," 36 "Reading Railroads," 52 pounds of flab, several clogged arteries, and no cool car! It's a great game…really!

When God gives you wisdom, He gives you the understanding to see through the rock walls of an issue.

There's one thing I can tell you about this Monopoly game—seventh graders are obsessive over it! Several years ago, while the Monopoly game was "on," I took our entire youth group to McDonalds for dinner. For the most part, we all bought our food, looked at our game pieces, and moved on with our lives. Not the seventh graders. They snapped! To this day, I can't really explain it psychologically, but it was quite a phenomenon.

I was just trying to calmly enjoy my order, when suddenly the seventh graders started running from table to table inspecting everybody's game pieces. Then they started collecting them—as though having more of everything increased their chances of winning! It was nuts, yet it went on for about ten minutes. It was like someone blew a whistle and started the great Monopoly game piece hunt. Very calmly I pulled one of them aside and asked him, "What are you doing?"

"We're getting Monopoly pieces," came the reply, without much solid reason behind it.

"Why?" I asked flatly.

"Because we want to win!!" he said with a bit of a maniacal glare.

"But having forty-two 'Park Places' doesn't increase your chances of winning!" I tried to reason.

"But we still want them," he said giggling and running off to ask the next table for their unwanted game pieces.

I sat there for ten minutes watching fifteen mindless seventh graders do something that made no sense. (That was the first time I began to think that perhaps we did come from monkeys!)

At that same moment it occurred to me, that somewhere in America there was an elderly man who would walk into McDonalds, as he does every morning, for his coffee and hash brown. I pictured him in my mind with his sweater, his newspaper, and his desire for some quiet solitude and a piping hot cup of coffee. He's not interested in Monopoly game pieces. He's not even worried about winning a cool car. He just wants his coffee and quiet. So, he finds a silent corner of the restaurant and takes his seat to read and enjoy his morning. This is his routine, his way of starting the day, every day. It works.

After thirty minutes of personal retreat, he quietly folds his paper up, sips the last of his coffee, gently slides everything but

the tray into the trash bin, and makes his way into another day—
completely unaware that he just threw away "Boardwalk" and one
million bucks!

He didn't even know there was a million bucks to be won, much
less think of how he might have used it. It was his, but he never
claimed it. He had it in his hands, but never realized it. How it might
have changed his family and friends, one can only speculate. But
now we'll never know. It's
gone—into the trash, into
a truck, out to the dump,
and soon to be recycled in
the "circle of life."

Millions of people
all over the nation are
saving "Park Place" so
that this guy can *throw
away* "Boardwalk"! Kind

> *"How much better is it to get*
>
> *wisdom than gold! and to get*
>
> *understanding rather to be*
>
> *chosen than silver!"*
>
> —Proverbs 16:16

of "gets you;" doesn't it? Who does this guy think he is anyway?
What kind of idiot gets a cup of coffee and a hash brown without
looking at the game piece. Doesn't he know that's the whole point?
Why, this guy oughta be...

Whoa there, stranger, settle down. It's just a story. But it
could happen.

Indeed it does happen every day in the spiritual realm! It's not
a game, and there are no cool cars to be won. It's real life, and the
stakes are life itself. The "seventh graders" (the simple minded of
life) spend all of their energies running to and fro trying to get as
many losing game pieces as they can! It's a no-win life. There are no
true prizes to claim, no spiritual blessings to be had, and no eternal
purpose to be fulfilled.

From job to job, toy to toy, relationship to relationship, they
run—looking for some kind of temporary fix to their emptiness.
They giggle, they play, they "party" the days away looking for their
reward, and there's not one shred of eternal rhyme or reason to any
of their madness. They seem happy at times, but if you stop them

in the middle of their mayhem, you'll discover that they're on a meaningless journey with no purpose.

Then there's a Christian young adult, maybe you, who is preparing to start his adult life with the winning element—the wisdom of God—right there on his tray. It's there for the claiming. It's there to be understood and applied. It holds all the answers for a successful life. It offers true understanding for godly success. Yet this Christian never realizes the treasure he holds or the wealth of wisdom to which he has access, and he starts his life with no thought of what he is neglecting! The greatest unclaimed resource of life has again gone unclaimed, untapped, unsought—and another life is destined to see things "the wrong way"!

Here's what the Bible says about the importance of wisdom in your life:

"For this cause we…do not cease to pray for you, and to desire that ye might be filled with the knowledge of his will in all wisdom and spiritual understanding" (Colossians 1:9).

"Then said I, Wisdom is better than strength…" (Ecclesiastes 9:16).

"Wisdom is better than weapons of war…" (Ecclesiastes 9:18).

"Wisdom strengtheneth the wise more than ten mighty men which are in the city" (Ecclesiastes 7:19).

"Through wisdom is an house builded; and by understanding it is established:" (Proverbs 24:3).

"He that getteth wisdom loveth his own soul: he that keepeth understanding shall find good" (Proverbs 19:8).

"How much better is it to get wisdom than gold! and to get understanding rather to be chosen than silver!" (Proverbs 16:16).

"The lips of the righteous feed many: but fools die for want of wisdom" (Proverbs 10:21).

"Get wisdom, get understanding: forget it not; neither decline from the words of my mouth" (Proverbs 4:5).

"Wisdom is the principal thing; therefore get wisdom: and with all thy getting get understanding" (Proverbs 4:7).

"The fear of the LORD is the beginning of knowledge: but fools despise wisdom and instruction" (Proverbs 1:7).

For you, the winning game piece is the wisdom of God! In God's Word, He tells you "wisdom is the principle thing"! He says to "get wisdom" and to "get understanding." He says that "fools die" because they don't have it and that wisdom is better than money or treasure! He says it strengthens and establishes! Words cannot describe the power and the impact that godly wisdom will have on your life; it will change the way you see and respond to everything. In some ways these thoughts relate closely to the pure heart in chapter seven, but there are some key principles that you must understand about wisdom.

Words cannot describe the power and the impact that godly wisdom will have on your life; it will change the way you see and respond to everything.

True wisdom is gained only from God.

The Bible speaks of two types of wisdom. In James 3:13–17, God says, "Who is a wise man and endued with knowledge among you? let him shew out of a good conversation his works with meekness of wisdom. But if ye have bitter envying and strife in your hearts, glory not, and lie not against the truth. This wisdom descendeth not from above, but is earthly, sensual, devilish. For where envying and strife is, there is confusion and every evil work. But the wisdom that is from above is first pure, then peaceable, gentle, and easy to be intreated, full of mercy and good fruits, without partiality, and without hypocrisy."

There are two distinct types of wisdom—an earthly, devilish way of seeing things and a heavenly, godly way of seeing things. The two are opposite; they oppose each other. They cannot co-exist in the same mind. They cannot agree. One is absolutely and undeniably true and the other is utterly false. The scary part is you will make your decisions through one of the two!

The Bible is clear that God's way of thinking is the opposite of the world's. In 1 Corinthians 1:20–22 and 24, God says it this way, "Where is the wise? where is the scribe? where is the disputer of this world? hath not God made foolish the wisdom of this world? For after that in the wisdom of God the world by wisdom knew not God, it pleased God by the foolishness of preaching to save them that believe. For the Jews require a sign, and the Greeks seek after wisdom: But we preach Christ crucified, unto the Jews a stumblingblock, and unto the Greeks foolishness; But unto them which are called, both Jews and Greeks, Christ the power of God, and the wisdom of God."

> *There are two distinct types of wisdom—an earthly, devilish way of seeing things and a heavenly, godly way of seeing things.*

Godly wisdom usually experiences worldly opposition.

If you see things God's way, through the eyes of spiritual understanding, it won't make sense to people who see things the world's way! Be ready for this. Almost every young adult knows friends or family members who have preconceived ideas of success. If you follow God by faith, it won't make sense to these people. In their eyes, you'll be throwing your life away. Stay the course! When all is said and done, you won't give account to these people, and they won't have to live with the consequences of your decisions. Their opinions of you or your direction mean nothing to your eternal destiny. I'm not saying don't listen to godly counsel; we'll get to that later. I am saying be prepared to be ridiculed for your faith and for seeing things that others don't. It won't make sense to those without God's wisdom.

The Bible says it this way in 1 Corinthians 2:14, "But the natural man receiveth not the things of the Spirit of God: for they are foolishness unto him: neither can he know them, because they are spiritually discerned."

When I chose to serve in ministry and went to Bible college, I had friends and family that thought I was making a mistake. They "jabbed" at me at times with hurtful remarks or innuendos. I'm sure they commented behind my back, but I knew I was following God, and that's all that mattered. Earthly wisdom just doesn't think like godly wisdom does.

Time always proves that godly wisdom was right and that earthly wisdom was wrong. Fifteen years down the road in my life, it's obvious that my decisions were right and that those of others (even some who "jabbed") were wrong. Let God and time be your "vindicator" and do what you know is right.

Godly wisdom is more valuable than elevated education.

Proverbs 4:7 says, "Wisdom is the principal thing; therefore get wisdom: and with all thy getting get understanding."

I've talked to dozens of parents and young adults about their futures and one of the most common replacements for godly wisdom is higher education. We live in a world that worships education. Education is power and influence. Education is the answer for all social and political ills. Education is the idol of many modern-day adults.

Please understand, I am not minimizing the importance of education. I'm not saying that wisdom replaces education. They actually work *together*, and you need *both*. I believe strongly that you need the best education you can get. Yet, education by itself will leave you lost in life. Granted, you'll be a smart lost person, but you will utterly fail without godly wisdom. First Corinthians 8:1 says, "…Knowledge puffeth up." What good is education if you don't know how to use it and apply it? What good is education if you cannot stay married or rear a godly family? The world is full of very smart people who do very dumb things; they know a lot, but they have no true spiritual understanding.

On the other hand, when you combine a well-educated mind with true heavenly wisdom, you're headed for godly success! It's extremely important that you get everything you can out of your high school and college classes. You will depend on this knowledge for the rest of your life! I echo the thoughts of God's Word to you—"with all of your getting, get wisdom and understanding." Yet, don't fall for the line that education alone is enough. You'll be sorely disappointed.

It seems that one of the goals of higher education is "open-mindedness." At secular colleges and universities you'll be taught that the Bible is closed-minded and that you should be more open-minded. Everything that you believe will be brought into question under the guise of being "open-minded." Most people think that the only alternative to being "open-minded" is being "closed-minded." Yet, this isn't true.

The goal of the Christian should not be either! The Christian's goal is to be "Christ-minded"! Philippians 2:5 says, "Let this mind be in you, which was also in Christ Jesus." Your heart and mind should be as opened and closed on every issue as is the mind of Jesus Christ. This is the bottom line, and this will take wisdom.

Wisdom is gained by asking for it continually.

Hey, wake up! This is the best part of this chapter. You've got to get it!

How can you get wisdom? Does it take some kind of special course of study or a lifetime search? Does it require that you graduate from a special school or pass some kind of "wisdom test"? No.

God says the way to get wisdom is to simply *ask for it!* He says in James 1:5, "If any of you lack wisdom, let him ask of God, that giveth to all men liberally, and upbraideth not; and it shall be given him." God promises that if you ask for wisdom, He will not only give it to you—He will give it *liberally*. Wow, what a great promise! This is far better than having "Boardwalk" on your Monopoly piece—and not asking for wisdom is far worse than throwing "Boardwalk" away! This is the world's greatest untapped resource—the Christian's most undiscovered treasure! The Creator of the universe, the Source of all wisdom, the Almighty God of Heaven tells you that you can have a liberal supply of heavenly wisdom—*if you ask!* What an *awesome* gift!

What would you do if I told you that the million-dollar winning Monopoly piece was in the back left corner trash bin of your local McDonalds right now? Nobody knows it's there, and you can have it if you want it—some guy threw it away without looking at it.

No doubt, you would find the fastest way to that McDonalds and dive head first into that trash bin. The food, the cokes, the ketchup, the trash wouldn't bother you…for a million bucks! You would figure that's a small price to pay! You would tear that trash bin apart, searching intently, until you found the treasure you were looking for. So would I.

Now, what would you do if I told you that the Source of all true wisdom has offered His wisdom freely and liberally to you if you will ask? Yawn? Fold your arms and doze? "Check out" mentally in Sunday school class or church wishing you didn't have to be there? Well, here's your wake up call, Einstein!

You have *huge* decisions just ahead; you have no idea which way to choose; and you need God's wisdom. So start asking. Ask now. Ask tomorrow. Ask the next day. Decide right now that you won't let a day go by without asking for this great treasure of life. Ask continually for wisdom and know that God will answer your prayer!

God's response to someone who seeks wisdom

God responds to a person who will ask for wisdom, and generally He's pretty kind to them. In 1 Kings 3:5–14, God came to Solomon in a dream asking him what He could give him. Rather than ask for riches or power, Solomon said it this way: "And now, O LORD my God, thou hast made thy servant king instead of David my father: and I am but a little child: I know not how to go out or come in. And thy servant is in the midst of thy people which thou hast chosen, a great people, that cannot be numbered nor counted for multitude. Give therefore thy servant an understanding heart to judge thy people, that I may discern between good and bad: for who is able to judge this thy so great a people?"

Solomon's request made God so happy that He said, "Because thou hast asked this thing, and hast not asked for thyself long life; neither hast asked riches for thyself, nor hast asked the life of thine enemies; but hast asked for thyself understanding to discern judgment; Behold, I have done according to thy words: lo, I have given thee a wise and an understanding heart; so that there was none like thee before thee, neither after thee shall any arise like unto thee. And I have also given thee that which thou hast not asked, both riches, and honour: so that there shall not be any among the kings like unto thee all thy days. And if thou wilt walk in my ways, to keep my statutes and my commandments, as thy father David did walk, then I will lengthen thy days."

While young adults your age are busy asking God for cars, spouses, jobs, and things, I urge you to follow Solomon's example. Rather than asking God to fulfill your plans or dreams; rather than asking Him to do what you want; rather than asking Him to reveal His will to you—start asking for wisdom!

Most spiritual young people are consumed with needing to know God's will. Every time they pray, they're begging God to show them what they should do with their lives. While seeking God in this way is commendable, this type of praying often misses the most important prayer. God will reveal His will in His time. He hasn't hidden it for you to hunt down like "lost treasure." This is not some kind of cosmic Easter-egg hunt. He will show you what He wants when He wants. What you need now is the wisdom to see and understand God today!

More than anything else, you should be asking God for wisdom. He will not only answer you fully, but He will also give a lot that you didn't ask for. I challenge you right now to permanently place wisdom at the top of your prayer list for the rest of your life; you'll need it every day!

> *Rather than asking God to fulfill your plans or dreams; rather than asking Him to do what you want… start asking for wisdom!*

You'll never feel like you actually have it.

The thing that makes it difficult to ask for wisdom is that it is intangible! Hey, if I ask God for a job or a car, and He answers—I can see it, touch it, experience it. I can tell everybody else to look at the answer to my prayer! It's a great experience. Asking for wisdom seems somewhat obscure in comparison; therefore, many people never get around to it. We're so distracted by our selfish prayers that we forget what we really need!

You'll never really feel like you have wisdom. You could spend a lifetime asking for it and never be able to pinpoint a moment when you actually felt "wise." Don't expect to ask God and *BOOM*—lightning strikes one day, and suddenly you're a "wise guy"! It's not a feeling or an electrifying experience. There's no magic moment, no arrival date, no special package in the mail, and no "paranormal experience." It's rather dry and "feelingless." You'll only know that God gave you wisdom when you've lived long enough to look back on His guidance in your life.

Here's how it works. Start asking now. Trust by faith that God is giving it to you, even though you don't know it or feel it. Keep on asking. Live twenty years. Turn around and look back. Suddenly you'll see decision after decision that you could have blown, but somehow every one of them was made right. That's wisdom! That's how God will answer your request for wisdom.

Wisdom is not a Christmas present that you can open; it's not a winning game piece you can claim; but it's just as real and far more valuable. The best part—you don't have to be some lucky "one-in-forty-billion" to have it. Just ask for it—anytime, anywhere, and *BOOM*—you can have it! (Without the *BOOM!*)

So, what will it be? Earthly wisdom? Are you interested in running around for the rest of your life collecting losing game pieces—spending your life on frivolous pursuits that mean nothing? Or will it be heavenly wisdom—gained by simply asking? You can live your life seeing things for what they really are—seeing them the way that God sees them.

Follow the pattern of Jesus in Luke 2:52, "And Jesus increased in wisdom and stature, and in favour with God and man." Go to God; go to His Word and start asking for wisdom today! Colossians 3:16 says, "Let the word of Christ dwell in you richly in all wisdom."

Don't be like the "seventh-graders" of this world. (If you're in seventh grade—sorry. Don't worry, you'll grow out of it.)

Don't be the guy with the coffee and hash browns either. Don't throw away the most valuable resource available to you. Decide that tool #4—the wisdom of God—is one that you won't miss out on. Start asking right now.

"Wisdom is the principal thing…"
—Proverbs 4:7

ten

Believing is Seeing
Tool #5 for Right Decision-Making—A Life of Faith

Up to this point, the decision-making process looks something like this: 1) Realize you can't do it alone. 2) Know you're in the mistake zone of life. 3) Believe you have an eternal purpose for God—your destiny. 4) Develop your desires and abilities but don't pursue them in the place of God. 5) Develop a serious mind. 6) Purify your heart. 7) Choose to have a courageous spirit. 8) Begin asking God for wisdom (spiritual insight).

Tool #5—A Life of Faith

There's yet one more tool to throw into your "belt" before we wrap up by talking about how to use these tools to make right decisions. In order to really find your destiny you must be willing to live by faith.

What is faith? Hebrews 11:1 says, "Now faith is the substance of things hoped for, the evidence of things not seen." Faith is the substance of the things you hope for—happiness, true success, purpose in life, God's blessings. If you will ever discover your true destiny you must realize that its very substance (its reality) will be found through faith.

Faith is the evidence for things that you cannot see. Think about that. You cannot see the family God will give you, the life He will let you live, the dreams He will allow you to fulfill; yet you know these things exist in God's mind. How? By faith. You believe in your heart that God has written your life's story according to His eternal purpose, and all you have to do is allow Him to reveal it to you. That belief is faith, and that faith is the substance and the evidence of your destiny.

Worldly wisdom doesn't understand this rationale! Most people would say "Show me, and I'll believe." God says, "Believe Me, and I'll show you!" Yet, in the mind of the typical unsaved man, it doesn't make sense that you would completely leave your destiny in the unseen hands of an unseen God. That's much too risky. It feels like a blind approach to life. Yet, that's the only way to truly guarantee yourself to find your destiny.

My personal lesson in faith

One of the most uncertain times of my life, from a human perspective, was my last semester of college. Dana and I had been married during Christmas break, enjoyed a wonderful honeymoon, and returned to school with great anticipation of beginning our lives together. I had five short months of school left and had no idea what would happen after that. Graduation was as far forward as I could see. Beyond the month of May my future was an unwritten script. It was as though we were heading into "nothingness"! Nerve-racking? Potentially.

I was twenty-one, newly married, barely able to afford the "payments" on my new bride, and had no idea where we would spend our lives or what we would be doing. I was planning to serve the Lord and that's all I could say! From a human perspective it should have been a very scary feeling, but from the faith perspective it was a completely secure position.

Years earlier, something had happened in my life that had prepared me for just such an "insecure" moment. As a junior in high school God placed a real burden in my heart that life was suddenly getting very serious. I was surrendered completely to His will, but I had no idea what that will was. That drove me nuts. It was a very frustrating thought. So, my response was to begin searching for God's perfect will in His Word. I was actually afraid that I would make a wrong choice and miss out on my destiny. I feared ending my life with regret rather than reward. Being in "no man's land" bothered me deep inside. When someone asked me what I was going to do with my life I simply said, "I'm going to serve the Lord somehow. I just don't know how."

Most mornings I would try to take a walk before school and pray. Mostly I asked God for wisdom and to prepare me for His will. Then, on occasion I would retreat to my bedroom, pull out my Strong's Concordance, and begin looking up any verse I could find about following the Lord.

> Most people would say, "Show me, and I'll believe." God says, "Believe Me, and I'll show you!"

I know it sounds spiritual, but most of the time it was out of sheer panic. I was one scared teenager. I knew that God had this destiny thing all pre-planned, and I didn't want to mess it up. I wanted to stand before Him and hear, "Well done!"

Then, the moment came when God gave my seventeen-year-old heart what it was looking for. In my reading, I came to Psalm 32:8 which says, "I will instruct thee and teach thee in the way which thou shalt go. I will guide thee with mine eye." Whoa! Vapor lock again! I stopped, I read it again, and I breathed one long sigh of relief. It was as though God personally spoke that verse directly to my heart. I sat there as a searching, nervous, scared teenager, and God reached out His hand to steady my fears and to relieve my pressure. He called an immediate halt to all of my frantic searching.

Suddenly it was clear that finding my destiny was not up to me. It was up to God. My responsibility was to simply trust Him by faith, wait on Him, and stay in a position where He could guide me. In that verse God personally told me that His eye was on me, He would guide me, and He would let me know which way to go in life. To me, it was a guarantee that so long as I was right with God, He would not let me make a wrong decision for my future. Mentally, I pictured that God was looking down on me, watching every turn in my journey, and promising me that He would not allow a wrong turn. What a relief!

In that moment, my fears and panic left, never to return, and all of the unknowns of the future were relegated completely to God's control. The central focus of my heart transitioned from finding God's will to being faithful to God so He could lead me into His will. The focus of my future became faith rather than sight. Suddenly it didn't matter to me if I could see or know what God's will was. I was content to know that He knew and He promised to guide me on the right path. Rather than feeling like God was "afar off" expecting me to search for His "hidden will," I realized that God was near me, leading and guiding my choices. Though His plan was a mystery to me, I accepted that it was no mystery to Him. As long as I was right with Him there was no way I could miss it!

Fast forward to my last semester of college. I still didn't know much about what the future held, but I was four years closer to it. When I looked at the horizon of my life, there were no specifics, and I was tempted to let the fear and panic return. From the perspective of a normal college graduate, my approach to life would have been sheer lunacy. But wait—it gets worse.

Dana and I began to pray that God would lead us and show us where to go. In five months our house lease would end, our schooling would be done, our savings would be gone, and we would be "street people" living in an old refrigerator box for all I knew. That was the sight perspective, but we didn't spend much time dwelling on that.

The catch is that we were completely surrendered to God's perfect will, and we were confident, by faith, that He would guide us. We knew that something would happen in God's time. To our great delight, something did happen! (Surprise, surprise!) In March of that semester, God began to answer the unknowns of our future, just as He had promised four years earlier—and right on time! It all started with a phone call from Pastor Paul Chappell of the Lancaster Baptist Church in Lancaster, California.

During my college years, Lancaster Baptist had grown from about 25 to about 600 in attendance, and Pastor Chappell asked us to consider joining the staff at the church. After an interview, a season of prayerful consideration, and a lot of discussion, we felt sure that God was opening a door for us to go to Lancaster, California. God told me exactly what I needed to know exactly when I needed to know it. He was faithful to His promise in response to our faith. This was an awesome experience!

...for four years I rested in not knowing my future. (That's the faith part.) In time, God revealed His plan just as promised. (That's the substance part!)

Consider this—for four years I rested in *not* knowing my future. (That's the faith part.) In time, God revealed His plan just as promised. (That's the substance part!) And there's more.

The decision to go to Lancaster was enormous! Words could never describe the mammoth implications that this one decision made on the entire outcome of our lives. Yet, there were still dozens of unanswered questions. In fact, the answering of one question became the birth of a hundred more!

When I asked Pastor Chappell what I would be doing at the church, he wasn't sure and said that he was praying about it. This means I had accepted a job that I knew nothing about. My salary never one time came up in our discussions, which means I had no idea what I would be paid. I didn't know where we would live or how our ministry would unfold. Could I use my gifts? Would I see my dreams unfold? Would I be able to do something I enjoyed? In addition to this, Dana had never been to Lancaster—a desert city in southern California. Would she even like it? Was there shopping there? On and on the questions could go, and we didn't have answers for any of them. We had blindly accepted a position we knew very little about—by faith!

Take the secular approach for a moment. Who in their right mind would graduate from a university and accept a position in a part of the country they had never seen, work for a firm they knew little about, with no idea what they would be paid or what they would be doing? You would call this person "out to lunch"!

In the secular world, you finish your degree and then begin hunting for the fulfillment of your career dream. When you find the place you'd like to live and work, you negotiate a salary package, discuss benefits, investigate a locale, and bargain for perks and position. It's a sight-based proposition, and you would be considered foolish to approach it any other way.

In the spiritual realm, it all happens differently. It happens by faith. It's not blind faith. Blind faith would involve trusting something with no substance or evidence. The intelligent faith that God commands us to live by is based on substance and evidence. This is a verifiable faith because it always moves God to action. When you trust God by faith, He is always pleased, and He will always honor that faith.

As a teenager, I chose my future based on my faith in God. Had I chosen my future based on sight and reason, my life would have unfolded in a completely different sequence—and it would have been wrong. Yet, by faith I chose to follow God. Time would tell the tale, and God proved Himself to be real and to be right in my life.

For eighteen wonderful years I have experienced the fruit of that decision as God has responded to my faith. In a nutshell, we moved to Lancaster not knowing what we would do, where we would live, or what we would be paid. Over the eighteen years to follow, Lancaster has become our home, our church has grown to more than 4,500, our family has grown to five, every bill has been

I found out that the script of my life as God saw it was far better than any script I could have imagined!

paid, and God has given us more privileges and opportunities in ministry than I would have ever dreamed. (And there was even "shopping" in Lancaster!)

I found out .that the script of my life as God saw it was far better than any script I could have imagined! Choosing the *faith* path (the path I couldn't see) was far better than choosing the sight path. I knew in my heart that God's plan would be better, I just couldn't predict how much better. Little did I know the awesome blessings I would have missed had I lived by sight rather than faith.

As a side note, let me clarify this. If God leads you into a secular career field, please don't think it's wrong to negotiate your salary or carefully select your locale. My personal illustration really applies more to ministry-related decisions, yet the guiding principle is the same no matter what you do. God's leading in your heart must be your first pursuit.

Whatever your future holds, God wants you to trust Him completely by faith. He wants to lead you into decisions where you must trust Him by faith, not knowing the outcome. He wants to be your full-time guide. If you have your life all figured out, well planned, and mapped in your mind, you're simply not living by faith. God will ask you to surrender your "life-map" and let Him create a new one—one you haven't seen! Sound too risky? Not at all. It just sounds like faith!

Faith chooses God before money.

My dad worked in secular sales positions during my entire childhood, and yet he still chose to live by faith with every major decision for our family. At age fifteen, due to a series of job changes and schedule changes that were straining our family, my dad began investigating a job offer that would move our family completely across the country. To say the least, I wasn't a real happy camper at the time. I had my friends, my sports, my school, my youth group, and I was facing the idea that it would all be taken away! It was probably the hardest time of my life up to that point.

The job my dad was being offered included a significant pay increase as well as future opportunity for advancement. From the sight perspective it was a "no-brainer"! As an adult, I've seen dozens of people toss their whole world aside and move to a new location in order to make a few more dollars. Yet, from my 15 year-old impressionable heart, I watched my parents approach this "no-brainer" decision with great faith!

The interview went well, the opportunity was huge, but my parents refused to accept the position until they had traveled to the West Coast looking expressly for the church and school that the Lord had for us. They told us that they would not even consider taking the new position unless God made it clear that there was a good church and school where we were headed.

To this day, it amazes me that my parents made two different survey trips together to three major cities on the West Coast for one reason—to find a church. They visited dozens of good churches yet were very close to turning the position down because God had not given them a peace about any particular church. At the last moment, through a strange series of events, God led them directly to a church and school that would eventually become our home.

You won't believe this, but that one "faith-based" decision on the part of my parents just happened to write the entire story of my life as I know it today. On my first day of tenth grade at my new school in northern California I met the two most significant people in my future: first, the man who would pastor my children and whom I would serve under, second, I met the girl I would eventually marry! (I didn't know it at the time, but I did think she was the prettiest girl in the class!)

To this day, I could never thank my parents enough for following God before they would follow money! That took real faith, and it taught me more than words could ever express. In blessing their faith, God also blessed my parents with the financial increase as well.

When God's demands seem outrageous, He is always right.

The Bible is filled with stories of faith and God's response to faith. Consider Noah in Genesis 6 when God commanded him to build an ark. Noah didn't live near water, had no idea what an ark was, and had never seen rain. Yet, in spite of all of this *sight-based* information, Noah chose the *faith* path. God's request seemed way out of line. His command to Noah was far beyond the bounds of normal reason. No matter how you look at it, it didn't make any sense! Nevertheless, God was right.

Consider that God asked Abraham to sacrifice his only son Isaac. This was the son that God promised to bless—the father of a "great nation," and now God was asking that he be killed! This sounds ridiculous. Though the request was bizarre, Abraham willingly trusted God by faith.

If you were Joshua preparing to fight the city of Jericho, what would you expect from God? You'd probably be looking for miraculous answers to prayer like tanks, machine guns, angel armies, and nuclear arsenals. Instead, God commanded Joshua to march around the city. March around the city? You've got to be kidding! What's that supposed to accomplish? It just didn't make sense, but he obeyed anyway, and God won the victory. I wonder how many armies around the world began "marching around cities" after that, thinking Joshua had discovered some kind of strange "seismic" advantage?

God commanded the leper Naaman to wash seven times in a muddy river to be healed. At first Naaman refused. Finally after some prodding from people who cared about him, Naaman dunked himself seven times in the Jordan River. He must have felt pretty stupid as people passed by. By about the fifth and sixth dunk he must have really been embarrassed that there was no hint of a cure!

Now that seventh dunk—that's the one that did the trick! Suddenly the leprosy was gone—all because of simple faith.

It wasn't the muddy water that healed Naaman. It wasn't marching around the city that made Jericho's walls fall down. God wasn't really interested in having Isaac killed or in teaching Noah how to parasail. He was interested in His faith relationship with each individual. Faith is the central theme of every intervention that God has ever had in human life.

He led Joseph into slavery and prison where Joseph's undying faith finally resulted in blessing and success. David chose to take on Goliath by faith. Peter chose to walk on water by faith. Daniel refused to defile himself with the king's meat—by faith. On and on the stories go. Person by person, you see God bless the faith of those who will trust in Him. God promises in Psalm 34:8, "O taste and see that the LORD is good: blessed is the man that trusteth in him." Again in verse 22 He says, "The LORD redeemeth the soul of his servants: and none of them that trust in him shall be desolate." The faith life is the most secure and sure way of living life. The way that makes the least sense actually makes the most sense!

> *Faith is the central theme of every intervention that God has ever had in human life.*

Why would God choose faith?

Could God have chosen to relate and interact with you by sight? Of course He could have. He does with the angels. He does with those already in Heaven. Why not with you and me? Why doesn't He just pull back the veil and let us see into eternity? Wouldn't it be great to see Heaven from Earth? Wouldn't it be great if, on every kid's fifth birthday, God came to the party? "Hello, Bobby, I'm God! Here's a gift for you! By the way, POOF—I just turned your water into milk to go along with that delicious cake and ice cream I made!"

Everyone would believe in God then. That would make everyone want to be saved. He could do these things if He wanted. So, why would God determine that our relationship with Him would be based upon faith?

The answer goes back to His eternal purpose. Outside of the boundary of time, God has an eternal purpose working all things together for good under the Lordship of Jesus Christ. Ephesians 1:10–12 says it this way, "That in the dispensation of the fulness of times he might gather together in one all things in Christ, both which are in heaven, and which are on earth; even in him: In whom also we have obtained an inheritance, being predestinated according to the purpose of him who worketh all things after the counsel of his own will: That we should be to the praise of his glory, who first trusted in Christ."

You are an intricate part of a timeless plan to "gather together in one all things in Christ." In other words, you are a part of God's eternal plan to reconcile all things back to Christ, to undo the effects of the angelic rebellion, and to restore perfect good back into eternity—for all of eternity.

The fact that you believe in God, trust Him fully, and follow Him in faith having never seen or heard Him brings great glory to Him in the courtroom of eternity! In order for your part in God's plan to even matter, your relationship to Him had to be based upon faith. He chose that faith would be the only "line of communication" between our physical world and His eternal existence.

In a sight-based universe, that's very difficult to comprehend, yet it's true. Somehow God's plan for you in eternity is predicated upon the fact that you must "relate" to Him in time and space strictly by faith. The rules of our existence and the purpose of our creation hinge upon relating to God without seeing or hearing Him physically.

Why? I believe that the biggest reasons for our *faith* existence go beyond our comprehension (remember "my ways are not your ways…"), but one reason may well be this. Consider how your testimony of choosing to love God by faith, having never seen Him, might weigh in the courtroom of condemnation of a fallen angelic host who rebelled against God "by sight"! Just a thought. (First Corinthians 6:3 says, "Know ye not that we shall judge angels?")

Think of it this way. The Bible is clear that God will "reward" our faith (1 Peter 5:4, James 1:12, 2 Timothy 4:8). When you stand before Him in eternity, at the culmination of His eternal plan, your faith will be a trophy that will glorify God and justify His judgment on sin. Your faith will be an inarguable testimony against Satan and his fallen hosts as sin is judged and cast forever into a lake of fire. Your willingness to trust God without seeing Him or hearing Him will be a witness in the courtroom of the universe to God's justice and goodness, and your faith-life will be recognized and rewarded by God.

Accept the fact and even enjoy the fact that you cannot see or hear God. That's what faith is all about. That's what your existence is all about. Anticipate the thought that in God's economy—believing is seeing!

Faith means trusting God when He doesn't make sense.

It's easy to believe in and trust in God when everything is going your way. Most Christians have no problem admitting that God is blessing them when they get a raise, a special gift, or a unique blessing. It's natural to believe in God and recognize His goodness when you have a new car, money in your birthday cards, good grades, and nice Christmas gifts.

In fact, there's a false teaching in some circles that faith is almost like a "force." Some people treat God like a genie, and faith is what binds Him to do what you want. If you have enough faith, you can make God do anything or give you anything, as though "your wish is His command"! If you are sick, God will heal you. If you are poor, God will make you wealthy. If you want something, simply have faith and claim it!

By this false theology, faith becomes nothing more than a self-centered tool of manipulation to get exactly what you want from God. In the end, this false brand of faith is very disappointing because you'll never feel like you have enough faith when things don't go your way. Eventually you will stop living for God and trusting Him at all.

No, faith is not a force, and having faith does not mean that everything will go your way. It's when things don't go your way that faith really "kicks in"! Up to that point you're trusting God by sight.

What do you do when God takes someone you love? What happens when you follow God with all of your heart and things don't go well? How do you respond to God when He leads you into a trial, controversy, or sorrow? Living the faith-life means you trust God fully and rely upon His strength regardless of what He chooses to do. Living by faith means you trust God even when your whole world is falling apart. Faith is knowing in your heart that God is working all things together for good when you can see nothing but bad!

Faith is Joseph wrongfully put in jail but never turning his back on God. Faith is Paul and Silas in jail singing praises to God. Faith is Noah being ridiculed for building a gigantic boat in his front yard, but trusting God anyway. Faith is Peter stepping out of the boat in the middle of a storm—the storm that God sent him into! Faith is three Hebrew young men being thrown into a fiery furnace not knowing what God would do, but trusting Him anyway.

Job had faith, even though God permitted the total destruction of his entire family and estate. Paul had faith, even though he was beaten, imprisoned, shipwrecked, and stoned. On top of that, God refused to take away his thorn in the flesh, but he still trusted Him.

Mary and Joseph had faith to trust God even though it meant their dreams and ideas for happiness would suddenly change. How would you like having to explain to your family that you were expecting a child from God? It didn't make sense that God would ask Mary and Joseph to endure the loss of their good reputations for His eternal plan, but they accepted His plan by faith. Mary herself said to the angel, "Behold, the handmaid of the Lord. Be it unto me according to thy word" (Luke 1:38). By the way, just in case it's never occurred to you, her decision at that moment affected you!

Faith is following God when He doesn't make sense, regardless of the outcome. Faith is knowing that this world is temporary and that reality is just one breath away in eternity. Faith understands that now we "see through a glass, darkly; but then face to face" (1 Corinthians 13:12). Faith is holding the physical world loosely so you can cling to the unseen eternal God!

Faith opposes human "reason."

God came to Moses in Exodus 4:21 and commanded him to tell Pharaoh to release the Hebrews. In the same verse, He told Moses that Pharaoh's heart would harden and he would not listen! Think about that. My question would have been, "So why go?" Why would God send Moses into a situation knowing that it wouldn't work! He deliberately commanded Moses to go on a failing mission. He knew the end from the beginning. He knew that Pharaoh would not listen. It didn't make sense for Moses to accept this command, but he did anyway.

This is a key characteristic of the faith-life. God will probably lead you into a situation that doesn't make sense. He will put you in a predicament where you are inadequate and unable to do His command. He may ask you to do something you just don't want to do. Often He will lead you directly into the face of impossibility!

Chances are, at first, His will for your life won't make sense by sight. In many ways, it will probably contradict all human reasoning and rationale. You won't be able to see the end from the beginning. When you come to the point that you will follow Him anyway— you will be living by faith! When you arrive at the determination that you will trust Him blindly,

This is a key characteristic of the faith life. God will probably lead you into a situation that doesn't make sense.

knowing "that he is, and that he is a rewarder of them that diligently seek him" (Hebrews 11:6), you are living the faith life.

When I got to Lancaster Baptist Church in July of 1990, you'll never believe what I was assigned. I became the supervisor of the third through sixth grade "video school"! Never in a million years would I have guessed I would teach elementary kids. I didn't study for it. I had no formal training. I had never dreamed of doing that. I had no advance warning. Had I known, I probably would have turned it down. I remember thinking, "God, you're making a big mistake here! You got the wrong guy!" If you had asked me to make a list of things I didn't want to do in the ministry, teaching elementary school would have been somewhere near the very top!

So, I had to make a quick determination in my heart. Was this God's doing? Obviously it was. Though it took me completely by surprise and didn't make any sense at all, I knew I must accept His leading by faith. I didn't enter ministry to set my own agenda, regardless of how mistaken I thought God was. (Boy, was I sure He was mistaken!)

I felt like Moses saying, "B-B-But God, th-th-this was n-n-never in the c-c-contract!" I felt like calling a "time out" to have a heavenly huddle to make sure I heard the call correctly. "Third graders? Are you sure? I mean—are you REALLY, REALLY sure?"

In my heart, all I heard was, "Yes I'm sure. Just follow by faith. It will all make sense later."

Well, I did follow by faith, and you'll never believe what happened. I LOVED IT! Two weeks into teaching that class I was convinced that I had discovered a hidden passion—teaching elementary kids. I had no idea it would be so much fun. Finally, I had the authority to call TWO recesses! That was awesome! (And I did—frequently!) God instantly changed my heart and my desires, and gave me a love for teaching. I learned more lessons that year than anyone else in that class, and to this day I look back on it as one of the best years of my entire life.

Since then, my job description and assignments have radically changed time and time again—and with every change the same faithful response followed from God. I've discovered that no matter what He asks me to do, He will give me a love for it and the ability to do it! I've also discovered that eventually He aligned my responsibilities more closely to my personal dreams and God-given desires—but not until He was sure I would follow Him when He didn't make sense.

Faith is always rewarded by God.

We live in a world where people want guarantees. Before you buy a computer, you'll probably check out the warranty. Before some people get married they make a "prenuptial agreement" to protect themselves "just in case." When you make a major purchase you read the fine print to safeguard that you aren't getting "ripped off." On and on it goes.

With the faith-life, the guarantee doesn't come until after you've signed the "dotted line"! But mark it down; it always comes! God's Word is true; His heart is good; and His promises never fail. He is faithful to those who trust Him. You will never read of a Bible character or meet a person who truly trusted God and was "let down"! It is an impossibility. It just cannot happen. After you've made the commitment to follow God by faith, He will always sustain you.

This is the process of the Christian life: life doesn't make sense, so you trust God. You step out by faith into the unknown. God responds to your faith and cares for you. You see God at work in your life in a real way. You believe more strongly that God is real and that He is right. Your faith becomes stronger for future steps of faith. The process begins all over again!

It's a wonderful progression of spiritual growth, but most people never take the first faith step to experience it. Most Christians never get very far in discovering the faith-life because they trust what they can see more than they trust God. As a result, their spiritual journey is stifled. So, I challenge you to step boldly into a life of faith. Expect that your future will hold many unknowns. Expect that God will deliberately "not make sense" to you. Expect Him to bring you into impossible situations where your faith can be expressed and enlarged.

Then, when you're standing on the edge of a sight-based life, looking into the "nothingness" called your future, have confidence that when you step forward, God will catch you. Have the boldness to follow what you cannot see, regardless of how stupid some people think you are. Then, when you follow in faith, and God leads you into a situation that has you scratching your head and wondering where God went wrong—trust Him anyway.

You will never read of a Bible character or meet a person who truly trusted God and was "let down"! It is an impossibility. It just cannot happen.

Just about the time you're thinking "Uh, Lord, I didn't see this in the fine print of our agreement" just tear up the contract, give God carte blanche with your life; and from that point, it will only be a matter of time before you see Him mightily at work in your life! That's when it really gets exciting.

Run the play as God calls it; the results will speak for themselves.

My ninth grade year was a rough one. I was about as insecure as any person on the planet ever has been. One of the ways I set out to prove my worth and strength to the world was by playing football. Looking back, it was a lot of fun and really built a lot of character within me. At the time, however, it was just my attempt to counteract my perceived deficiencies in the human race.

Somehow, I managed to end up at the position of quarterback for our junior varsity team and tackle dummy for the varsity practices. I was a much better tackle dummy than I was a quarterback. We were a small team in a small league, and our season was nothing that you'd want to write home about. I think we did end up winning two games—out of about eight. It's still hard for me to imagine that there were two teams in that league that were *worse* than we were.

One of the games we won provided a "life-lesson" and a "faith-lesson" that I have never forgotten. I don't remember the team or the location. I just remember the play that was called.

Being the fine quarterback that I wasn't, the coach never allowed me to call the plays. Instead, he would send a runner in to tell me the play during every huddle.

On this occasion we were at about mid-field, in our offensive huddle, and the runner comes huffing into the huddle and says "Coach calls a 'fake 34, 17 boot!'"

If you don't know much about football, that simply means, that the quarterback (me) was supposed to fake a handoff to a running back on one side of the field, and then personally do an "about face" with the ball and run around the other end of the field. I knew so little about football, that this call didn't make sense. I quickly figured that by the time I faked the hand off and turned around to run, everyone on the defense would know exactly what was going on. I didn't think it would work.

Well, our time in the huddle was limited and I had to make a decision. This couldn't be the correct play. This kid must be low on oxygen and must have mixed up the call. Surely the coach meant to call a "fake 34, 18 boot." That would mean I fake the hand off and keep running in the same direction around the right end of the defense. Surely that would make more sense. So, I did the unthinkable. I changed the call.

"Fake 34, 18 boot, on two. Ready BREAK!!" and we were off to the line.

Well, the next thing I remember was picking the grass clippings from my face mask, about five yards behind the line of scrimmage, just a few steps past my "fake 34 hand off"! It wasn't pretty.

Have the boldness to follow what you cannot see, regardless of how stupid some people think you are.

That didn't work so well, I thought and went back to the huddle. I actually thought "what a dumb call, coach"!

The next runner came in, breathing heavily, and whispered loudly, "Coach calls a fake 34, 17 boot."

What? Again? This couldn't be. Two guys in a row mess up the call like that? It just didn't make sense, but neither did that call. This can't be right. So, in my childish stupidity, I did the unthinkable—a SECOND TIME! I changed the call.

"Fake 34, 18 boot, on three. Ready BREAK!!" and we were off to the line again.

This time I only lost three yards on the play, and there wasn't nearly as much grass in my face mask. It was mostly just mud. The one difference was the loud, distinctly angry voice shouting my name from the sideline. Now, my mom can shout loudly, but I knew immediately this wasn't her. This voice was thunderous and murderous.

"SCHMIDT!"

I looked at Coach, as innocently as I could as he continued.

"WHERE'S THE '7' HOLE?" His neck veins were quite large, foam was spewing from his mouth, and the entire defending team could hear him clearly!

In the split second before I answered, I realized the runners had called the play correctly both times, and I was in deep trouble.

Lamely, I pointed to the left side of the offensive line and stared at coach wondering if I was about to die.

"THEN RUN TO IT!!!!" This time he shouted loud enough for the opposing team's fans to hear him. Now the whole world knew exactly what play we were going to run, and I had to run it any way, just to bear the humiliation.

"Fake 34, 17 boot, on two," I said sheepishly in the huddle, "ready break."

You'll never believe what happened. I took the hike, faked the hand off to the right side of the offense and then turned around as quickly as I could to run around the left end of the field expecting to be destroyed by a wall of defenders. As I turned, I saw a sight I had never seen in all of my extensive two-year football career.

Pasture. Green, open grass—and nothing else. Nothing. And there in the distance, about 60 yards down field—the goal line. It was beautiful.

A few seconds and sixty yards later, the whole world forgot about the previous two plays and started celebrating our touchdown—except for Coach.

As I came to the sideline, he grabbed my facemask, and intensely said, "that's what would have happened two plays ago if you would have done what I said." Then he smiled, and I knew I would live another day. It was a lesson I'll never forget.

You're the quarterback, God is the coach, and sometimes He's going to call a play that just doesn't make sense to you! Do yourself a favor. Save yourself the embarrassment, and potentially the ruined life. No matter how strange you think the play sounds, no matter how backwards it seems to your psyche, no matter how mixed up you think it is—don't do the unthinkable. Don't change the call. Just run the play. God knows exactly what He's doing!

"…I being in the way, the LORD led me…."
—Genesis 24:27

eleven

Only Weird People Wear Their Pants Backwards

Step #1 for Right Decision-Making—Refuse to Trust Yourself

He was three years old, as cute as they come, and for him, life was full of "firsts"—getting his first Happy Meal toy, taking his first trip to the dentist, riding his first bike (complete with training wheels and a helmet twice the size of his head), and on the list could go. On this particular occasion, the "first" was that of dressing himself.

It was a typical early evening. I had just arrived home from a long day, and Lance had spent most of the day playing in his pajamas. Just before I arrived home however, he decided to get dressed—by himself. He was somewhat over-confident for a three year old and felt that this new task was well within his gift mix.

As I walked in the door, he proudly stepped out from the hallway holding his head high and wearing a smile from ear to ear. "Hey, Dad. Guess what?" he asked expectantly.

I stood, stared, and immediately knew what was coming next, "What, buddy?"

"I got all dressed all by myself!" He seemed to stand wider to flaunt his new found ability and his good taste for fashion.

I was impressed, and it showed, as I looked him over. I mean, I was genuinely and sincerely impressed. I've been in a skit or two over these past years when I was required to put on a pair of pants backwards, and I'm here to tell you it's no easy task! I don't know if you've ever tried to zip a pair of pants and snap them while they are on backwards, but it's nearly impossible. Yet, standing there in front of me, my first-born son had been gifted with the unique ability to accomplish this amazing feat of dexterity at the tender young age of three! WOW! I had always hoped my kids would be smart, but I would have never guessed that my family would be blessed with such giftedness.

I paused for a moment in disbelief. I spun him around to check the authenticity of this amazing accomplishment, and sure enough the zipper was up; the snap was snapped.

"That's great buddy, I'm very proud of you!" I tried to sound sincere while at the same time coughing back a laugh and watching my wife do the same. Lance was oblivious to his mistake and swelled all the more with pride and joy at our pleasure. It was truly a defining moment for him.

That's when it hit me. My son has his pants on backwards.

This is not good. Girls won't date him. His high school peers will never accept him. He'll never be able to get a decent job. I couldn't bear the thought of his eighth grade graduation, his first baseball game, his first date, or his first job interview—with his pants on backwards. Even if this did require amazing skill and dexterity, the world would never see it that way. He would be rejected and ridiculed—the object of scorn and mockery. As his father, I couldn't allow this. Something had to be done. As painful as it was, I had to say something.

Be gentle, I thought. This could really set him back. That's not good. I had read books and heard lectures that his brain develops more in the first three years of life than at any other time in life. I knew I had to be careful not to upset the delicate balance of his toddler psyche. I envisioned him withdrawing for the rest of his life all because his dad was a perfectionist when he was three. That would be bad. Be gentle, act quick, but be gentle, I thought again.

I swallowed; I cleared my throat; I spoke very deliberately and very gently, "Lance, buddy, that's really great that you got dressed. I'm really proud of you. You did a good job." I hesitated, almost chickening out.

"Uh…but…uh…buddy, there's just one little problem." I waited for him to ask what.

"Nuh, uh." He said matter-of-factly.

"Yes, there is buddy. There's just one thing wrong that I think we should fix before we go out anywhere." He was shaking his head in denial as I continued, "Your pants are on backwards."

There. I said it. Then I waited. No tears. That's good. No psychological set back. That appears good. No deep-seeded anger from feelings of rejection. That seemed good. I think we're in the clear here.

Then he spoke again shaking his whole body the way most people just shake their head, "nuh, uh."

I paused, taken back a little. Up until that time, no one had ever argued with me about how to put on a pair of pants. The little attorney guys in my head started scrambling for evidence to prove my case. This is one I had never dealt with before, so they didn't come up with much useful material.

"Lance, really, buddy. I wouldn't lie to you. These pants are on backwards. You did a good job getting them on, but we need to turn them around."

He wasn't buying it. He just shoved his hands deep into his back pockets (which were in the front) and continued to shake his body with a stern "no" motion. He was resolute—firmly convinced— that his pants were on correctly. I, on the other hand, had spent twenty-five years learning how to put on pants, and my wife had worked hard to dress me well—I was sure they were on backwards. I glanced at Dana just to be double sure. She gave an approving nod that indeed I was right.

With a new reassurance I took Lance by the shoulders, looked deep into his eyes and said, "We're not going to argue about this. You did a very good job getting dressed, but let's go to your room so I can show you how to fix these pants." I spoke with that familiar "this is going to hurt me worse that it hurts you" tone of voice that parents like to use.

About that time, he stopped arguing, and we went to his room to fix his pants. I'll never forget his face when we finally put them on correctly. It was that "oh yeah" kind of face. Then he made a funny little giggle sound that seemed to say "that's a lot more comfortable anyway. Thanks, Dad," and life has been good ever since.

Many teenagers and young adults are very much like my three-year-old son. They are making decisions, taking steps, and moving forward in life—on their own. They are so proud of the fact that they are "grown up" that they've completely missed the fact that they still don't know much. They are doing things like accepting jobs, enlisting in the military, choosing colleges, buying cars, getting credit cards, dating strangers, falling in love, getting married, and having children—but they're doing them all the wrong way. They're doing them with no biblical direction, no prayer, and no godly counsel.

The first step to actually making a right decision is to refuse, absolutely refuse, to trust yourself.

Obviously, *doing* these things isn't wrong, but it is possible to *do* them wrongly. It's possible to go about these things in all the wrong way, to "put life on" backwards.

The crazy thing is these people are always "right in their own eyes," but their mistakes are glaringly obvious to others around them. The decisions they are making are as obviously backwards as Lance's pants were, but they are firmly convinced that everything's okay! And you usually can't reason with this type of person. You can see as plain as day that they are making a wrong choice, but they are completely oblivious to it. They are blinded by their own ignorance and unwilling to listen to anyone else. In fact, if you try to intervene and lovingly interfere, you might even become the object of anger or resentment.

What's the problem? Two words—trusting self. Lance was trusting in himself to get his pants on properly, and he was wrong. In his limited view of life and his minimal understanding of the clothing industry, he had credited himself with far more knowledge and understanding than he really had. He was self-confident.

Many young adults have this same problem. They are completely self-confident. They fail to see how much they don't know and how vulnerable to mistakes they really are. (By the way, we're all vulnerable. It's just that young adults seem to have a tough time admitting that.)

Refuse to trust yourself.

So, let me be completely honest with you. As painful as this may be, you'll be way ahead of the game if you'll take this bitter pill and swallow it now. The first step to actually making a right decision is to refuse, *absolutely refuse*, to trust yourself. I know it sounds backwards when the world is screaming at you, "It's your life, do whatever feels good!" But it's the Bible truth.

Remember that the Lord calls us "sheep." When is the last time you heard of a major NFL team or a college team named "the mighty, mighty *Sheep*?" I don't think so. Why? Sheep are known for being the dumbest animals on the planet. They are easy to scare, easy to prey upon, and very easy to mislead. Sheep must be led to safety, led to water, and led to food. They must be carefully watched over and guarded, and the Bible says that we are just like them!

We are weak and helpless, and we cannot guide or protect ourselves. When it comes to the reasons and intricacies of God's eternal purpose, we're just plain dumb. We're easily deceived and misled, and we are utterly dependent upon the Good Shepherd to watch and guide over us.

Proverbs 3:5–6 says, "Trust in the Lord with all thine heart; and lean not unto thine own understanding. In all thy ways acknowledge him, and he shall direct thy paths."

As we've explored the tools of a sober mind, a pure heart, a courageous spirit, a life of faith, and the wisdom of God, they all begin to be applied in this principle. All of these "tools" should lead you to the conclusion that you cannot and will not see things the way that God sees them, and this conclusion leads you to a decision. Who will you trust? Who will you rely upon? Whose viewpoint will you adopt as you make decisions in your future?

If anything that you've read thus far has sunk in, hopefully you are instantly thinking, "God, of course. Who else?"

That's good, but keep reading.

Deceiving yourself—the lie of emotions

The implication of Proverbs 3:5–6 is that we all have the tendency to lean to our own understanding. It's natural for you to just rely on the way you see and understand something. We all tend to assume that *our* perspective is the *right* perspective. When left with a choice, we naturally trust our own perception and reasoning as being truthful. We trust that deep inside we're being honest with ourselves, but believe it or not, this isn't always the case.

It's possible for you to deceive yourself. Sound crazy? Maybe, but it's true. It's actually possible for your heart to mislead you, to lie to you, to misguide you. James teaches in James 1:14 that "every man is tempted, when he is drawn away of his own lust." In this case, we draw *ourselves* away from the right path. We lead *ourselves* into danger. We bring *ourselves* into sin and pain.

Paul taught in Romans 7 that there was a war going on within himself. This war was between his righteous desires and his sinful flesh—or the new man and the old man. Even though he wanted to do right, he often found himself being led astray by his sinful flesh. Apparently this struggle was quite frustrating for him, and he concludes the chapter by crying out "who shall deliver me…?"

His answer is found in the next verse when he says "I thank God through Jesus Christ…."

The principle is the same in each of these passages. There is a part of all of us that can actually lead us away and deceive us into danger and sin. It was this struggle in Paul that caused him to completely abandon himself to the power of Christ. In Galatians 2:20 he said, "I am crucified with Christ: nevertheless I live; yet not I, but Christ liveth in me: and the life which I now live in the

Emotions were never meant to be trusted.

flesh I live by the faith of the Son of God, who loved me, and gave himself for me."

I once heard a fantastic illustration of the fact the we can all deceive ourselves. It goes something like this.

Imagine that you're lost deep in the woods. You're scared, alone, and looking for help. Suddenly, in your wandering, you happen upon a gigantic, hungry grizzly bear. At that precise moment, your brain begins drawing immediate conclusions. In the flash of an instant you would conclude something like this.

"This is a grizzly bear. He looks hungry. Grizzly bears eat meat. I'm made of meat. While I'm thinking of other options, I could at least start running."

So, you would immediately start running, and instantly your fear factor would be at about fifteen on a scale of one to ten! You would be instantaneously terrified and your pulse rate could prove it.

Now, imagine that, as you're running through the woods praying, you miraculously happen upon a concrete bear shelter built deep into the side of a large mountain. It's absolutely impenetrable. So, to save your hide, you run inside and bar the door, just barely escaping the claws of the bear who was hot on your heels.

The scientific fact of the matter is—you're now safe. You're well blockaded into the side of a mountain and the bear cannot harm you. Yet, for some reason, you find yourself huddled all the way to the back corner of the shelter, heart still pounding, chest still heaving, and fear factor still topping 14.5 on the Richter scale.

Your emotions are now lying to you. In your conscious mind you know that you are safe, yet your emotions are still telling you to be afraid—be very afraid! Even though you know the facts, your body is still responding in contradiction to the facts. It would probably take any normal person thirty minutes or more for their emotions to settle down and accept reality. In the case of someone like my wife, it might be a week or two!

Emotions were never meant to be trusted. They were given to us by God to season life's moments with feeling, but they make terrible guides because much of the time they just don't tell the truth. Yet many people base their decisions on emotions. They trust themselves, and they make life-long mistakes based on the misinformation of the moment!

I know teen girls who have fallen in love with and married the wrong guy. Everyone knew it. It was an obvious mistake, but they were closed to anyone's opinion but their own. They were trusting themselves alone! In this type of situation, friends and family have really only one choice—grin and bear it. Very few people, especially parents, would take an opposing side when a child is making a grave mistake. Every parent wants to be thought of as supportive, so usually, they smile silently, hoping that somehow everything will work out. Unfortunately, things rarely do just "work out."

In this case, the girl has been blinded by emotion and cannot see reality. Usually just a few short months or years into this type of marriage, reality hits hard (sometimes literally), and one or both partners are running for their lives with broken hearts.

Who do they run to? It never fails; they always go running back to the people they wouldn't listen to in the first place. These are the people that were there all the time (even though their wisdom was silenced), and they always will be there to love and restore a broken life.

Trusting self is always a very dangerous path. It never works out. It's so easy to follow emotion or feeling. It's so easy to rely on your own understanding, which always seems so true and real. It's natural to rely on the way you see things, but it's also deadly.

As a side note on this thing of emotion, remember this: Feelings will always follow obedience. Emotions will always fall in line with reality eventually. There will be times in your life when your emotions are way out of whack, maybe during a hard break up, a personal failure, or a time of trial. During these times, you must determine to cling to what you know to be true—God and His Word. And in time, your emotions will settle back down and fall in line with reality.

Don't run away, kill yourself, or freak out on drugs—no matter the despair that your emotions may bring. Remind yourself that these are just emotions talking, and that there's something greater than emotion—TRUTH. This is what God says about it in 1 John 3:20, "For if our heart condemn us, *God is greater than our heart*, and knoweth all things."

As you obey God, your emotions will eventually catch up, and you'll be glad you listened to the steadfast voice of truth rather than the unstable voice of emotion.

Perhaps the biggest lesson on trusting self that I've had to learn revolved around my first car purchase. In the second summer of our marriage we were blessed with our first baby. It was a hot summer, and suddenly my wife was very interested in driving the air-conditioned car most of the time. We were blessed to have two used cars, but only one had air conditioning. Even though the other one was a beautiful red '67

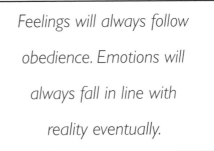

Feelings will always follow obedience. Emotions will always fall in line with reality eventually.

Mustang, it may as well have been a sauna in the high desert heat of southern California.

While my wife hated parting with her "cool" car, we both concluded that it just wasn't practical for a young family. So we decided to trade it in. One problem—we didn't have any money saved and couldn't really afford a car payment.

In all of my grand brilliance, I set out on my own, determined that I knew exactly what I would do (total "self-trust" trip). The thought occurred that maybe I should get our parents' advice or perhaps the advice of my pastor or friends, but I concluded I didn't need to. My idea would work—I just knew it.

I knew, somewhere in our area, there was a used car dealer who would be more than happy to make an EVEN trade for a used car with air conditioning. I didn't care what kind of car—just that it had air and that it would be an EVEN trade. I was right. The used car salesmen were only too happy to rip me off in all of my glaring ignorance.

It's embarrassing to share this, but I actually traded a beautiful red '67 Mustang for an '86 Renault with air conditioning! I had no idea that Renault was synonymous for "car that no one wants"! I didn't know that Renault makers were out of business. I couldn't have predicted that the car would need more than $2,000 work within a few months. I didn't know that Renaults were perhaps the worst cars that have ever broken down on American freeways. But a lot of good people around me could have told me those things. I just didn't give them the chance because I was working this one on my own! I was grown, married, and now ready to prove my "headship" in my home. In so doing, I proved my own stupidity.

The funny part is that, when I began to explain the trade to my friends and family, they all sounded so supportive. I hadn't really given them a choice to say otherwise, so what else were they going to do? I had made the decision on my own, forcing everyone else to just "hope for the best." I'm sure my father-in-law was cringing when I told him the news. I'm sure both of our dads could have warned me not to make that trade. But I chose the path of trusting self, and I lived to regret it.

When you put yourself in the prideful position of needing to prove your own self-reliance, you're headed for the mistake zone every time!

Put your trust to the test.

So how do you know for sure whether you're trusting yourself or God? How can you test your trust?

Let me encourage you to do a little assignment that will help you put this command into practice. Take a few moments at the end of this chapter and get some blank paper and a pen. Find a quiet spot and write these words at the top of the paper: "The Way I See It" (my own understanding).

Then, begin to write out your best description of how you think your life should unfold. Don't play mind games with yourself; just write what comes to mind. Describe things the way you envision them. Be specific. Be transparent. Be honest. Dream big. Hope for the best. Be realistic. Don't just think it—actually write it down. It won't take that long. What college do you want to attend? Who do you want to marry (or what kind of person)? Where would you like to live, and what would you dream of doing? What kind of house would you like? How many kids? Even write down the things that you believe are "God's will" for your life.

There's probably more of this stuff under the surface of your heart than you realize. You might be amazed how much you actually do write down in just a few moments. It might surprise you that you've thought of all this but never quite so clearly. I've had many teens share with me that this experience was one they will never forget! So, be sure to do it.

Once it's all out on paper, read it. Take a good long look at it, like when you're saying goodbye to a friend that you won't see for a long, long time. Savor the moment. Read it a few times, and then find a big red marker and write these words boldly across the page: DO NOT TRUST THIS!

Now realize—it's not necessarily that what you wrote is wrong for your future. It may not be right either. Simply put, it's your own understanding, and you must not trust it for now. This is the best way to articulate from your own heart what the Bible means by the phrase "thine own understanding" as stated in Proverbs 3:5–6. It's the way you see things, and it is exactly what the Bible tells you not to trust or lean on.

In order for your future decisions to be right in God's eternal plan, they must be based on faith, and they must come from Him, not yourself. In order to fully lean upon Him, you must come to a release point of your own understanding. You must come to that moment when you consciously decide that you don't trust YOU!

Strange isn't it? All your young adult life you've wanted people to trust you and now I'm telling you not even to trust yourself. Actually, God is telling you from the Bible. I'm just reminding you.

Change the direction of your "lean."

Finally, let me encourage you to seek God's help in making one more change in the years ahead.

Wouldn't it be great if, over time, you could just get in the habit of "leaning to God's understanding" rather than your own. It's natural for all of us to lean to our own, but I believe, over time, God can help you change this natural tendency. I believe every Christian's first thought in any situation should be, "Lord, what is your understanding of this situation?"

Whether it's your next meal or your next major decision, ask the Lord to help you develop the habit of instantly thinking of His way before your own. First Corinthians 10:31 says it this way, "Whether therefore ye eat, or drink, or whatsoever ye do, **do all to the glory of God.**"

By the way, save that sheet of paper. You might even need to hang it somewhere prominent to remind yourself what not to trust. You might turn around thirty years from now and be pleasantly surprised at how much of it God brought to pass. You might turn around thirty years from now and be happy that none of it came true. Either way, thirty years from now, you'll want to know that you're living your destiny, and you'll never get there by trusting yourself or leaning to your own understanding.

And don't forget, when you're in the mistake zone, trusting yourself is about as obvious as wearing your pants backwards—at least to those older than you. It really looks pretty goofy!

"Thou wilt keep him in perfect peace,
whose mind is stayed on thee:
because he trusteth in thee."
—Isaiah 26:3

twelve

Chapter Twelve
Dimples, Donuts, and Destiny
*Step #2 for Right Decision-Making—Seek and Surrender
to God's Will*

It was high noon. I was off for the day, and Lance was just being dismissed from another grueling day of kindergarten. As my wife and I waited in the "car-line" in front of the school, we were both pretty excited. We had a great day planned, and we couldn't wait to tell Lance about it.

When Lance saw us, his face lit up. He quickly grabbed his backpack in one arm and his "craft" for the day in the other (some sort of weird looking thing made of pipe cleaners), and he jumped into the back seat. Having waited all day to tell him the good news, I was about to burst with excitement!

"Lance! Guess where we're going today?"

For a moment his brain was searching his "fun places archive" then, he said, "DIMPLES?" (This was the only "fun place" he knew of at the time.)

"Dimples" was a storefront fun center for small children that Lance had come to love. Quite often we would take him to bounce in the balls, play games, and just goof off for a few hours. Dimples had become one of our favorite "young family" hangouts. For Lance, any day that included Dimples was a good day! At his young age, his imagination couldn't conceive of any place being more fun.

"Nope." I answered, with a knowing resoluteness to my voice. "We're not going to Dimples today. We're going someplace better!"

My excitement was building, but his wasn't.

"I want to go to Dimples." At that point, he sat back as if nothing in the world could move him.

So that was it—Dimples or nothing. It was seemingly impossible that any place on the planet could be as much fun as Dimples, but I didn't give up.

"Lance, we're not going to Dimples because we're going to…" anticipation was building "…we're going to…DISNEYLAND!!" I announced with great fanfare. Little trumpets were playing in my head, confetti was falling, and a whole mental parade was about to start!

Frown. Nothing else. Just a frown. No wild-eyed "WOW!" No "You're the BEST, Dad!" No "Yahoo!!" Nothing but a bad attitude.

Maybe he didn't hear me correctly. Let's try again. Rewind the trumpets and parade.

"We're going to…DISNEYLAND!!" This time my mental fanfare was louder and happier.

Still nothing. Then…

"I don't want to go to Disneyland. I want to go to Dimples!" He was upset, belligerent, and quite arrogant about it.

What's the deal with that? How could a five-year-old possibly want to spend a few hours at some half-baked, storefront game center when he could spend a day at Disneyland? I was really lost for a minute, until it finally hit me. (My wife knew all along and I think she was enjoying this whole experience.)

This kid doesn't even know what Disneyland is! That's the problem. He doesn't remember going as a baby, and he has no idea what he's turning down. So I pressed on. I knew I could win this thing.

"Lance, Disneyland is where Mickey Mouse lives!"

Still no progress. By this time, he was actually pouting! My well-planned, surprise day was going downhill fast, and it was time to move into crisis mode to try to save the moment.

"Lance, trust me, man. Just TRUST ME! You're gonna love Disneyland so much that you'll never want to go to Dimples again." I laughed at the insane idea that I was arguing with a five-year-old about something so ridiculous!

"I want to go to Dimples." Now he was demanding, and that was enough.

"Lance," I stated sternly in that pointed, parental voice that you've heard so many times, "we are going to Disneyland, whether you like it or not, and you're going to have fun and that's the bottom line. Stop crying, Lance. I mean it. Stop the crying RIGHT NOW. YOU'RE GOING TO LIKE DISNEYLAND!"

By this time, my wife was reaching back to console him. I was beside myself. I gave up trying to convince him. In fact, I almost just took him to Dimples to save the money, but I was too excited about Disneyland. (I guess I forgot that I wouldn't get to ride any good rides!)

He cried for a few more minutes, and then fell asleep for a long afternoon nap while we drove to Disneyland.

It wouldn't be hard for you to imagine the rest of the story. We got to Disneyland, took one step into the park, and Lance never looked back to Dimples ever again. In fact, a few weeks later, when our budget called for some "affordable family fun" at Dimples—he was crying for Disneyland. It seemed I just couldn't win at this "plan Lance's fun life" game.

I will never forget that day with Lance at Disneyland. I recognize that some are against Disney, and certainly I don't endorse much of what the Disney Corporation is about. So don't hold this against me, but we had a great time. We met Mickey, Minnie, Pluto, and Pinocchio! We played. We rode rides. We ate churros and cotton candy. We watched the electric light parade, and we made a host of great memories as Lance enjoyed these "first experiences."

By the day's end, Lance had learned that Dimples could never compare to Disneyland.

Why some people resist God's will

God's will. Those words echo so often in the halls of a Bible-believing church or school. If you've grown up in a Christian home you've heard them all of your life. Those two words are so mysterious, so intangible, so hard to grasp. What is it? Why is it? How does it affect my life today? How do I find it? When will I know I've found it? What will it be like? What if I don't like it?

All these questions make a fairly simple issue so complex and intricate that many young adults have one of three negative reactions to it.

First, this vague concept, "God's will" seems so intangible that we just give up trying to understand it—let alone seek it or surrender to it. Out of sheer ignorance, we miss God's best simply because we "don't understand it." This boils down to self-centered rebellion.

Second, this "will" (whatever it is) seems to threaten our hopes and dreams, so we run from it as fast as we can (another path of rebellion). We don't want "God's will" to ruin our lives and shatter all of those well-laid plans we talked about earlier.

Third, those of a spiritual mindset can begin weaving an intricate maze of mental questions, theories, and personal puzzles that lead them in frustrating circles of thought. They wonder what is God's will? They theorize if it's this or that. They exhaust themselves, entertaining a myriad of possibilities. They jump to radical conclusions for weird reasons. It's like a psychotic Easter egg hunt—and we're not finding any eggs!! This circular reasoning drives us spiritually insane with this question: "What is God up to and why won't He tell me?"

This response feels like a desperate "spiritual quest," but in reality it is exhausting, frustrating, and can often lead to depression, despair, and even spiritual failure. This self-centered quest can easily turn into serious disappointment with God and with the spiritual growth process, which can drive us away from God altogether. Perhaps you can identify.

Simply put, people who resist God's will or who deliberately reject it just don't understand what it is. Similarly, people who reject God simply don't understand who He is and what He is like. People run from God because they perceive Him to be a threat rather than a Saviour. They believe Him to be a tyrant rather than a loving Father.

Even so, people who resist God's perfect will in their lives have the same condition. They believe the lie that His will is a danger to their desires. They think of God's will as a terrible detour to their personal dreams. They fear that if they seek or surrender to God's will, He will surely send them to some far corner of the globe to eat bugs and to be killed by cannibals.

In short, people resist God's will by choice—because they do not understand that His will is better than they could ever imagine.

Regardless of whether I give up on God's will because of ignorance, perceived threat, or sheer frustration—it all boils down to a decision to rebel against God. Resisting God's will is a sheer act of defiance against Almighty God—regardless of my reasons. Rather than trust Him by faith, I choose to rebel. I choose to fight back—to protect my "turf" from God's encroachment.

In short, people resist God's will by choice—because they do not understand that His will is better than they could ever imagine.

Think of it this way—God's perfect will compared to your selfish will is like Disneyland compared to Dimples. One is so blatantly better than the other that the comparison is ludicrous! There really is no comparison. God is our loving, heavenly Father, and He has spent an eternity conceiving a master plan for our lives (destiny). We are the children in the back seat of life with scarcely the ability to imagine what God might have in store.

God offers us a "surprise" (by faith) plan that He knows we're going to love, if we just trust Him. The moment we fully understand His plan, we're going to thank Him for all of eternity. But we're demanding, arrogant, and ignorant. Beyond that, we're clinging to our feeble and meager plans as though we're holding the exclusive recipe for happiness and success.

There we sit in the back seat—just like Lance—arms folded, frowning, demanding our way. In childlike ignorance we refuse to trust the Father and wait out His timing. All the while, God is offering us a perfect will that far exceeds and surpasses the selfish ways for which we fight.

What is God's will?

Jeremiah 24:5–7 says, "Thus saith the LORD, the God of Israel; Like these good figs, so will I acknowledge them that are carried away captive of Judah, whom I have sent out of this place into the land of the Chaldeans for their good. For I will set mine eyes upon them for good, and I will bring them again to this land: and I will build them, and not pull them down; and I will plant them, and not pluck them up. And I will give them an heart to know me, that I am the LORD: and they shall be my people, and I will be their God: for they shall return unto me with their whole heart."

In this passage, God is describing His plans or His will for His people. These verses uniquely show God's awesome heart of compassion and goodness. Notice that God says, "so will I acknowledge them" indicating that He knows, recognizes, and is interested in His people. He acknowledges you, right now!

Then He says, "I will set mine eyes upon them for good," showing that His plans are always good and working for eternal good. This means God isn't planning to ruin your life! He has good things in mind for your future! Have you ever considered the fact that God likes you and that He has good plans for your life?

He goes on to describe His plan to lead His people, build them, plant them, and fellowship with them. What an awesome, loving Heavenly Father we have! It's humbling to think that the Creator of the universe would go to such detail in His feelings, thoughts, and plans for each of us!

What is His will? Well, I cannot tell you the specific details of His plans, but I can tell you His promise. He promises that His will is good. He promises that He will lead you. He promises that He will provide for you and bless you with true success.

Simply, God's will is the daily unfolding of your life as designed by the perfect, infinite, loving, awesome mind of God. It's so wonderful you cannot imagine it. It's so joyful, that the Psalmist simply said, "Thou wilt shew me the path of life: in thy presence is fulness of joy; at thy right hand there are pleasures for evermore" (Psalm 16:11). It's so intricate that you can only take it in "daily doses." It's so right that once you experience it, you'll never look back.

> *God isn't planning to ruin your life! He has good things in mind for your future!*

It isn't problem free, carefree, or painless. It isn't easy, effortless, or lighthearted. Sometimes it's uphill. Sometimes it involves tears or trials. Sometimes it leads through valleys. Sometimes it involves burdens or disappointments. But life in general includes all of that as well—without the promises of God attached.

God's will isn't some rosy life of bliss and blessings. God never promises a perfect, problem-free path. His will includes a vast array of life experiences that range from the pleasant to the painful—and everywhere in between.

The difference between God's will and your own is this. Your will might provide temporary joy from time to time—His will provides fullness of joy. Your will might lead through painful experiences that you must face alone—His will provides strength, provision, security, and love during painful experiences that He foreordains. In addition to this, through every trial, in His will, you'll have the sustaining peace that He is there; He is in control; He is carrying you through; and He is weaving something good in your life. Your own will offers no such promise.

Living in your own will leads you to a lonely, barren place where you must be your own god. You must provide for yourself, sustain yourself, and depend upon yourself. In the face of tragedy, job-loss, or disaster, you are alone; and you are forced to find your own solution. Something impossible for mere "sheep."

In God's will, whether on a mountain top or in a valley, you can rest in knowing that God is leading you, and your soul "shall not want" (Psalm 23). In God's will you will find true success, purpose in life, and internal joy. In God's will you can have confidence that even the most mundane details of your day align somehow with God's awesome design! In God's will you will know what life is all about and how you fit into His eternal plan. In God's will, you can pillow your head each night with true peace and satisfaction, and you can face death with confidence. Wherever His will leads you, His grace will sustain you, and His power will keep you.

Finally, from the deathbed of your own will, you will look back regretting a life of bad choices and missed blessings. Yet, from the deathbed of God's will, with a full heart of joy, you will look back on a rich legacy of spiritual blessings with no regrets!

God's will for you is a detailed account of your life, pre-written in eternity past. He will unveil this plan to you moment by moment along your life-journey. At every turn, He already knows what is around the next bend, and He has already provided what you need when you get there. God's will takes you from birth through a series of decisions and choices (both yours and others) leading to the ultimate fulfillment of your purpose for existing. God's will is your life lived by God's leading, for God's glory, and within God's control. It's awesome!

In all of life's desired experiences, God's will is the one experience that you don't want to miss!

How does God reveal His will?

So many young adults struggle with the concept of God's will. Some struggle with surrendering to something they cannot see or comprehend. They feel as though they are "leaping in the dark."

Others have no problem surrendering to it, yet they struggle trying to find it or hoping to understand it. They worry needlessly about it and often work themselves into an emotional frenzy trying to reason it out.

A good look at biblical accounts of God's leading in the hearts of His people will help you deal with either of these issues. If you are struggling to surrender, you only need to see that God never fails, never falters, never lies, and never lets you down. This will compel you to surrender and give you confidence that His will truly is the "only option."

If you are struggling with finding it, needing to know it, or worrying about it, you'll find in Scripture that God always reveals His will in bite-size pieces. Think of the stories we've already talked about—Moses, Abraham, Joseph, Peter, etc. God led all of these individuals one *nerve-racking* step at a time! (Emphasis on *nerve-racking*!) There's not one person who knew the whole story up-front. There's not even one person that knew *some* of the story up-front. They were all led one step at a time, one moment at a time—but don't let this escape your realization. They *were* led! God has never failed to lead *one* of His followers!

The key is they were all listening! They all had listening hearts and ready minds. They were all surrendered and ready to follow His lead. They knew how to walk with Him, wait on Him, trust in Him, and recognize His hand at work. We'll talk more about that in a coming chapter, but for now, take note—God never fails to lead those who are of willing hearts! He wants to! He's waiting to! He *will*!

Perhaps you have been searching, worrying, and even panicking over finding God's will. Relax! If you are willing and surrendered, He will guide you! He won't let you make a wrong move (Psalm 32:8). He's not hiding it from you. Just wait on Him, seek Him, and in His time everything will fall into place.

Perhaps it drives you crazy that you cannot see more than a "few steps" down the path. Relax. That's how God works. So long as you know you're following Him, what does it matter? He sees tomorrow; He knows the future; and you'll get there in His time. Worrying about it, stewing over it, and working yourself into a frenzy serves only to rob your joy and minimize your trust.

Second Timothy 1:7 tells us, "For God hath not given us the *spirit of fear*; but of power, and of love, and of a sound mind." If you are fearful or anxious about not knowing God's will, perhaps you're not really living by faith. True faith will rest in God's good promise and truly trust Him with the future.

Relax! If you are willing and surrendered, He will guide you! He won't let you make a wrong move.

Think of it this way. It's not up to you to *find* His will as much as it's up to Him to *lead* you into it. Your primary responsibility is to be lead-able—to stay soft, sensitive, surrendered, and right with Him so that He can guide you day by day.

Can I miss His will?

When I was in my later high school years, this was my big fear. I didn't want to miss His will. I didn't want to end up on my deathbed having taken too many wrong turns. The thought literally scared me.

Surely, you *can* miss God's will for your life, but the question is how? In Psalm 32:8, God taught me that missing His will was more related to me denying His leading than it was to me missing His clues.

I had this mental picture that God had created a perfect will, hidden it among all the other options of life, and then sent me out into young adulthood to find it for myself. My idea was that it was a scavenger hunt for my destiny, and I was truly hoping to find it. I was afraid of missing it.

The promise in Psalm 32:8 taught me that there is NO WAY for a *surrendered* person to miss God's will, apart from God breaking His promise. (That's impossible!) He has promised to lead you and guide you, so long as you are lead-able. He says in verse nine, "Be ye not as the horse, or as the mule, which have no understanding...." In other words, if you choose to resist, if you choose not to be led, like a stubborn mule or horse, you *will* miss it. So, God says, "don't be that way!"

If you're spending a great deal of time worrying about God's will—stop. Focus more on drawing close to Him, walking with Him, and knowing Him. Concentrate on having a surrendered heart. Consume yourself with being lead-able, and God will take care of everything else.

Seek His will first.

There is a difference between seeking God's will and fretting over it. Hebrews 11:6 tells us that God rewards those who diligently seek Him. Matthew 6:33 tells us to seek first the kingdom of God. Other verses command us to draw nigh to Him, seek Him early, and give Him first priority in our lives. Obviously God wants us to seek Him, to seek His will, and to make His kingdom the primary pursuit of our lives. In light of these Scriptures, when it comes to God's will, I challenge you to begin seeking!

By now, hopefully you recognize that God's will is wonderful! It is not something to fear, but it is something to anticipate! It is not something to run from but to run to! It is not something that threatens our futures, but rather holds our futures. Hopefully, by now, you want God's will!

I firmly believe that God is pleased when His people seek Him and seek His ways. I believe He delights when we choose to pursue Him, to know Him, to understand Him, to learn of Him. I believe that He reveals Himself most fully and intimately to those who truly seek Him personally.

If God's will is something you desire, then you should begin communicating that desire to God through a seeking heart. You should begin deliberately studying, praying, and meditating on truths that teach you of God's will and ways. Begin a quest for God and for His truth. At this point, this quest is not merely a self-centered *need to know the details*. It's far deeper and richer than that. This is a quest to walk with, to understand, and to know the heart and mind of God.

Think of it this way. Right now, in your life, you are seeking something. It may be something intangible like acceptance, friendships, popularity, or prestige. It may be something tangible like a car, a job, a driver's license, or a status symbol. Chances are you woke up this morning with something on your heart and mind—something you are seeking. It may be a dating relationship with some special person, a grade point average in a certain course, or a promotion at work. What are you seeking?

I submit to you, based upon the Scriptures, if God's will is something that you really desire, you must seek it *first*, above all else. This might seem like a high-hurdle for you to get over at this point in life, but you must. If God's will is not your first priority, it may as well be your last. You'll never experience it.

Perhaps the toughest decision of my teenage years was which college to attend. I knew my college decision had enormous consequences, and it was not something that I took lightly. I truly wanted to do God's will.

The tough part of the equation was that I was dating a girl that I really, really loved. I had this gut feeling that we were made for each other. I really believed that we would one day be married, and I think she felt the same way, though I couldn't say for sure. For several months I had a very real quandary. I wanted to follow God more than my feelings for this young lady, and I feared that my emotions would dictate my college decision! If this happened, I knew it would be the mistake of my life.

So, by God's grace, this young lady and I had a talk, and came to the conclusion that we would not discuss college with each other, at all. She felt the same way I did. We both wanted God's will for our lives more than we wanted each other, and we deliberately chose to protect ourselves from our own blinding emotions. We determined that she would choose a college based upon God's leading in her own heart and with godly counsel from her parents and others, and I would do the same. We would not be a part of each other's decision in any way, and we would not disclose our decisions to each other until both were finalized. Talk about nerve-racking!

If God's will is not your first priority, it may as well be your last. You'll never experience it.

Well, judgment day finally arrived. Several months later, the time came when each of us had made our decisions, apart from each other, and it was time to reveal the outcome. I was as nervous in that moment as I have ever been. Yet, in both of our hearts, as much as we liked each other, there was a calm resolve that God's will would prevail. We knew if God led us apart, it was for a good reason. Silently, we both hoped that God would lead us together.

"Okay, you go first." I said.

"No, you go first." She said.

"No, you go first." I said.

It didn't take a rocket scientist to figure out that this was going nowhere, so one of us finally gave in. I don't remember who, and it didn't matter. God led us both, independently, to the same Bible college!

At that moment I wanted to grab her, wrap her up in both arms, and shout "I knew it, I just knew it. You ARE the one for me!" I wanted to hug her, kiss her, and tell her I loved her, but her dad would have killed me, shortcutting the whole destiny thing. So I opted to smile real big and say, "cool!" (A few years later, we were married, and now we kiss all the time—it's our destiny!)

Here's my point. We both made a conscious decision to seek God's will first, no matter how strong our personal desires were. And we were both serious about that commitment. Had God led us apart, we were truly willing to part ways and follow Him down separate paths for our lives.

Looking back on that time, I know that one reason God made His will clear was that we were both seeking Him first in our lives. This pleased God and prompted Him to guide us just as He promised.

I challenge you to do the same. Seek God's will first above every pursuit and desire of your heart. Make Him preeminent. Make His plans your priority. Show him, in your seeking, that you are hungry to know Him and to follow Him every step of the way. In so doing, you will not only please Him greatly, you will know Him personally.

How should a person seek Him?

There are many ways to seek God and His will, but here are a few practical ways that you could begin right now:

1. Read, study, and meditate on the Bible. Do character studies, word studies, or topical searches on following God and knowing God. Study how Bible characters followed Him. Study those who rebelled. Read everything in Scripture that you can find about God's leading and God's will.

2. Walk with God in prayer. Take a walk with God literally. Sometimes it's hard to stay awake if you pray kneeling or in bed. Get up a few minutes earlier and take a walk around the block before school. Slip out of the house at sunset and walk the neighborhood. While you do, talk to God. Give Him your undivided attention and ask Him the questions that are on your heart. Communicate your true desires and thoughts to Him.

3. Make church a priority. It's a priority with God, so it should be with you too. If church is unimportant to you, then so is God's will. Don't work on Sundays. Go to church and listen with an open heart to every lesson, every song, and every message. You'll be surprised how much God will address your specific questions or thoughts during these times if you have an open and seeking heart.

Show God, in your seeking, that you are hungry to know Him and to follow Him every step of the way. In so doing, you will not only please Him greatly, you will know Him personally.

4. Read good books and biographies. Ask godly mentors in your life what books they've read that have impacted them greatly. Read biographies of great Christians who walked with God. Read books about spiritual maturity and growth. All of these resources will equip you for the journey ahead and mature you in God's grace. Each tool will be useful in the hands of the Holy Spirit as He speaks to your heart and molds you for God's glory.

5. Listen to godly music. Godly music will lift your heart towards the Lord. It will motivate you to love Him and to listen to Him more attentively. This kind of music will nourish your soul and sharpen your mind. God will use it to lead you forward in your spiritual journey.

6. Deliberately separate from worldly influences. We've talked about a pure heart, but think of it this way. Each worldly influence serves to deaden your spiritual senses and dull your understanding. At this time in your life, you need every spiritual insight that you can get. Get rid of things that take your heart away from spiritual things.

There are probably many other ways, but this is a start. If you want to live God's will day by day, then you must begin seeking

God as your first priority in life. Truly, He's the only One worthy of that preeminence!

Surrender to His will completely.

Question: Why should God feel obligated to reveal His will to someone who has no intention of following it? Answer: He shouldn't. Fact: He won't.

So, let me cut you off at the pass. If you have the intention of *seeking* His will and then determining *if* you will do it or not, forget it. You cannot choose to do His will *after* you see what it is. This choice must be made before He will ever reveal it to you. That's what faith is all about. God doesn't make deals. He knows your heart before you ever begin seeking. If you are seeking His will with ulterior motives, God won't play that game.

It's not about finding out what God wants to do with your life. It's about choosing God and knowing that *He* is enough. It's about knowing that He is your life and your only hope of true success and happiness. When you make that realization, you'll choose Him, and His plan will simply become a by-product of your intimate walk with Him. At that point, you won't need to know *what* He wants you to do. You'll just be glad to know He's yours and you're His—and everything else will be just fine!

Romans 12:1–2 says, "I beseech you therefore, brethren, by the mercies of God, that ye present your bodies a living sacrifice, holy, acceptable unto God, which is your reasonable service. And be not conformed to this world: but be ye transformed by the renewing of your mind, that ye may prove what is that good, and acceptable, and perfect, will of God."

God expects unconditional surrender prior to revealing His will. In His economy, this kind of surrender is reasonable. He expects you to sign a blank sheet of paper so that He can fill in the details. He is looking for complete abandon and total trust.

You might be thinking, "Are you kidding? God expects me to just abandon everything *before* I even know what He's going to have me do?"

Exactly. That's what the disciples did when Jesus said, "Follow me." That's what Abraham did when God said, "Leave your homeland." That's what Joseph did when God said, "Go to jail. Go directly to jail." That's what Mary did when God said, "Surprise, you're expecting!" That's what every great Bible character did at some point in life. They abandoned themselves in total surrender to God's plan. They truly loved God more than anything or anyone else!

This is directly opposed to what your social science teacher will tell you. You won't get this advice from your public school guidance counselor. You won't find it on *Oprah*, and it won't be featured in *Seventeen* magazine or in any other worldly resource. It's still true. It's still the right way to live.

Simply put, God will not guide you or lead you until He knows that you are fully surrendered to Him.

Have you ever come to that vital moment when you knelt down and completely gave your life to God? If not, now is the time. What's holding you back? What is it about God that you don't trust? What are you afraid of? Why do you feel that God is such a threat?

Question: Why should God feel obligated to reveal His will to someone who has no intention of following it? Answer: He shouldn't. Fact: He won't.

Face that fear. Call it what it is—faithless defiance. Call it distrust. Call it an accusation that God is not truthful or faithful. Call it pride and arrogance. At the very least, call it a lie that you should stop believing. Then let go—surrender. It's not hard. It's not some impenetrable fortress. It's just a choice.

Bow down on your knees; confess to God that He is everything He claims; and then surrender completely to His every desire. Tell Him you will do whatever He wants you to do. Tell Him you will follow wherever He leads and obey whatever He says. Tell Him you belong completely to Him—it's your "reasonable service."

You are not your own (1 Corinthians 6:19–20). You were bought with the blood of Jesus Christ, and you exist for the purpose and glory of Almighty God. Give God what is rightly His and stop laying claim on His purchased possession—your life.

There is sweetness in surrender that touches the deepest reaches of our beings. There is deep, incomparable joy in letting God have control. There is an intimate and consuming peace that passes all understanding when you finally reach the point of giving in.

When you completely surrender to God's will, not knowing what it is, you are truly expressing a very genuine faith, and you are on a collision course with destiny!

God won't force His will on you.

One final thought about God's will. God will not force His will on you. He doesn't force Himself on anybody. He has always given man a free will in matters relating to eternity. Even Jonah, though relentlessly pursued by God, had a choice. You must choose Him. You must seek Him and surrender to Him. You must initiate the process of surrender, and He will most definitely respond.

There was another time that I planned a fun day for Lance and Larry. It was about five years after the "Disney vs. Dimples" incident, and I'll never forget it.

Haylee, our daughter, was about a year old at the time, and Dana decided to take her to San Jose to visit Grandma and Grandpa. Her flight was on a Thursday morning, my day off, and on a sheer whim I opted to take the boys out of school for the day. Lance was ten, and Larry was seven.

We woke up early, loaded everybody into the car, and headed to the Burbank airport about an hour away. Over the course of that hour, Lance and Larry both asked about our plans for the day. Not wanting to give away the secret, I avoided the questions.

"Oh, we'll probably just go home and go back to school."

My plans were to drop Dana off at the airport, take the boys to Krispy Kreme Donuts (my home away from home) and then to surprise them with a day at Universal Studios (not that I endorse Universal Studios movies, but it is a fun theme park).

So, we dropped Mom off at the airport, said our good-byes, and began our "trek" through Burbank to Krispy Kreme. This time Lance and Larry had no idea where we were going, and neither of them seemed to mind too much. They were just glad to be out of school and with Dad.

There is sweetness in surrender that touches the deepest reaches of our beings. There is deep, incomparable joy in letting God have control.

I was trying to imagine the best way to reveal my surprise. I love to plan surprises for these kids just to watch their excitement. It's something I never get over! By this time I was dying to tell them what the plan was, but I waited. Just a few more minutes.

Suddenly, I saw the sign. That lovely, red and green neon sign. Then, in the window, the red flashing sign—"Hot Donuts Now!" Oh, how I love that sign. It beckons to the soul.

As I pulled in, I adjusted my mirror so I could see their faces. "Hey guys."

"What?"

"How about if we go to Krispy Kreme to get some donuts?" I waited, knowing there was more.

Their faces came alive, "All RIGHT!" The backseat broke out in cheers of joy and anthems of delight.

"AND THEN," I raised my voice to capture their attention, (dramatic pause) "THEN, we're going to UNIVERSAL STUDIOS!" I shouted with triumph.

You would have thought we won the Publishers' Clearing House Sweepstakes. They exploded with a chorus of high fives, "*all right's*," and "*yes's*" that would have rivaled any Super Bowl championship. It was a moment I shall cherish for the rest of my life. I was a hero. In one fell swoop I had managed to free them from the tyranny of school, reveal the promise of hot donuts, and deliver them into the welcoming arms of fun and fanfare for one full day. I was "cool." I was "great." I was "the best." I was "awesome." They hugged me; they kissed me; they danced on each other's heads; and they played gleefully for all of fifteen seconds.

Then, they both pensively sat back in a moment of stark realization. I was confused. Where did the fanfare go? I was enjoying the acceptance. What happened? I waited, and it only took a second or two. This time, it was Larry who spoke. His voice was innocent and searching. His tone—sincere but inquisitive.

"Hey Dad, what's Universal Studios?"

Lance followed, "Yeah, Dad, what *is* Universal Studios?"

I laughed. I mean I laughed hard, and so did they. They laughed because I laughed! Here they were, in the back seat, having a party for ONE REASON ONLY. The sound of my voice had convinced them that Universal Studios, whatever it was, was something they should be happy about. So, for all of fifteen seconds they chose to live by faith, to trust Dad, and they had a celebration. I mean they were out of control. They didn't know *why*, but they knew it must be GOOD!

What innocence! What trust! What a perfect picture of surrender and faith.

I tried for a few minutes to explain the rides, the animal shows, the fun—but I finally just said, "Guys, trust me, you're going to have a great time. Today is going to be an awesome day."

Guess what? They did!

That day is one of the most memorable days I've ever had with my two boys. I'm sure all three of us will remember it for the rest of our lives. We ran all day long. We laughed, played, and had a big time. We bought souvenirs and made great memories, and they slept all the way home. As long as I live, I'll never forget the moment that they were made so happy, just by the tone of my voice.

Do you think we could be that way with God? Do you think we could explode with joyful anticipation at the mere mention of His good and perfect will for us? Do you think we could celebrate His plan, even though we don't know what it is? Do you think we could be that childish? I sure hope so. Something tells me that would make God very, very happy.

So, while you're chewing on all this "God's will" stuff, mainly remember to sit back, relax, and know that you're going to have a great life so long as God is planning it.

Now let's go have some donuts…

Last one in is a rotten egg!

"Blessed is every one that feareth the LORD;
that walketh in his ways."
—Psalm 128:1

thirteen

Chapter Thirteen
Speak Up, God; I Can't Hear You!
Step #3 for Right Decision-Making—Pray About Your Decision

Looking back for a moment, right decision-making starts with five vital tools. To make right choices you must have the following:

1. A Serious Mind
2. A Pure Heart
3. A Courageous Spirit
4. The Wisdom of God
5. A Heart of Faith

Then, decision-making moves forward with these critical steps:

1. Refuse to Trust Yourself
2. Seek and Surrender to God's Will

This brings us to a very important step three in the process.

Once you've come to a point of total surrender to God's unseen will, you are ready to begin seriously **praying** about your decision. How do you pray? Why pray? What happens when you pray? What will God do in response to your prayer? What are you hoping to get through prayer? All of these questions will be addressed in the next few pages, so stay with me.

Silencing the voices without

I need you to work with me in this section. Since I cannot physically communicate with you in these next few pages, I need your help in imagining some things that might help you understand how prayer plays a part in decision making.

Imagine that you are standing in a room called "life" and there are four people standing around you—one in front, one behind, and one to either side of you. For the sake of illustration, these people will represent four opportunities for your future. For now we'll just call them "voices." These four people represent things you could do, opportunities that will open up to you, and influences that will try to persuade you to choose one way over another.

The first person in front of you is the person you might date or fall in love with. Imagine that he or she is standing directly in front of you talking loudly about plans for your future. This person will represent voice #1.

Now, let's imagine that the person behind you represents your current employer. For the sake of illustration, let's assume that for the past two years you've worked at Wendy's hamburger restaurant. You've become an expert at flipping burgers, frying French fries, and pouring large frosties. In fact, you've done so well, management has promoted you. They like you. They would love to keep you on the Wendy's team and make you a permanent part of their organization. Imagine that this man is promising you further training, management promotions, and higher pay in your present job. He represents voice #2.

With one person in front of you talking loudly and one person behind you talking loudly, the person to your left starts shouting too, trying to be heard over the other voices.

For the sake of being absurd, let's imagine that one of your highly acclaimed skills is ballet. (C'mon. Work with me here.) Let's imagine that ever since you were little, you excelled at ballet. In fact, you have become one of the finest ballerinas or balladeers in the nation. (The guys in my Sunday school class really cringe when I use them for this illustration.)

To your left stands a representative of the New York ballet. He is offering you a highly acclaimed position. He is loudly promising you a high salary, worldwide fame, and a host of other incentives. He is compelling you to come and join his award-winning team of ballet professionals. In fact, imagine that he has grabbed your arm and is forcefully trying to pull you in his direction.

To your right is a representative of the University of California in Los Angeles (UCLA). This man is here to offer you a full four-year scholarship for a pre-med degree from UCLA with the promise of medical school, residency, and a lucrative practice in the years to come. He is loudly shouting and touting his offer, trying to convince you to choose his school, and he too has grabbed your arm and is actively pulling you his direction.

There you stand, surrounded with *promising* opportunities. By the way, you don't have to go along with my absurd illustrations. You could fill in the blank faces with whatever opportunities are currently trying to persuade or pull you in a direction. You could fill in the blanks with whatever your interests, hobbies, or academic skills lend themselves to.

These four (or more) voices are now shouting loudly, competing with each other for your future, pulling for you to move their direction, and actively trying to recruit you. It's confusing. It's loud. It's frustrating. It's a very difficult choice.

This is where you will be—sooner or later. You will have opportunities. You will face these voices in one form or another. The faces will be different, but they will be there trying to pull you, to monopolize your attention, and influence your future. You will have job offers, college offers, and relational opportunities; and these "promising opportunities" will come your way when you least expect them. Most importantly, they will attempt to confuse your decision-making process, and you must be prepared for them.

One senior who recently graduated from my youth group had surrendered his life to Jesus Christ. He had been called to serve God in the ministry, and he had been hearing these principles in our twelfth grade Sunday school class. Oddly enough, the very week I mentioned these distractions in class, this young man received a $5,000 check in the mail from a bank he had worked for. They needed his bi-lingual ability and the check in the mail was their official offer for him to return to work for them. The catch? He would have to forego Bible college and would have to put off serving the Lord with his future. His schedule with the bank would not allow for these commitments. (Hmmm…)

Once you've come to a point of total surrender to God's unseen will, you are ready to begin seriously praying about your decision.

Think about that for a minute. A $5,000 check makes for a pretty loud "voice" when you're a high school senior!

By the way, these voices may not all be wrong or sinful. In fact, eventually God's calling for your life will come in this same way—as an opportunity. I'm not saying that every voice is wrong. I'm just calling your attention to the fact that every opportunity has a voice, and many times those voices drown out God's voice.

When this young man came to me for advice about his $5,000 check, I must admit, I was hopeful that the bank would work with his schedule so that he could keep the check and stay in Bible college. At the same time, I was suspicious that the check was a loud voice trying to pull him away from God's perfect will.

After some talks with the bank and a lot of prayer, thankfully, this young man returned the check and "stayed the course" for a future in ministry! His decision was a good one, but it wasn't easy.

Not every voice will come in the form of a $5,000 check, but they will come! Be ready for them and recognize them for what they really are—loud voices that often drown out God's voice.

Back to our illustration—imagine that, outside of the circle of voices that has surrounded you stands your Heavenly Father. He's not speaking, shouting, or pulling. He's not a part of the chaos. He's just waiting. He's waiting for you. He waits patiently and silently.

Having seen Him and recognized Him—imagine that you deliberately look at voice #1, and you silence it. You intentionally turn a deaf ear to the demands of this person you're dating. Then you forcefully pull your arms from the grasps of voices #3 and #4 and turn a deaf ear to them as well. You're letting go of these opportunities. You're making a conscious effort to silence their influence in your heart, for the moment.

Finally, you turn and face Wendy's (voice #2) and deliberately still that voice as well. Now, all the voices are quiet, all of the opportunities have been put on hold, and you stand alone in silence.

This is a picture of surrender. Now it's just you and God, standing in an empty room called life, and He's standing there waiting for you.

At this point, you move to where God is, you kneel down before His presence, and you begin to ask for His guidance and help. You pour your heart out to Him. You rehearse all of the things the voices were shouting at you, asking for His insight and opinion on each opportunity. You have bowed before His presence with an open heart. You're not clinging to any single hope or dream. You are empty handed—having truly let go of all the things that were calling for your life. Now, you're finally ready to begin praying for God's direction.

Until you come to this powerful point of surrender, you're simply not ready to pray for God's guidance. Why should God answer the prayer of a person who isn't really planning on obeying the answer in the first place? Why should God feel obligated to reveal His will to someone who isn't completely committed to following it?

If you're still struggling with this idea of surrender, you should still pray, but your praying should focus on seeking God's help to surrender. In other words, your prayers should say something like "God help me to trust you" or "God give me the courage to surrender to you."

On the other hand, once you finally silence the voices and let go of the opportunities, you are truly ready to bow before God and ask for His guidance and leading.

Understanding how God speaks to His children

I said in an earlier chapter that God will never force Himself or His will upon you, yet He will always try to speak to you. So how does God speak?

Primarily, God speaks today through His Word. He doesn't speak audibly, and He doesn't appear in burning bushes or through "weeping" crucifixes. He speaks through the Word of God to your heart. At the same time, He speaks through His indwelling Holy Spirit in your heart. But understand, His still small voice within will always be consistent with the final authority of His preserved Word.

Many people today elevate some personal experience to be equal to the Word of God, but this is a dangerous path. Even Peter in 2 Peter 1:16–21 declares that the Word of God was "more sure" than his own eyewitness or his own personal experience. While the bulk of this chapter will be about hearing and discerning the voice of God within, you must realize that this "inner guidance" must never come above the authority of God's Word in your life. To truly understand and hear God speaking, you must be in His Word first and foremost.

In 1 Kings 19:9–15, the prophet Elijah experienced God's leading in a very special way. The Bible says, "And he came thither unto a cave, and lodged there; and, behold, the word of the LORD came to him, and he said unto him, What doest thou here, Elijah? And he said, I have been very jealous for the LORD God of hosts: for the children of Israel have forsaken thy covenant, thrown down thine altars, and slain thy prophets with the sword; and I, even I only, am left; and they seek my life, to take it away. And he said, Go forth, and stand upon the mount before the LORD. And, behold, the LORD passed by, and a great and strong wind rent the mountains, and brake in pieces the rocks before the LORD; but the LORD was not in the wind: and after the wind an earthquake; but the LORD was not in the earthquake: And after the earthquake a fire; but the LORD was not in the fire: and after the fire *a still small voice.* And it was so, when Elijah heard it, that he wrapped his face in his mantle, and went out, and stood in the entering in of the cave. And, behold, there came a voice unto him, and said, What doest thou here, Elijah? And he said, I have been very jealous for the LORD God of hosts: because the children of Israel have forsaken thy covenant, thrown down thine altars, and slain thy prophets with the sword; and I, even I only, am left; and they seek my life, to take it away. And the LORD said unto him, Go, return on thy way to the wilderness of Damascus: and when thou comest, anoint Hazael to be king over Syria."

His still small voice within will always be consistent with the final authority of His preserved Word.

In this passage we learn something very significant about the leading of God. God doesn't speak through loud voices. He doesn't compete for your attention. He won't try to shout louder or longer than all of the other opportunities in your life.

No. He will simply speak with a still small voice.

You may be wondering, "What does all of this have to do with prayer?"

The answer—"*everything.*" Why pray about your decision? Because God commands you to diligently seek Him! God intends for you to be the initiator of the seeking, and in turn He will respond to your faith. He will speak to your heart. He will indeed lead you, guide you, and impress you through the still small voice of His spirit within your life.

The catch is, if you don't silence the outside voices and seek His voice alone, you will never hear it.

In Mark chapter six, Jesus deliberately sends His disciples across the sea and directly into a storm. You probably know the story, but there's an interesting detail in verse 48 that many people completely miss. In the middle of the night, Jesus came walking on the water to the frightened disciples, and in verse 48 the Bible says that Jesus "would have passed by!" Think about that. He was literally going to pass right by them, if they didn't notice Him and cry out to Him.

In this verse, once again, we see the nature and character of God. He refused to force His help or assistance upon His followers. Yet, when they noticed Him, He immediately talked with them and helped them.

Consider this. Jesus Christ will stand in the shadows of your life, ready to guide and help you. He will not force His will upon you or forcibly require your obedience.

You may be sailing through the middle of a storm of decisions and confusing opportunities. You may be so busy dealing with the mess that you completely miss Him. You may spend the rest of your life trying to calm your own storms and find your own way home. And all the while, Jesus will be there, quietly waiting to come to your side, calm your storm, and guide you to safety in His perfect plan. Will you notice Him? Will you go to Him? Will you seek Him in prayer and listen for His still small voice? He's waiting to speak if you will place yourself in the position of truly listening. Praying about your decision is all about placing yourself in a position where God will speak to your listening heart.

Remember this, God will not line up among all of the other voices in your life and shout to be heard. He will not compete or settle for partial surrender. He doesn't speak that way. He speaks with a still small voice to a surrendered and listening heart.

Many people have never heard this voice; therefore, they cannot identify with it. If you've never come to a point of full surrender and sincere prayer, then you've probably never heard it either.

Yet, if you will silence the voices and come boldly to the throne of grace—something very wonderful will happen. God will speak to your heart.

We have this swing in our backyard. It's really great. First of all, it fits all five of us—which makes for some interesting family fun. Second, it's really comfortable after a long day. Third, it's a great place for family talks. Something about the tranquil setting of our backyard in the evening just makes that swing a nice place to "be with God." That is, until the guy on the other side of the fence starts yelling at his dog or slamming his trash can or something. Generally it's a really nice place to be.

A few days ago, I grabbed Haylee and called for the boys, and we headed for the swing. Something we hadn't done in a while. It was a nice evening, quiet outside, and the last rays of sunlight were just disappearing. On top of that, this just isn't *any* swing. It's the best one that Wal-mart sells. It just sort of swallows you. It's great!

Not long into our conversation Dana joined us, and we were all sitting there just discussing our favorite things about being Christians. I was surprised at the great things Lance and Larry thought of.

Then, in a moment of quiet thought, Lance asked, "Dad, what if I don't remember being saved?"

His question was deep, so to clarify I said, "Do you mean you don't remember praying the prayer because you were little?"

"Yes," he said, "What if I don't remember getting saved? Am I still saved?"

The theologian guys in my head panicked. Then they started running around crazily searching for answers. I paused for a moment, hoping they would come up with something quick. Fortunately, with the Holy Spirit's help, they did.

"Well, Lance, there are several ways to know that you're saved. Remembering when you got saved is pretty important, but that's not the only way."

"What are some others?" he asked.

"What about when you do something wrong? Does the Holy Spirit convict you?"

"Oh yes." He said with an absolute tone and a laugh.

I continued, "And the Bible says that His Spirit bears witness with our spirit? Does His Holy Spirit tell your heart that you're saved?" I knew I was sticking my neck out on the line. *Dear Lord, don't leave me alone in this.*

God doesn't speak through loud voices. He doesn't compete for your attention. He won't try to shout louder or longer than all of the other opportunities in your life.

"What do you mean?" He said.

Dana was sitting there with this look like, "Where are you going with this?" Larry was just glad that it was Lance's problem and not his. Haylee didn't seem burdened at all for Lance. I think she was looking for the moon.

A little hesitant, I continued, "Have you asked the Holy Spirit, in your heart, if you are saved? The Bible says that He will bear witness with your spirit and tell you if you are or not."

Lance laughed like, "You've got to be kidding," and I just looked at him.

"What, you mean like right now...just ask Him...right here?" He was beside himself.

"Sure, why not?" I said flatly, "If you need to know, ask Him."

At this point, Larry really laughed. Dana hushed him, and I just looked at Lance and said, "Well, go ahead. We'll be quiet for you."

Again he glanced at me like I was half crazy, but then he bowed his head, and everything was quiet for about ten seconds. Suddenly, he looked up and said, "Wait, wait…just like right here…just ask Him?" Apparently, he really felt weird about it.

"Sure, go ahead. He will either tell you that you are saved, or He will convict you that you should get saved, one of the two. Go ahead. We're being quiet."

Dana's hand was over Larry's mouth, who was letting out little snorts and sniffs like he was about to explode with laughter. He really thought this was funny.

At this point, I just began to pray, "Lord, I'm sticking my neck out here, please speak to His heart like only you can."

Another ten seconds passed, and Lance looked up with a big smile.

"Well, what did He say?" I asked.

He sort of let out a laugh, "Well, my mind said yes, but then it said no, but then it said yes again."

"Well, who do you think is speaking to your heart and saying 'yes'?" I asked resolutely.

"Wait, wait, let me try one more time." With that he bowed his head and we entered another time of quiet prayer. I winked at Dana who was still trying to keep Larry from ruining a good thing.

A few seconds later he looked up and loudly stated "Okay, He said 'YES!'"

I smiled, "How do you know?"

"I asked Him for a final answer!" He laughed, we all laughed, Larry really laughed, and for the first time, Lance understood what it meant to seek God in prayer and listen for an answer.

"Lance," I said with my hand on his shoulder, "You just learned a very important lesson about the Christian life. God will speak to your heart like that for the rest of your life, if you will listen and if you will obey."

I'll never forget that night. There have been many such moments in my own heart, and I'll never forget the look on Lance's face when he realized how accessible God really is and how easy it was to enter His presence and hear from His heart.

Now, it might sound like I'm oversimplifying it, but for a surrendered heart, it's about that simple. The Lord is waiting for you to seek Him. He's eager to answer you, and He's ready to speak to your heart. The problem is we rarely acknowledge Him with our questions; therefore, His voice is foreign to our hearts. The other problem is sometimes we're not really willing to hear His answer.

By the way, I'm not saying to listen to your heart above God's Word or to "let your heart guide you." There's a vast difference between following your heart and following God's voice at work in your heart. One is self-centered; the other comes through real surrender and spiritual seeking. One leads to despair while the other leads to blessing. Be careful that you don't confuse the two.

Feigning prayer to soothe the conscience

Have you ever known someone who made a bad decision, yet they claimed to have "prayed about it"? People do this all the time. As human beings, we have the unique ability to deceive ourselves, and this is one of the most prevalent ways that young adults do so. The recipe for self-deception goes something like this:

Trust your own desires and emotions and decide you're going to do something. Godly friends and counselors may know that you're making a wrong decision, but disregard their opinions. Think about what you want and just make up your mind. Now, pray. Sure, go ahead and actually ask God if you should follow through with your decision. Pray for a few seconds, a few minutes, or for weeks if you want to. It doesn't matter at this point, because your prayers are useless. They are simply a "prop." God doesn't respond to this kind of prayer, and He doesn't lead this kind of heart—so your prayers only serve two legitimate purposes.

First, they serve to soothe your conscience. Deep within your conscience, you will recognize that you have made up your mind without God and that you've completely disregarded His principles, and "praying" will make you feel better about your rebellion.

Second, they will serve as your defense in the face of godly counselors. You're going to need a spiritual reason for defending what ultimately are *your own selfish desires*. These "prayers" make a great defense against those who would caution you or warn you that something's not right about this decision. You can counter all resistance with those pious words, "Well, I've prayed about this, and God has given me a peace about it."

Of course, what you really mean is you've made up your mind, and you've closed your heart

There's a vast difference between following your heart and following God's voice at work in your heart. One is self-centered; the other comes through real surrender and spiritual seeking.

to the matter. The "prayer" talk becomes a convenient shroud to cover up your blatant disregard of spiritual principles.

You can use this "prayer" talk to get or do just about anything that comes to mind. I've heard of adults who "prayed" about leaving their spouse to marry someone else. I know young adults who "prayed" about getting out of church to follow some career path. Pregnant girls have "prayed" about getting abortions, young men have "prayed" about being immoral, and rebellious teens have "prayed" about running away from home to live with another parent. It's actually pretty amazing that God has "led" so many people to do so many things in direct opposition to the principles of His Word.

You see, once you set your mind to follow your own path, "prayer" talk is a great way to cover your tracks. After all, who's going to argue with that kind of defense? Hey, if you've prayed about it, what else can anybody say—right?

Beware of this kind of prayer. It's not real seeking. It's not genuine. It's simply a cover up for a rebellious heart, and it will lead you to a point of utter despair.

How should I pray about my decisions?

In previous chapters we've talked about praying for wisdom, but at this point, I challenge you to begin praying for guidance. Begin asking God to show you His direction and lead you in His perfect will. Let Him know that you desire only His best and remind Him of His promises to guide and direct your paths (Proverbs 3:5–6; Psalm 32:8).

Practically speaking, there are a lot of ways to pray, and sometimes we get psyched out about praying to the point that we do very little of it. Let's face it. It's pretty hard to actually pray on your knees with head bowed and eyes closed for any serious length of time. Maybe I'm more human than you, but it's during these times that my knees hurt, my brain falls asleep, and my thoughts wander. It's often during these times that I'm more focused on the discomfort of my physical position than I am on walking with my wonderful Saviour! (How's that for sheer honesty?)

Now, don't get me wrong. There's also something very scriptural about falling to your knees or on your face in humility and worship before God. You should do this as a regular part of your walk with God. There should be frequent private times when you literally bow before Him in adoration, confession, and thanksgiving. I'm simply saying that the physical obstacles in this often keep us from praying to God at all because we think that prayer only counts if we're on our knees. It's hard to motivate ourselves to *want* to spend a lot of time in this physical position of prayer.

In addition to this we're commanded in 1 Thessalonians 5:17 to "pray without ceasing"! The Bible also says that God wants to be in "all of our thoughts" (Psalm 10:4). When you take this into consideration, it becomes obvious that there are ways to pray that don't involve dark closets or difficult physical positions.

Genesis 5 teaches us that Enoch "walked with God." Genesis 6 teaches us that Noah "walked with God." The Bible is replete with occasions of godly men carrying on their daily, moment-by-moment relationship with God in a very personal and intimate way.

So, let me encourage you to do the same in your prayer life. Make prayer a part of your daily walk, your daily life, and your moment-by-moment thought processes.

I taught my Senior High class recently that prayer is as simple as thinking. Did it ever occur to you that you are always thinking? Your brain never really stops thinking. The more that you and I can begin capturing those thoughts and directing them to God in prayer, the more we are truly following the teaching of God's Word to "pray without ceasing" and to have God in "all of our thoughts."

You can pray while you drive, pray in the shower, pray while you get ready in the morning, and pray while you eat breakfast. (It sure beats helping Captain Crunch through the crunch-berry maze on the back of the cereal box for ten minutes every morning!) You can pray while bike riding, exercising, or walking. For me, one of the best ways to pray is to simply take a walk!

There is a multitude of ways to pray, and I encourage you to begin praying in and through everything you do. Make your praying a way of thinking, and specifically pray each and every day that God will guide you moment by moment into His perfect will.

As for *what* to pray, our pastor and others have taught a simple little four-point guide for prayer. Just remember the word ACTS when you pray. The letters stand for the following kinds of prayer:

Adoration—First, spend time adoring and worshipping God for His greatness, power, and love.

Confession—Then, ask Him to bring to mind anything that's not right in your life. Confess sin and make your heart right with Him. Ask Him to cleanse your heart and purify your life (Psalm 51).

Thanksgiving—Spend time thanking God for everything in your life. Thank Him for the blessings and the trials at the same time.

Supplication—Finally, bring your requests to God. Ask Him to help you, mold you, change you, guide you, and lead you. Ask Him to intervene in the special needs on your heart and mind. Bring the requests of friends and family before Him and trust Him to answer these prayers.

That little acronym—ACTS—could be your guide for any personal time of prayer. Adore Him, confess to Him, thank Him, and then bring your supplications.

One final thought—keep a prayer journal. I dare you to write down a list of specific requests with an entry date. Keep the list, pray through it regularly, and then write down the date that any request on your list is answered.

You're going to have a "jaw-dropping" experience about twelve months later. If you will consistently ask God for answers for one solid year, you'll be amazed at the ways He will answer specific prayers in your life over a twelve-month period. This is one of the single greatest "faith-building exercises" that you can do as a young adult.

In conclusion, prayer is a critical "step three" in your decision-making process. First, silence the voices. Then come before God regularly to ask for His guidance and help. Then, simply listen. God will speak to your heart with a crystal-clear voice—a still, small voice. You will know it is Him, and you will have a very clear understanding of what He wants you to do—at least for the next step on your journey. Remember He will lead you on a "need-to-know" basis. He's never going to unveil the whole thing at once, so don't get your hopes up.

> *Remember He will lead you on a "need-to-know" basis. He's never going to unveil the whole thing at once, so don't get your hopes up.*

One of the saddest verses in the Bible is Job 33:14, "For God speaketh once, yea twice, yet man perceiveth it not." Wouldn't you dread standing before God only to look back on a life that ignored His still, small voice? Imagine the regret that you will have one day to realize that God was trying to speak to you your whole life through, yet you never perceived His voice.

To the contrary, one of the happiest verses in the Bible is the account of Samuel hearing God's voice for the first time as a young boy. First Samuel 3:8 says, "And the LORD called Samuel again the third time. And he arose and went to Eli, and said, Here am I; for thou didst call me. And Eli perceived that the LORD had called the child." One of the greatest experiences of the Christian journey is to perceive the voice of God speaking to your heart. Many Christians never hear it because they never silence the "noises" of life long enough to discern it. But for those who will consistently enter into His presence, seek His leading, and listen—God still speaks quite undeniably and clearly.

If you will come to God with a surrendered, listening heart, you too will perceive when He is speaking to you. And believe me—He will!

"For God speaketh once, yea twice,
yet man perceiveth it not."
—Job 33:14

fourteen

Tight Ropes, Safety Nets, and Stupid People

Step #4 for Right Decision-Making—Seek Godly Counsel

Everything I've said up to this point in this book is intended to kick start you on the journey of seeking God, loving Him, and craving His will personally. Up to this point, it's all been about your personal, private walk with God. As we near the end, we're going to turn a big corner, and it's all predicated upon the fact that you must personally be seeking God. No one else can do it for you. Step four is to seek godly counsel. It will not be about giving up your personal search so you can blindly follow another person's plans. No, it goes far deeper than that, as you'll soon see.

Have you ever been to the circus? When I was a kid, one of my favorite "circus" experiences was watching the tightrope walkers. I don't know if it ever occurred to you, but there are two kinds of tightrope walkers in the universe—smart ones and dumb ones. And it's actually very easy to tell the difference. The smart ones are still alive because they realize the importance of using safety nets. The smart ones usually become "grand champion ropewalkers" while the dumb ones usually end up just being "stuff on the floor."

Several years ago, I was watching a documentary story about some tightrope walkers who had fallen to their death while performing. (Wow, what a show!) My first thought was, "Well, who didn't string the net up properly?" I assumed that they had fallen into a net that apparently "gave way" under them and dropped them to their deaths. Not so. These particularly brainy ropewalkers never used a net.

I laughed. I know I shouldn't have. It's not funny when somebody dies. (My wife reminded me.) I just couldn't believe that somebody could have such a small brain for a human.

I've heard of people killing themselves in stupid ways—like the guy who pulled a Coke machine over on himself while trying to shake loose a free can of Coke. Or, the lady who broke the law by parachuting over a cliff to prove how "safe it was." She died when her parachute didn't open. People all over the world die for stupid reasons, and tightrope walkers who die without safety nets should be right at the top of the list. The gene pool must not have been kind to this crowd.

Really now, if you're going to choose circus performing at significant heights for a career path, how much training does it take to figure out that you need a safety net? The word *splat* must not mean anything to these people!

I don't feel sorry for circus performers who die stupid deaths without safety nets. Maybe I just don't have the "gift of mercy." Pray for me.

Likewise, I don't feel sorry for young adults who make bad decisions without getting advice either. Godly counsel or "advice" is literally the "safety net" that God has given you to undergird your decisions. It's the "system of checks and balances" to verify that your heart is pure and that your direction is truly biblical. It's the last thing that's going to catch you just before you drop to a mistake zone of bad choices.

Think of it this way—just in case you've deceived yourself, and you're headed down a dark road with a bridge out, godly counsel is the last warning sign along the road that's going to cause you to turn back. Proverbs 19:21 says, "There are many devices in a man's heart; nevertheless the counsel of the LORD, that shall stand."

On the flip side, godly counsel is the final confirmation of God's true leading and direction in your heart. It's His way of proving Himself to you, and it's the safest way to absolutely know for sure that you're doing the right thing. Proverbs 20:18, "Every purpose is established by counsel: and with good advice make war."

What do I do after God speaks to me?

When you finally reach the point of sincere, surrendered prayer, good things are about to happen. God is going to speak to you and lead you. You won't get struck by lightning or see a 500-foot Jesus standing at the end of your bed. You won't feel warm and tingly, and you won't pass out with convulsions.

His leading may not be immediate, but it will be *in time*! In other words, God will speak to you when it's time. Until He does, don't sweat it. For instance, if He hasn't completely confirmed His will for college, that's okay. Don't get uptight about it. Just keep a listening heart. In time, He will confirm His leading in your heart.

This fourth step in decision-making, getting godly counsel, is absolutely one of the most important principles you will read in this entire book. Without it, you are in grave danger. While you can most certainly get counsel at any point in your spiritual growth, this step must absolutely follow the moment that God speaks to your heart. In other words, in between the moment that you hear God's still, small voice and the moment that you finalize your decision, you must seek the counsel of godly influences in your life to verify what you believe God has said to you.

The most critical time to get godly counsel in your life is after God has put a direction on your heart—but before you finalize your decision. At this point, you have done everything personally to seek God first, and now you're going to verify God's leading though a "multitude" of counselors.

Remember how I promised you that there is a way to "know for sure" that you're making a right decision? There is a biblical way to know for sure that you're marrying the right person, choosing the right college, and following the right career path. Well, this is the key step in getting that assurance. This is the litmus test of a pure heart, sincere motives, and true Holy Spirit leading. After all that we've learned and studied up to this point, this is the capstone—the final confirmation that you need before you "leap"! If you get anything in this book, get this.

Two types of counsel

In the Bible, the word *counsel* simply refers to advice or purposes, and the scriptures are clear that there are two types of counsel—just as there are two types of wisdom. The Bible refers to **godly counsel** and **ungodly counsel.**

Psalm 1:1 says it this way, "Blessed is the man that walketh not in the counsel of the ungodly, nor standeth in the way of sinners, nor sitteth in the seat of the scornful."

As you stand at the edge of your next decision, you will be surrounded by both types of counsel—godly and ungodly. There will always be those who try to advise you against God's will and those who try to advise you towards God's will, and it's up to you to choose who you will listen to.

In fact, I know many young adults who "play" ungodly counsel against godly counsel, or those who deliberately choose to hear ungodly counsel because they know they will be told what they want to hear. This kind of "game" is not what the Bible is referring to when it challenges us to get counsel.

Remember this, if you have chosen to follow your own will, it will be very easy to find people who will side with you. Usually it will be your friends—other young adults who don't know any more than you do about life. (Probably less!) They will say things like "It's your life, do whatever you want" or "Come on, everybody's doing it."

Here is the key principle—ungodly counsel will always find *you*. Godly counsel is just the opposite—you must find *it*!

In 2 Kings 12:3–8, we read the account of a young king faced with a tough decision. Rehoboam made the mistake of his life in this passage. It reads like this, "That they sent and called him. And Jeroboam and all the congregation of Israel came, and spake unto Rehoboam, saying, Thy father made our yoke grievous: now therefore make thou the grievous service of thy father, and his heavy yoke which he put upon us, lighter, and we will serve thee. And he said unto them, Depart yet for three days, then come again to me. And the people departed. And king Rehoboam consulted with the old men, that stood before Solomon his father while he yet lived, and said, How do ye advise that I may answer this people? And they spake unto him, saying, If thou wilt be a servant unto this people this day, and wilt serve them, and answer them, and speak good words to them, then they will be thy servants for ever. But he forsook the counsel of the old men, which they had given him, and consulted with the young men that were grown up with him, and which stood before him:"

> *Ungodly counsel will always find **you**. Godly counsel is just the opposite— you must find **it**!*

Read the rest of the story. Rehoboam forsook godly counsel and chose instead to follow the ungodly advice of his peers—the young men—his "friends." It was literally the mistake of his life. It was all down hill from there. In 2 Chronicles 12:14, God sums up Rehoboam's life with these words, "And he did evil, because he prepared not his heart to seek the LORD." From early in his life, his decision to listen to ungodly counsel took him down a path of no return. He knew what was right, but deliberately made a choice to ignore godly counsel. Your story will be no different if you make such a choice.

"But ye have set at nought all my **counsel**, and would none of my reproof:" (Proverbs 1:25).

Mark it down—godly counsel will only come from people who unselfishly want only God's perfect will for your life. You won't find good godly counsel from those who do not know and walk with God. It's impossible.

Why do I need counsel?

If I were you, right about now I'd be wondering this. If I am so careful to apply all of these principles of faith, trust, surrender, and seeking—then why does it all come back to needing advice?

You might wonder, "If God is leading me, why should I get advice about it." It's simply about three key principles.

The first is the principle of confirmation. You're not looking to godly counsel to "divine" your future like a fortune teller, a guru, or a palm reader. In truth, even the godliest of counselors has no more access to God than you do. Looking to a counselor in this way is not only unbiblical—it's spiritually lazy because it causes you to avoid all of the personal seeking of God that you're commanded to do. This is the sort of blind follower-ship that cults and false religions teach.

You don't need a priest to stand between you and God and reveal His will to you. That's a form of Nicolaitanism, which means, "to conquer the laity." God makes it clear in Revelation 2 that He actually hates this. Revelation 2:6 says, "But this thou hast, that thou hatest the deeds of the Nicolaitans, which I also hate."

Over the years, I've had a few friends who were too lazy to seek God for themselves. Rather than put forth the personal spiritual effort, they chose to just "go with the flow" and do whatever their parents or pastor told them to do. That looks and sounds noble on the surface, but it's rotten at the roots. It's noble to follow authority, but it's negligent to "ride on someone else's coat-tails." It's negligent to forsake seeking God's purposes personally.

This lack of personal depth and commitment may initially lead a person to *appear* to be following the Lord, but ultimately this plan will unravel from within as the devil wreaks havoc on this ungrounded individual. This person will not be like a "tree planted by the rivers of water" (Psalm 1). Rather, he will be easily uprooted and blown away.

So, you must not put your life in "auto-pilot" to blindly and indiscriminately be led around by the voices of others. These kinds of decisions never last.

Yet, you *do* need godly people, God-given authority, who want God's best for you. You need their guidance and advice, and you need their sound insight into the paths you are praying about. You need the collective wisdom of parents, pastors, and other spiritual leaders to confirm God's leading in your heart and to provide insight as to how to best follow that leading.

You need the collective wisdom of parents, pastors, and other spiritual leaders to confirm God's leading in your heart and to provide insight as to how to best follow that leading.

And on those occasions when you come to a point that you simply don't know what God wants you to do, you need to be able to fall back on their authority in your life, which leads us to the second principle.

The principle of God-ordained authority. In your life, God has given you key authorities who love you, pray for you, know you, and perhaps understand you better than yourself! In the case of your parents this is absolutely true. If you have faithful Christian parents, they know you better than you know yourself at this point.

God has given these authorities the wisdom they need to guide you. The Bible also calls this "understanding" or "perception."

Your parents have an amazing God-given perception that you must trust and listen to. Your pastor will also have a godly perception as well as a vast wealth of biblical knowledge and personal insight gained over years of dealing with crisis counseling and ministry situations. God has placed these divine authorities in your life on purpose. They are to be heard and followed (obeyed). Hebrews 13 teaches us to honor and obey them that have the rule over us. Ephesians 6 teaches us to obey and honor our parents.

At this point you might argue that you are a legal adult, but that's irrelevant. God has placed all of us under some sort of authority, and He expects us to obey and honor the biblical authorities in our lives regardless of our age. One of the biggest mistakes I see young adults make is that they think they have the legal right to stop listening to their parents when they turn eighteen. You may have the legal right, but that doesn't mean it's a smart thing to do! This is when you need their counsel and guidance the most!

God designed authority to be a hedge of protection in our lives to protect us from the fiery darts of Satan. Check this out. In Job 1:10, the devil is talking to God about his inability to get to Job. He wants to hurt Job, but he is literally admitting to God that he can't get to him. Job is too safely protected within a "hedge." Look at it, "Hast not thou made an **hedge** about him, and about his house, and about all that he hath on every side? thou hast blessed the work of his hands, and his substance is increased in the land."

God-given authority in your life is just like that hedge in Job's life. So long as you stay in the hedge, you are protected from the attempts of Satan to ruin you. But beware, the moment you break out of that hedge, you are target practice for the devil! Ecclesiastes 10:8 says it this way, "He that diggeth a pit shall fall into it; and whoso breaketh an **hedge**, a serpent shall bite him." You should be mature enough to voluntarily place yourself within the safe hedge of authority and to stay there by choice!

Authority is something that most young adults in our culture are trying to escape. It's not cool to be eighteen and to be under "authority." After all, you're free now! Rebellion is rampant! Perhaps you've seen the bumper sticker that says, "Question authority."

I'm sorry to be the one to break it to you, but rebellion causes people to do stupid things! The sooner you get over your need to prove your independence, the sooner you will be able to avoid some serious mistakes. Being under authority is not about being treated like a "kid;" it's about being a responsible adult. The fact is God has gifted you with some godly authorities in your life—so go ahead and question them! Ask them things like, "How did you make it through this?" "What would you do if you were in my situation?" "Would you pray for me in this area?" "Could you help me understand this situation?" Sure, go ahead and question authority and then listen to their answer and follow it!

I've often had young adults tell me "I don't just want to do what everybody thinks I should do." While I understand their reasoning, it's a mistake to have some inner aversion to following godly advice. That's nothing more than pride. If your heart is sincerely seeking God, you'll have no problem following the advice of godly people. I've seen some young adults do some amazingly ridiculous things out of sheer rebellion against authority and live to regret it. Authority is God's gift to you—so embrace it.

The third is the principle of self-deception. We've already studied that you can deceive your own heart, and godly counsel is the last line of defense to sift through all of your heart's emotions and verify that you truly are yielding to God's best.

Think of it this way. God's Holy Spirit is not divided. If you are truly seeking and surrendered and if your counselors are truly godly and Spirit-filled, then you will all reach the same God-led conclusions about your decisions and your future. The same Holy Spirit that leads you to one conclusion would not lead a multitude of other godly counselors to different conclusions. That's why this step is called the "safety net"! It's God's way of protecting you from yourself.

In other words, if you come to a conclusion that you feel is right for your future, and multiple godly counselors feel differently—you have to draw one of two conclusions. Either you are wrong and deceived…OR…your counselors are wrong and deceived. At this point, a choice is made to either trust yourself against counsel or trust godly counsel against yourself. Confused? Good. Stay with me.

In summary, God expects you to seek counsel because:

1. He will use godly counselors to confirm His guidance.
2. He has ordained godly authority for your own protection.
3. He knows you can easily deceive yourself.

How do I go about getting godly counsel?

There is a right way and a wrong way to seeking godly counsel, and it's very easy to miss the boat on this.

I've known of many occasions where an individual determined to take a course in life, and much like feigning prayer, they chose to "feign" getting counsel. It goes something like this.

Start with a desire. Perhaps I want to get married or start a career or purchase a coveted possession. Perhaps I just want to get out of the house and on my own. Soon this desire is so strong and my craving is so consuming that I make up my mind to do something about it. I make a wrong decision, even though I'm convinced that it's right.

After feigning prayer so I can make myself feel better, I decide to feign counsel to further salve my conscience. So, I set an appointment with a spiritual leader or determine a time to talk to Mom and Dad about my course. At the appointed time, I sit down, take a deep breath, and tell my "counselor" what I intend to do. At the end of my discourse I wrap up with "I've prayed about this, and I feel it's God's will." (Every time I say it, it makes me feel better—eventually I even start believing it.) Finally, I say something like "So, what's your opinion?" At this point I feel really good about myself.

After all, I'm obeying the Word of God in seeking godly counsel, right? Wrong.

Actually, all I've done is backed my potential counselor into a corner and forced them with one of two difficult options. Support me in this and watch me mess up my life, or try to oppose me and get ready for World War III! I haven't asked for guidance, advice, or insight. I haven't come with a seeking or surrendered heart. I'm not prepared to hear *any* answer, especially an honest one, and I'm ready to move on with my decision regardless of what anyone thinks. This is not what getting godly counsel is about—at all!

What parent or pastor in their right mind is going to stand in strong opposition against a mind so firmly made up? They may initially try to talk some sense into you, but eventually they will choose the "support" avenue and simply hope for the best. In other words, if you choose to marry a person your parents do not approve of, they may try to resist at first, but eventually they will do what all good parents will do—support you and hope it works out somehow. It never does.

The same Holy Spirit that leads you to one conclusion would not lead a multitude of other godly counselors to different conclusions.

I'm saying this—it's very easy to convince yourself that you are getting counsel when really all you are doing is insisting on approval for a decision you've already made. It's easy to corner your authorities into supporting your decision whether they like it or not. What other options do they have—disown you? Never see the grandkids at Christmas? Start a relationship with their future in-laws with war paint on? I don't think so. Forcing your counselors to "grin and bear it" is not what the Bible teaches you to do.

It's tricky, isn't it? It's subtle. This thing of decision-making can very easily become a cunning game of self-deception and conscience-soothing. It can very easily become a selfish pursuit shrouded in cloaks of spirituality. At every turn you have to be brutally honest with yourself, and you have to follow God's principles for verifying that honesty!

Sincerely getting godly counsel is the exact opposite of what I've just described, and it is one of God's quickest ways to verify your true heart and direction.

So, now that you know how "not" to get counsel, here's what you should do:

First of all, have a multitude of godly counselors. The Bible principle in this is very clear. Proverbs 11:14 says, "Where no counsel is, the people fall: but in the **multitude of counsellors** there is safety." Proverbs 15:22 shows us, "Without counsel purposes are disappointed: but in the **multitude of counsellors** they are established." God wants you to have a number of godly people that you will turn to for advice, and at the top of the list should be your parents and your pastor.

In addition to this list you could add godly teachers, assistant pastors, grandparents, deacons, etc. Just take a minute and look at the landscape of godly leadership in your life. God has probably given you a good number of godly people who would be more than happy to give you biblical advice. So, go to them. Set up appointments, make phone calls, get as many people on your team of godly counselors as you can. You're going to need all the insight you can get.

Most importantly, make sure that your counselors are truly godly people. I don't mean perfect, just faithful in walking with God and seeking Him. You are about to entrust your future to these people, so choose people with a proven track record of faithfulness. Choose counselors who will approach giving you advice with fear and trembling. This needs to be someone who would literally be absolutely terrified of counseling you with anything but biblical, Christ-centered advice.

Second, listen with an open heart. Proverbs 12:15 says, "The way of a fool is right in his own eyes: but he that hearkeneth unto counsel is wise." Proverbs 19:20 states, "Hear **counsel**, and receive instruction, that thou mayest be wise in thy latter end."

When you step into a counseling appointment, don't have your mind made up. That's a terrible mistake, not to mention a waste of time. Have an open heart and a willing spirit. Don't sit down and start to "sell" your point of view. Don't even present your point of view. Just lay out the options, explain your search for God's will, and then ask for honest insight and advice.

In that moment of counsel, what you need the most is to know the impressions of the Holy Spirit on this person's heart in regards to your situation. You want to hear the Scriptures that this person brings to the table. You want this godly counselor to speak freely and openly of what the Lord is guiding him to say. You want him to be totally and completely honest, and you want to be ready to hear and receive *any* answer—not just the ones you want to hear. Your counselor needs to be willing to even hurt your feelings if that's what it takes to be truthful and transparent. And you should want the truth so bad, that you're willing to take it.

Ask for honesty. Alleviate his fears that you might not want the full truth. Ask for this person to be brutally transparent if they sense any danger, deception, or error in your circumstances.

Finally, ask this person this question, "If the decision were yours to make for me, what do you really believe is God's will in this?" The Bible principle for this is stated this way, "Counsel in the heart of man is like deep water; but a man of understanding will draw it out" (Proverbs 20:5). Work at drawing out the real scriptural opinions and admonitions of your counselors.

Whoa. Now that's vulnerability! Are you brave enough to take that kind of medicine? Are you courageous enough to ask for that kind of feed-back? Can you deal with hearing what you may not want to hear? If so, then you are ready for true, godly counsel.

At this point, when your counselor speaks, one of two things will happen. Either the counsel will confirm God's leading in your heart or it will contradict it. As you talk to a multitude of counselors, this same thing will happen over and over—either **confirmation** or **contradiction**.

Here's the best part! If you have truly surrendered to God, and if you have honestly sought the advice of godly people, your multitude of counsel will fall directly in line with the internal voice of God (which your counselors may or may not know about).

Godly counsel—what a wonderful gift from God! Next to wisdom, it's probably the most untapped resource in the Christian life.

Do you get it? God will use the voices of a multitude of counselors to independently confirm what He placed on your heart in the first place. This forms a closed case for a right decision. At this point, you can have the final full peace that you are making a right choice, *and* you have the full authority of Scriptures and the full support of God's promises backing you up. You're now in good hands with God's Word, God's truth, and God's promise for a bright future!

Break out the pop-tarts and ice cream! Somebody make a cake! You're there! You've confirmed what you thought was God's direction, and now you can go forward in full faith and confidence! It's awesome! It's full proof! It's the *best* way to live life.

For me, the best lesson I've ever had in this was in making my college decision. I prayed and felt that I knew God's heart, but I knew I had to put that knowledge to the test. One of the key counselors in the equation was my dad, and I chose the "blind test."

"Dad, I'm not going to tell you what I think God might want. It's your decision, you make it *for* me, what do you think is God's will?" Now, that might sound like a wimpy retreat—like I was afraid to make a decision. It wasn't that I was afraid to make it. I was just willing for God to prove me wrong, and more than that, I wanted Him to confirm what was right.

Guess what happened! Amazingly enough, my dad made the call, and it lined up exactly with what God had put on my heart. Once again, when I was the most vulnerable to being wrong, God proved Himself and His truth to be absolutely undeniable in my life.

Godly counsel—what a wonderful gift from God! Next to wisdom, it's probably the most untapped resource in the Christian life. Imagine the wealth of knowledge and insight that young adults all over the world turn away from every day!

Along these lines, be careful about "shopping counsel" or "comparing counsel" to try to find what you want to hear. The principle of hearing a multitude of godly counselors is that the same Holy Spirit will impress the same leading on all of their hearts. In addition to this, different counselors will give you different insights and varying vantage points that will all prove helpful as you make your decision.

In the rare situation where the advice from two or more "godly counselors" comes into direct contradiction with each other, be careful about casting judgment or forming a premature opinion. For example, you may have a spiritual leader who gives advice that contradicts your parent's advice. It could easily happen if that leader doesn't know what your parents have advised.

At this point you should hear the counsel, weigh it carefully, discuss it with your parents or other "authority," and fall back on the authority principle in knowing how to apply the counsel. In other words, depend on your closest authority to guide you through the questions. Whatever you do, don't pit one counselor against another. Don't withhold critical information that could put them in opposition, and don't negatively compare them against each other (i.e., "Well, so and so said this…").

As a youth pastor, I give a lot of counsel to graduating seniors. In those appointments, it is my policy to always ask what other counselors (parents, pastor, etc.) have shared with them. Why? Because I believe in the principle of godly authority and I would never advise a teenager against what their parents have advised them. Yet, on many occasions there were "gray" areas where I could have unintentionally seemed to advise differently than parents would. In those cases, I've always said to the teen, "If your parents feel differently about this, then follow them—or at least talk it through from this perspective."

The point is, when talking to multiple people about the same issue, you must avoid getting into a "counsel debate." That will derail the whole process all together and potentially hurt some good people in your life.

Whatever you do, don't defy a multitude of godly counselors.

In conclusion, mark this down. If you have determined a course of action that your godly counselors do not concur on—don't make a move. You cannot walk the tightrope outside of the safety net and hope to survive. There is something terribly wrong with this picture. Somewhere along the path you got off course—guaranteed. If you can talk to godly person after godly person who feels that you are making a wrong decision—you are! Just ask yourself this, "If the Holy Spirit is confirming this in me, why isn't He confirming this in others?"

By the way, it may not mean that you're totally "off your rocker." It may just mean that God wants you to wait for His timing.

Remember my "Mustang for Renault" story? (I'm embarrassed to bring it up again.) That was the time I didn't get counsel. The next time I went to buy a car, I was smart enough to ask my dad (a car-buying expert) to go along. It was the smartest purchase I've ever made, and I learned a wealth of valuable principles that I've used over and over again. Godly counsel made all the difference and saved me a lot of money!

Don't be afraid of getting godly advice. Be afraid not to! Don't be so arrogant as to think that you can walk the tightrope of life without ever making a wrong decision. Get counsel! Your circumstances are not new! There are many people who have stood where you stand and felt what you feel! So, go get their advice and follow it. You'll save yourself a lot of heartache!

String that safety net across your path, tie it down tightly, and then don't be afraid to fall into it and find out that you were about to make a wrong decision. In fact, be like a trapeze artist—get real comfortable with falling into the safety net. There's nothing to fear about it!

When godly counsel contradicts the intents of your heart, walk softly stranger! You're on very thin ice and you need to re-think, re-pray, and re-search this whole process.

Psalm 33:11 says, "The counsel of the LORD standeth for ever, the thoughts of his heart to all generations." Proverbs 21:30 says, "There is no wisdom nor understanding nor counsel against the LORD."

There are many people who have stood where you stand and felt what you feel! So, go get their advice and follow it. You'll save yourself a lot of heartache!

Don't dare move forward until you have undeniable confidence that God has first confirmed His will within you—and then without—through the godly voices of a multitude of counselors! Those who learn decision-making with the safety net of godly counsel beneath them always survive to eventually become the "grand champions" of decision-making. Those who don't usually end up just being "stuff on the floor." What a mess!

**"Hear counsel, and receive instruction,
that thou mayest be wise in thy latter end."
—Proverbs 19:20**

fifteen

Don't Just Stand There; Set That Ship On Fire!
The Testing of a Well-Made Decision

Well, you've come a long way in this journey, and here's what the roadmap looks like. Discovering your destiny in God's perfect will looks something like this. First you must have:

1. A Serious Mind
2. A Pure Heart
3. A Courageous Spirit
4. The Wisdom of God
5. A Heart of Faith

Then, you must follow the scriptural principles that lead to these critical steps:

1. Refuse to Trust Yourself
2. Seek and Surrender to God's Will
3. Pray About Your Decision
4. Get Godly Counsel

At this point, you should very clearly understand what God has led you to do, and you should be ready to finalize your decision. If you have truly followed the principles of God's Word, you will not only have clarity of heart, but you will also have the support of godly authorities in your life and the promises of Scripture as the foundation of your decision. In addition to this, you should have deep purpose and commitment to the path that God has led you down.

Move it or lose it; it's time for action!

Now you have a choice. Either follow God or retreat. It's quite simple really. You've come to the "precipice" of action, and now it's time to "leap"! It's literally time to take a deep breath and step forward in faith without wavering.

It doesn't matter if you *want* to do what God has led you to do. Your emotions will catch up later, and God will work all that out. It doesn't matter if you can't see *how* it's all going to work out—that's the faith part. It doesn't even matter if it makes sense. The point is you have sought the Lord, and He has led you and confirmed His leading—so it's time to do it! It's time to muster up the courageous spirit that Joshua had and step out across the Jordan River!

It's at this point that many young adults come so close to following God, and then suddenly for some unforeseen reason, they chicken out. They get so close to tasting the reality of their faith, and like a scared animal, they turn and run. DON'T DO THIS!

Rather, determine that you will proceed forward. Determine that you will not retreat or run. With a fierce commitment and fiery certainty, choose to commit wholeheartedly to God's leading in your life. Say with the Apostle Paul, "But none of these things move me, neither count I my life dear unto myself, so that I might finish my course with joy, and the ministry, which I have received of the Lord Jesus, to testify the gospel of the grace of God" (Acts 20:24).

There is a season of time between *God's* confirmation and *your* action when the devil will do everything within his power to "spook" you out of following God. This is when he will work overtime to deceive, distract, and detour your future.

In addition to this, he will bring to your mind every negative thought you could ever have about the possibilities of God's will. He will remind you of all the things you "don't want to do." He will be ruthless and relentless, raising questions and doubts and doing everything he can to cheat you out of the greatest happiness you could imagine!

Don't fall for it! Stay the course. Commit to God's will and follow Him with unyielding passion. Determine that God's leading will not come into question, and quickly turn your decision into action. Immediately begin doing what God has told you. Obey right away and leave no time for reconsideration. Reconsidering would simply give place to defiance against God, and defiance is not an option.

Honestly, in spite of the spiritual opposition you might sense, my guess is that you will be pretty eager to go forward at this point. After all this time of seeking and praying, you finally know God's will—at least for the immediate future. What a relief! Now, rather than anticipating your future, you can begin fulfilling it!

Helping Mark to "grow in grace"

I hadn't been there for five minutes when my brother Mark came up and boldly said, "You're not going to get me this time."

I acted innocently ignorant. "What ever are you talking about?"

"You know exactly what I'm talking about, and you *will not* get to me this trip. I have covenanted with God, and I have grown in grace—I will not give in."

Truthfully, I knew exactly what he was talking about, and he may as well have given me a straight up challenge one-on-one to see who would come out "on top."

It was family vacation, and we had flown the whole family to my parent's home in Baltimore. Both of my brothers and their families were joining us for a long week of fun together, and we were all very excited to see each other. It had been years since we had all been together.

If you have little brothers or sisters, you'll identify with this. I love pestering my little brothers. It was fun growing up, it was fun as a teenager, and it's still fun! (I'm now in my thirties.) Now, Matt was never much of a challenge. For some reason, he just didn't "bait me" as well, or something. I never really got "addicted" to pestering him. But Mark—Mark was a different story all together.

Since we're a lot alike, it just came naturally. I knew exactly what to say at any moment to really "set him off." In fact, it came so naturally that quite often it would happen with no advance planning whatsoever—sort of like getting an extra recess in elementary school. You didn't expect it, but you sure enjoyed it when it came! Honestly, I think I have a special giftedness for being able to "get under his skin." It's a God-given talent, and I've always tried to be a good steward of that gift.

This is what Mark was talking about when he said I "wouldn't get to him." He had made a spiritual decision to avoid confrontation on this particular trip. And, in all honesty, I had no intention of "getting to him." I was just glad to see him, glad to see his children, and looking forward to some time together—which is why I say this is a natural "gift." What happened next just came *naturally* and made it clear to me that the Lord wanted me to be a "help" in putting Mark's decision "to the test."

I could tell he was really nervous and serious about his decision. Actually, it was a little amusing. I couldn't believe that well into my thirties, I still had this "spiritual gift"!

I really couldn't understand why he was so jumpy about it. Perhaps it was a few years before when I untied his golf bag *three* times in a row as we golfed together. He wasn't playing so well that day, which already made him a little testy, but when he jumped into his cart, punched the gas pedal in anger, and launched his golf bag ten feet into the air—he really came unglued. As the clubs sprawled on the cart path with a glorious "thud," I was already speeding down the fairway, holding back my laughter, with my dad in the passenger seat.

"What else can go wrong today?" Mark loudly pleaded in disbelief, thinking he had failed to secure his own clubs. We stopped, stared, exuded a sigh of disbelief, and no one was the wiser.

It was so perfect that it worked two more times—in a row!! By the third time I just couldn't hold it together any longer. Boy, was he upset at me. Talk about the testing of a decision. I'm lucky to still be alive after that one. Don't mention it to him; his face still twitches when it's brought up.

I'm not sure, but maybe that's why he was so jumpy on this particular vacation. All I know, is that somehow, unintentionally, the little boy in me was awakened by the challenge, and I found myself intrigued with the "testing" of Mark's resolve. I wouldn't have to wait very long for the Lord to open a door.

A few evenings later we found ourselves at Camden Yards to watch the Orioles play. Several of the grandkids were ready to have their first "major league" baseball experience, and the whole family was pretty excited. There was only one problem—a massive torrent of rain kept us huddled outside the park waiting to see if the game would be played. Somebody had the brainy idea to ride the subway to the park, so we didn't have the option of "waiting in the car."

*There is a season of time between **God's** confirmation and **your** action when the devil will do everything within his power to "spook" you out of following God.*

So, picture this. About twelve of us are huddled under a six-inch ledge with two umbrellas and some rain ponchos for an hour and a half. We were cold; we were crowded; but for the most part—we were staying dry. Lucky for me, I was one of the blessed individuals to be wearing a poncho AND holding an umbrella—which placed me toward to center of the dry zone. And also lucky for me, Mark was unlucky enough to be "poncho-less" and standing under my umbrella—much closer to the wet zone. It was poetic. I knew my time had come.

While Mark and the rest of the family were engaged in trivial conversation, the world around began to fade into a blur as my attention became riveted to Mark's position. Suddenly, I was in a world of my own. A mission had been divinely handed to me. It was beckoning to my soul.

Directly above Mark's shoulder (which was partially exposed to the rain) was the ledge under which we had huddled. Beneath that was the wire of the umbrella that was conveniently catching and funneling water down its spine and dumping it just beyond Mark's right shoulder. My world shifted into slow motion as I began to calculate how to shift my movements at precisely the right moment.

All around me the drone of trivial conversation continued as I feigned participation. An occasional laugh or "uh-huh" was all it took to make them think I was still listening. In reality I was *in rare form*. No one suspected what was about to happen. No one knew I had retreated to a covert offensive. No one suspected Mark's vulnerability—least of all—him!

At just the right moment, I shifted the umbrella just slightly to catch a little more water, and then in one more swift and skillful motion—dumped it straight down Mark's neck. The water beautifully cascaded down the inside of his shirt while I simultaneously re-entered the conversation, looking the other way, and laughing at some joke I hadn't even heard.

Out of the corner of my eye I saw Mark react. He jumped, ducked, and dried—with not one hint of what had just happened. Like I said, it was poetic. On the outside I was looking totally and completely innocent. But on the inside, I was loving life! On the inside, the sun was shining!

Again and again—four, five, six times the Lord looked down upon me with His good pleasure, and Mark never suspected a thing.

My movements were swift and subtle, my actions—deft and daring. What a gift!

I'd better quit while I'm ahead, I thought. By now, he was really soaked, and he had no idea that all of it was intentional. He really thought that it was simply a series of small but unfortunate accidents. He really thought he just had a bad spot to stand in and he was really lost in the conversation. I should have quit right then. I could have carried this whole thing to my grave, but it was too late.

I must have been enjoying it too much. I must have crossed some subliminal line that resurrected some repressed boyhood intuition within him. I really thought I was in the clear, but something went wrong. He glanced my way, looked away, then suddenly back again.

He's on to me, I thought. I glanced down to the ground, and then looked around trying to appear inconspicuous. I tried to avoid his eyes. I must have shown some inconsistency in my cover. Perhaps I shifted the wrong way or gave a hint of "gotcha" in my face. I'm not sure. But, in a moment of harsh realization, he knew. I could see it in his eyes. He looked up at the umbrella, looked at the hand holding the umbrella, looked at my eyes again, and then looked at the ledge.

He knows. It's over. It's so over.

No one else in the family had any idea what happened.

Suddenly, with a glare that only a little brother can give, Mark spoke with a loud, pointed tone, accenting every word with disdain, "Cary, you are such a jerk!"

The family was shocked. This outburst seemingly came from nowhere, and I put on the most innocent face I could muster up, trying to appear as shocked as everybody else. But, I couldn't hold it together. In an instant I doubled over with laughter, Mark was angry, and I quickly let the whole family in on my devious bit of fun.

My mom scolded me, Mark glared, Matt laughed, and my dad was actually very appreciative of my ingenuity. We all had a good laugh that day—at Mark's expense. To put it mildly, his decision was "put to the test." It took him a few hours, but he finally came around, and we've lived to love each other in spite of my "gift." In truth, we're pretty good friends today, and I deeply respect and admire him as a friend and brother. (Bad recovery—I know.)

In truth my testing of Mark's decision was all just a brotherly joke, but there are tests coming in your life that aren't at all funny!

In your time of decision and resolve, the devil will quietly, shrewdly, and cunningly be devising a test for your decision.

In your time of decision and resolve, the devil will quietly, shrewdly, and cunningly be devising a test for your decision. He will be "out to get you," and you better believe that the stakes are a lot higher than they were for Mark that day. He will sneak up on you and fight against you in ways you won't suspect. In fact, you might be drenched with the rain of testing before it even occurs to you that you're facing spiritual adversity!

The immediate testing of a decision

In 1485, Hernando Cortez was a newborn baby. By 1511, he was a political leader on the newly conquered island of Cuba, and by 1519 he was a pyromaniac! It's true. On April 21, 1519, Cortez landed his ships and army on the coast of Mexico near Veracruz. His intent was to capture and conquer the Aztec empire, and he was determined to be victorious! He was so determined, that he literally commanded his men to burn the ships that brought them to this unconquered land! As the men went ashore, their only hope for retreat literally "went up in smoke" before their very eyes.

This radical act of commitment and determination left Cortez and his army with only one option—move forward. It was an act of total abandon and surrender to the pursuit of power and wealth—regardless of the cost.

Friend, it's time for you to go ashore in God's will for your life, but before you do, you need to set fire to the ship! You need to determine there is no retreat in the will of God. There is no reconsidering the direct leading of God in your life. You must obey with absolute abandon, leaving yourself no room for withdrawal. Paul said it this way in Romans 11:29, "For the gifts and calling of God are without repentance." In other words—there's no turning back!

There's a reason that this commitment is so needful at this point. You are about to enter into a critical proving time for your decision and for your future. I call it "the testing of the decision." It's not the testing of God's leading. (That's already been taken care of.) The testing of the decision involves the proving of your commitment and resolve in the decision. In other words—just how committed are you to seeing this decision through to fruition? Before you will enjoy the mountain top experiences of God's will, you'll have to climb the mountain of testing.

You see, the devil will not only work against you before you finalize your decision. He will also fight you shortly after you've made your decision. Here's what I mean.

Almost every major decision of your life will be followed by an immediate time of testing that either solidifies or uproots the decision. The strategy is that the devil will try to question your direction and reverse your decision before you've had time to really settle in and begin to experience the long term fruit of doing right!

Don't expect your world to be perfect and your path to be effortless the moment you decide to follow God. In fact, you should expect the exact opposite. You should expect spiritual opposition (Ephesians 6:12) and even emotional upheaval. (Wow, following God sounds exciting, doesn't it?) You should expect trials—intended by God to strengthen and settle you, but intended by Satan to discourage and frustrate you. Again, Paul referred to this testing in 2 Corinthians 4:16–17, "For which cause we faint not; but though our outward man perish, yet the inward man is renewed day by day. For our light affliction, which is but for a moment, worketh for us a far more exceeding and eternal weight of glory."

Throughout your spiritual journey, you will face spiritual opposition, but perhaps never as intense as during this time, and perhaps never at such a critical moment as this. The moment you set out to obey God, you will enter into a proving time that tests you, prepares you, and paves the way for future blessings.

It's as though your decision is a seedling tree that will one day become a mighty oak—solid and unmovable. Yet, while it is young and fragile, the devil wants to step on it, crush it, and destroy it. It will take the forces of the elements and a lot of time for your decision to become rooted deep, and there will be many times along the journey that you will want to look back and question the validity of your decision, but don't!

Every marriage experiences times of questions like this. Some people entertain the doubts and give up too early. Others cling to the truth of God's plan, and they eventually make it through the testing with a stronger and happier marriage.

Every pastor faces times, especially early in the ministry, where the devil would discourage and brings doubts. At this point that pastor will either press on through the test or retreat to "another opportunity" somewhere. Those who press on always find greater fruit and blessing just beyond the test!

Sadly, the spiritual landscape is littered with casualties from this "crisis point." Many people follow God, only to be scared back into the ship of retreat because of unexpected battles or trials. Many Christians hear God's voice and obey Him only to turn and run for the hills at the first sign of spiritual opposition. No, the "promised land" of God's will is not intended for the weak or faint-hearted. It is intended for those who are fully committed to pressing forward with the ships burning behind them.

Now, I don't want to scare you. When you choose to obey God you are certainly in store for happiness, blessings, and awesome joy—but first you're going to have to pass some tests. You're going to come to your own "crisis point" where you will be tempted to entertain doubts and questions. You should expect this, and you should determine to silence the doubts immediately.

Your "major" decisions of life may take years to mature and come to full fruition, but don't let that discourage you—it's going to be well worth the journey!

What kind of "promised land" is this?

Remember our chapter about courage and our talk about Joshua? Well, Joshua *was* courageous, and he *did* follow God across that Jordan River, but what he found on the other side was certainly no "promised land." "War-land" or "Battle-land" would have been a more appropriate name.

His decision to be courageous and follow God led the children of Israel into a series of spiritual tests and physical battles unlike any they had ever faced. They had never been so close to the fulfillment of God's promises and never so tested either!

City after city, battle after battle, Joshua repeatedly followed God and did exactly as he was told. He was clinging to God's promise that this land of battles would one day be conquered, and a "promised land" could be claimed.

Before the nation of Israel could ever enjoy the "milk and honey" of the Promised Land, they had to deal with the "blood and guts" of the battlefield. Even so, as you follow God into a faith-based decision, you can be sure you will fight some spiritual battles before you experience the real blessings of such obedience.

...the "promised land" of God's will is not intended for the weak or faint-hearted. It is intended for those who are fully committed to pressing forward with the ships burning behind them.

Right about now, you might be asking, "Why would God answer my obedience with such testing?" I'm glad you asked. There are several reasons.

First of all, God's best blessings are more than you can handle right now. Though you've surrendered, you're nowhere near being prepared to properly handle all that He plans to give you. His goodness will be so abundant and His blessings so awesome, that He's going to have to strengthen you and prepare you for them. Every battle and every testing will take you one step closer to being able to properly enjoy the blessings God has in store.

Second, God's best requires a steadfastness and stability that only spiritual tests can prepare you for. Without the testing of your decision, you'll never experience the blessings! No pain, no gain.

As a side note, it's not all bad. I don't want you to get the idea that as soon as you follow God, life gets miserable and difficult. It's not like that at all. You simply get "put to the test." Before you can really savor the blessings, your resolve and commitment are going to be tested and tried. Your decision will endure a spiritual "refining" process that will solidify it deep within.

My personal ministry testing

Remember how I described the process of coming to Lancaster Baptist Church and following the call of God? It sounded so easy didn't it? Well, looking back, I can honestly say that our first three years in the ministry were literally our "testing time." These were the "make-it-or-break-it years"! If we were ever going to quit, leave, or give in—it would have been during this time. I feel as though the devil threw everything he could at us in an attempt to knock us off course.

We were newlyweds with preconceived visions of what "ministry" would be like. We were adjusting to life together, life in the ministry, and life in a new hometown. In addition to this, we were a part of a young dynamic church that God was preparing for greater blessings than any of us imagined. I really believe God was taking that young staff team during those years and putting us through "ministry intensive training" to prepare us for what was ahead.

Looking back from where we are now, it's easy to see the fruit of our decisions. But at the time, we couldn't see that far down the road. It would have been easy to endure if we could have seen the future, but that was not possible. The enduring had to be "by faith." We had to go through a season of "boot camp" testing in order to prepare for the real victories ahead—and there have been many!

The testing came in the form of simple things that seemed *huge* at the time—financial pressures, schedule challenges, broken cars, intense life changes, productivity challenges, and on the list could go. Looking back, I know that every young family in ministry would face these same tests, but they sure seemed hard at the time! And in fact, these tests are not unique to ministry, though the devil would have had us think that. Every young family faces these same issues in one form or another.

With every potential problem, the devil tried to take us down a road of "false reasoning" that could have led us into retreat. He will do the same in your life. He will try to get you to blame the pastor, the ministry, or the schedule you keep at church. If you go *into* ministry, he will tell you that it's easier *out* of ministry. If you're *not* in the ministry, he will tell you that it's easier *in* the ministry!

In addition to this, he will try to take small problems and wedge them deep between your family and your spiritual leadership. He will try to drive a wedge between your ministry/job and your family. The list could go on, and you'll be much more prepared if you'll expect these things and see them for what they are—spiritual battles.

I guess I'm confessing that these things caught me a little bit off-guard. I should have been more prepared for these tests, but I wasn't. Please let my ignorance in this be your fair warning.

While we never really entertained the thought of leaving or quitting, I know that the devil tried to take us there. He consistently tried to make us think that we had made a mistake by following God.

There were times of confusion, frustration, and discouragement during those first three years that could have been used against us—but God meant them for good! God was strengthening our hearts, establishing our lives, and solidifying our faith in Him. He was preparing us for blessings that we knew not of! He was paving the way in our lives for some amazing, unimaginable experiences and "fruit-bearing"! If we had given in, we would have missed it all! That's a scary thought!

> *Know that the devil will try to get you to turn back, but know that God will use these tests to prepare you for awesome blessings!*

Honestly, these seasons of growth were hard! They were strenuous, arduous times of spiritual consternation. They led to late-night talks, tearful times of prayer, and long walks, but they were all a part of God's molding process in our lives. Without them, we could never have experienced effectiveness in ministry.

Thirteen years later, it's easy to see the blessings now, but it was impossible to see them from within the storms! So get ready! As you cross your own Jordan River, you will face some tests. Recognize these as the good hand of God molding you, preparing you, and stretching you for future blessings.

Every Bible college student must face the despair of homesickness before they can gain the benefits of ministry training. Every marriage must withstand the test of relational disagreements before a stronger love can be forged. Every ministry intern must withstand the tests of personal sacrifice before real fruit can be seen.

So, expect the testing of your decision. Expect doubts to come and hesitation to invade your heart. Expect discouragement and frustration from time to time. Expect to lose some sleep dealing with issues of spiritual growth. Know that the devil will try to get you to turn back, but know that God will use these tests to prepare you for awesome blessings!

Lest you think that our early years were all rough, that's not the case at all. The fact is, the tests were minimal compared to the blessings, the joys, and the incredible fun we had in the early years of our lives together. I could keep you busy for hours sharing the unforgettable memories and special moments we shared as we stepped out by faith to follow God. Every day was a new adventure with multiplied blessings. We've never regretted one step of the journey. I'm just trying to help you expect some things that might otherwise "blind-side" you.

Three critical areas of tests

Dana and I opened our home last week to some of the recent graduates of our youth ministry who are currently preparing for ministry. About thirty-five Bible college students gathered for a wonderful evening of testimonies, memories, and fellowship. It was real joy to spend an evening with so many young adults who were applying truths that we had taught them.

During the testimony time, I asked a simple question. "How many of you, as you entered Bible college, found that the devil tried to test that decision and get you to turn back within the first year or two?"

Every hand went up.

One young man told how he packed his bags and planned to leave college at night when no one would know. Another talked about family trials that tried to pull him away. Others indicated a variety of ways that their decision had come "under fire." It was evident to everyone in the room that right decisions always go through times of testing and adversity.

After the testimonies, I shared three primary periods of life, thus far in my walk, when the devil really tested my decisions. No doubt, he will try to test you in these same three areas, so be ready.

The first is your first year or two of college. When you choose to follow God to the right college, you can be sure that the first year will be a proving time. You will face many opportunities to retreat, rethink your decision, and renege on your surrender to the Lord.

The second is your first few years of marriage. As wonderful as those first few years are, they also include many times of intense "life-shaping" as two become one. Any time you blend two individual lives into one, you're going to experience some testing. Most people enter into a marriage completely ignorant of the storms that they will sail through together. Then, rather than face the storms together, they jump ship. They forget that when the storm is over, sunny skies return and sailing skills are stronger.

The third is your first few years of faithfulness to God. This may be in reference to your faithfulness to God as a layperson in your local church, or it may be your faithfulness in full-time ministry. Whether in ministry or secular work, you can be sure that your faithfulness to the Lord will be tested when you are "on your own."

In my life, these three periods were critical times of testing. That's not to say that there weren't blessings during these times, and it's not to say that I won't still experience future tests in my life. It's just that these periods seemed to be more intense. It's as though the devil was deliberately trying to destroy my direction early in the journey.

Stand guard over your heart during these seasons when your decisions are still "fresh" or "new." Once the "cement dries," once you survive a few storms—you won't be nearly as easily moved.

How do you pass the tests?

How do you pass these decision tests so that you can really see the long-term fruit of your decision? Here are a few suggestions.

1. Refuse to entertain doubts. If God led you, then don't ever let anything bring that leading into question! You may have heard the saying "Don't doubt in the night what God gave you in the light." Simply refuse to entertain any thought that you made a wrong decision. I really believe the devil gives these initial thoughts as "bait." If you don't "bite," you won't get reeled in!

2. Renew your commitment. When tests come, simply renew your commitment to Christ and to following what you know to be right. Strengthen your stand and deepen your roots. Stand strong in what you know is right, and your storm will eventually subside, leaving you stronger and more prepared.

3. Return to Scripture. God's Word will renew your strength, settle your doubts, and help you to mount up with wings (Isaiah 40:31). Rather than doubting your direction, go to the Word of God and seek His power.

4. Remember the promises. God has given you hundreds of awesome promises to sustain you through times of testing and proving. Here are just a few that might help to strengthen you during the testing of your decision.

"Nay, in all these things we are more than conquerors through him that loved us" (Romans 8:37).

"Therefore, my beloved brethren, be ye stedfast, unmoveable, always abounding in the work of the Lord, forasmuch as ye know that your labour is not in vain in the Lord" (1 Corinthians 15:58).

"Therefore seeing we have this ministry, as we have received mercy, we faint not;" (2 Corinthians 4:1).

"We are troubled on every side, yet not distressed; we are perplexed, but not in despair; Persecuted, but not forsaken; cast down, but not destroyed;" (2 Corinthians 4:8–9).

"Therefore I take pleasure in infirmities, in reproaches, in necessities, in persecutions, in distresses for Christ's sake: for when I am weak, then am I strong" (2 Corinthians 12:10).

"For the which cause I also suffer these things: nevertheless I am not ashamed: for I know whom I have believed, and am persuaded that he is able to keep that which I have committed unto him against that day" (2 Timothy 1:12).

"Wherefore seeing we also are compassed about with so great a cloud of witnesses, let us lay aside every weight, and the sin which doth so easily beset us, and let us run with patience the race that is set before us, Looking unto Jesus the author and finisher of our faith; who for the joy that was set before him endured the cross, despising the shame, and is set down at the right hand of the throne of God. For consider him that endured such contradiction of sinners against himself, lest ye be wearied and faint in your minds" (Hebrews 12:1–3).

"My brethren, count it all joy when ye fall into divers temptations; Knowing this, that the trying of your faith worketh patience. But let patience have her perfect work, that ye may be perfect and entire, wanting nothing" (James 1:2–4).

"Watch ye, stand fast in the faith, quit you like men, be strong" (1 Corinthians 16:13).

My pastor recently said in a sermon, "Anything that moves forward will face friction." This is true in the spiritual world as in the physical. Anything that moves forward will face adversity and friction. Adversity in your spiritual life proves that you are moving forward, and also puts the power of God into motion in your life. He will sustain you, strengthen you, comfort you, and renew you. Just like He promised Joshua—He will be with you through every battle!

This is serious stuff. If you're not careful, you'll seek the Lord carefully for your future only to be disappointed by the tests you face when you get there.

Take hope—the testing is worth it. For every test that God leads you through, there is an equal or greater reward. For every storm your marriage endures, there is a stronger love to be gained. For every ministry obstacle you overcome, there is a greater fruit to be harvested. For every personal doubt you settle, there is a personal reward to be treasured—in the perfect will of God. For every year you stay faithful to God, there is a truckload of blessings and fruit that you will enjoy somewhere down the line.

So, get moving. If God has brought you to the point of confirmation, then it's time to leap! Go for it! His promises will sustain you through every test, and His grace will sustain you through every doubt. The testing of your decision will simply be a pathway of preparation for God's greatest plans.

And don't forget my brother, Mark. Just about the time you make that solemn resolve, you can probably suspect that the devil will be quietly positioning himself against you. He's preparing to drench you with the rain of testing. Just remember, he's a jerk—and a little rain never hurt anybody. Expect the tests, dry off, and stand strong.

So, are you ready to leap? More importantly, are you ready for the tests that will come once you make it to shore? This is the "make-it-or break-it-time." But before you jump in, there's something you must do.

Grab a lighter, a match, a blowtorch, a flamethrower—whatever it takes—and take a good look around your ship, because this is the last time you'll see it. Grab your things and light a fire. Then, jump in and start swimming for the sand. Once you get there, enjoy the view! There's nothing quite like the ocean breeze, the swaying palms, the call of the gulls, and the "campfire" smell! There's nothing quite like the breaking of the waves on the beach of God's will—with a big, beautiful ship burning behind you!

It's time to set your ship on fire.

"But he knoweth the way that I take:
when he hath tried me,
I shall come forth as gold."
—Job 23:10

sixteen

What Do You Do With a Pet Chicken?
Returning to God's Will from Bad Decisions

I made a really, really bad decision when I was in fifth grade. I had a pet chicken. I thought it would be cool. I thought all the kids would like me. I thought I could start a new fad in my state—domesticated chickens. I pictured taming my chicken, putting him on a leash, taking him for walks, teaching him tricks. I didn't even know that chickens aren't "hims" at all—they're "hers"! It was a sad day when I realized I had named my *female* chicken with a *boy's* name. I even remember looking for a book on "How to Tame Your Pet Chicken." Never found one.

Somehow, I talked my parents into letting me keep a chicken. I know, it sounds crazy, but it really happened! To this day, I'm not sure how, and I'm not even completely sure of where it came from. All I remember is that our dog had recently died; our dog pen was empty; and I was convinced that the pen was perfect for raising a "house-chicken"! I knew it would work, and no one could tell me any differently.

At first my parents were against it, but I finally wore them down. And with three boys in the house and five acres of land, one chicken would never do. So, within a day or two, we had *three* chickens, and our empty dog pen was once again alive with pets—pet chickens.

The school day couldn't pass fast enough! All day long I couldn't wait to get home to my pet chicken! My brothers felt the same way. We would run into the house, throw our stuff down, and make a beeline for the "dog-pen" turned "chicken-pen." We would spend the whole afternoon playing with our pet chickens. It was truly a sight to behold. It was wonderful—everything I had hoped for in a pet, all the fun I had imagined—for about a week. That's about how long it took for reality to begin setting in.

No one told me that chickens are about 90% poop. I hate to be crude, but that's just the fact. It only took about a week for that beautiful, fenced-in dog-pen to look like a "white Christmas" on a frosty December morning. Seemingly over night, that place went from being green grass to being the chicken-dung *capital* of the world! Even the rectangular fence was "white-capped"! It's no wonder we began to lose interest in playing in the pen! Suddenly our "beloved" pet chickens seemed more like clucking caulking guns!

With all of that, came a smell unlike any cow pasture I've ever smelled. It was unbelievable. Just being in the mere vicinity of our backyard became an unpleasant nasal experience.

In a matter of a few days these chickens went from being the most loved and well cared for chickens on the planet to being the most neglected, renegade fowls imaginable. Our backyard pen became a sort of "chicken slum" for unwanted and abandoned chickens. We hated even the thought of throwing feed into that pen! It seemed like such a waste of good feed! Emphasis on "waste"!

I'll never forget the moment my mom suggested that we get rid of the chickens. I'm sure she thought she was going to break our hearts, but we were only too willing to reclaim our backyard for childhood play. It took all of two seconds to talk us into giving them up to some hungry families who lived in the vicinity of our country property. In a few short days we were able to hose down our "winter wonderland" and reclaim our childhood territory; while at the same time, some hungry stomachs were filled with our sumptuous pets! It was a win-win situation!

I learned a valuable lesson through that experience. Simply put, chickens are not pets—they're food. Chickens were not designed to be domesticated; they were designed to be battered and fried. They were not made to tame and train; they were made to dip and devour. My personal preference is barbecue sauce. Chickens were not given to be guided; they were given to be grilled!

Chickens cannot be domesticated, and when some poor soul tries, he's going to end up with more "poop" than he can deal with. It's a fact of life. It's a law of nature. When you try to domesticate chickens you upset the delicate balance of the "circle of life" and the whole "ecosystem" gets out of whack.

For the sake of all that's green and wholesome in your backyard—DON'T TRY IT!

The main lesson I learned from my pet chicken incident is that poop doesn't have to be permanent! Deciding to *have* pet chickens didn't mean we had to *keep* pet chickens. It's too bad it took my mom's prompting to help us learn that lesson, or we would have been rid of those chickens a lot sooner. The fact is I had to deal with that "white Christmas" for about three weeks longer than I wanted to because I was too afraid to tell my mom that we had made a grave, grave mistake!

So, what are you going to do with your mistakes—your bad decisions? Perhaps you've already made some. Perhaps you're standing up to your neck in "bad decisions," and you're not sure what to do. Well, hopefully you can learn the same lesson I did. Let's talk about it.

Bible failures

Rahab the harlot, David the adulterer, Peter the denier, Jonah the runner, Moses the murderer, Mark the deserter, Paul the persecutor—do these names ring any bells with you? They are

Bible characters that all, at one time or another, made some tragic decisions.

If you had known them during their time of "bad choices," you wouldn't have given them much hope. You wouldn't have wanted to be their best friend, and you wouldn't have voted them the "most likely to succeed."

Yet, somewhere, somehow in all of their lives, they were given a second chance. In the midst of their bad choices, God touched their lives and redirected their futures by His grace. You probably know most of the stories, and in fact I'm sure there are many more in Scripture, but I want you to look closely at one in particular.

Is there a second chance in God's will?

John Mark was a young man who was serving the Lord under the ministry of the Apostle Paul. You could call him an "intern." Acts 13:5 says that he was serving with Paul and Barnabas as their minister. Apparently he made a decision to follow God into the ministry. Later, the book of Acts tells us that John Mark had left the ministry at some point. Here's the story:

"And some days after Paul said unto Barnabas, Let us go again and visit our brethren in every city where we have preached the word of the Lord, and see how they do. And Barnabas determined to take with them John, whose surname was Mark. But Paul thought not good to take him with them, who departed from them from Pamphylia, and went not with them to the work. And the contention was so sharp between them, that they departed asunder one from the other: and so Barnabas took Mark, and sailed unto Cyprus;" (Acts 15:36–39).

For whatever reason, John Mark apparently deserted the work and later wanted to re-enter the ministry. He made a bad decision and wanted to return to the perfect will of God for his life. Paul refused him, but Barnabas took him back. This caused a division between Barnabas and Paul that caused them to part ways.

Here's the rest of the story. Fast forward to the end of the Apostle Paul's life and look at what he says about John Mark. The Bible says in 2 Timothy 4:11, "Only Luke is with me. Take Mark, and bring him with thee: for he is profitable to me for the ministry."

God not only restored John Mark to the ministry, but he apparently used him in a unique and effective way. John Mark did indeed have a second chance, and so do you if you've already made some bad decisions.

God's perfect will starts today.

Perhaps as you've read this book, you can look back at mistakes you've already made in the mistake zone. Perhaps you've already passed through many of the major decisions we've talked about, and you're wondering exactly where you are on the "road map" of God's will. Maybe you feel like you're not even on the map anymore.

That could potentially be a depressing and discouraging feeling in light of all the principles that we've studied. Please don't allow yourself to feel that despair. Rather than revisit "what might have been," let's take the advice of one of the Bible's biggest "come-back-kids"—the Apostle Paul.

Here is a man who literally tried to destroy the church of Jesus Christ. He was a persecutor and a murderer. The new Christians of the first century were terrified of him! Yet, God reached out of Heaven, saved him, and gave him a new mission in life.

Can you imagine the guilt, the discouragement, the despair that the Apostle Paul could have constantly lived with? Can you imagine how the devil must have constantly dredged up the past, reminding him of the Christians he had killed or persecuted? This could have potentially had a crippling effect—a paralyzing impact—on the future ministry of Paul! Think about that!

Had Paul continued to dwell on his past decisions, he could have literally missed all that God had in store for the future! Here's what he said about his past, "Brethren, I count not myself to have apprehended: but this one thing I do, **forgetting those things which** are behind, and reaching forth unto those things which are before, I press toward the mark for the prize of the high calling of God in Christ Jesus" (Philippians 3:13–14).

There is a beautiful principle about God's will in this passage. God's perfect will for your future always starts today! In other words, what's behind you cannot be changed, but what's ahead of you most certainly can be! Wherever you are in the journey of life, there is never a time when God doesn't have a perfect will for you from this day forward. There's no use crying over spilt milk! There's no sense in throwing away His blessings in the future because of bad decisions in the past. Thanks to God's awesome plan, we can literally put the past behind us and anticipate a bright future in His will.

> *God's perfect will for your future always starts today! What's behind you cannot be changed, but what's ahead of you most certainly can be!*

God has a way of dealing with your bad decisions. It's called the Cross! He sent Jesus to die in your place on the Cross so that He could forgive and forget your past. And, if you have trusted Him as your Saviour, then He truly has forgotten your past! Have you forgotten your past? Of course not, and the devil will continually try to use your past to keep you from surrendering your future! The sad part is many people fall for this deception.

Perhaps we could sit and talk about what God's will for your life "might have been" if only you hadn't (fill in the blank). Perhaps you've been thinking these thoughts as you've read this book. So get this—there is nothing productive or spiritual about such thinking. It can only be destructive.

There is nothing about your sinful past that God remembers, and there is nothing about your future that He doesn't want to bless! That's how great His grace really is. That's how wonderful it is to belong to Him!

Your only choice in the face of this kind of "self-incrimination" is to either wallow in the past for the rest of your life or accept God's unconditional forgiveness and start living in His perfect will right now! Don't fall for the lie that you missed it. You haven't missed what is yet to come! If anything, let your bad decisions of the past be the catalyst that keeps you from "missing out" on anything else that God might have waiting for you! Let the lessons you learned yesterday be your turning point today.

Remember how we talked about God's eternal plan? Well, the fact that your heart is still beating is evidence that you still have a role to play in that plan! God hasn't left you on this earth for no reason! If you're breathing, then you still have a second chance—you too can be a "come-back-kid" in the story of God's unfolding purpose!

So, quit listening to the lies of your past and start surrendering to God's perfect will today. I don't care what you've done—it's still going to be awesome! The choice is yours, and your track record for "right decision-making" could start right now.

Lingering damage from the mistake zone

If you've made some bad decisions in the past, be aware that there may be some lifelong consequences that cannot be removed. That doesn't mean that God hasn't forgiven you or that He cannot use you. It simply means that bad decisions cannot be undone.

I could write for hours of the hundreds of "come-back" stories that I know of. These are amazing stories of people who made tragic decisions, experienced the tragic results, and then determined to be restored to God's purposes by His awesome grace! The pain and regrets of the past are a very real part of their lives, but the hope and blessings of their present lives in God's will are something they wouldn't have missed out on!

Yet, bad decisions often have bad consequences. When a young lady has a baby out of wedlock, that new life will bring a reminder of a past failure for many years to come. When a family experiences a divorce, there are multiple lingering effects of that separation. When someone experiences substance abuse, pre-marital sex, or a hedonistic lifestyle, there are long-term consequences emotionally, mentally, and physically.

I bring this up not to "rub it in your face" but simply to say the presence of these lingering effects do not in any way negate the possibility of future blessings or usefulness to God. In fact, God's promise to you is directly opposed to that thinking.

Romans 8 shares an awesome passage about the purposes of God, and right in the middle of this passage, God says to you "Likewise the Spirit also helpeth our infirmities: for we know not what we should pray for as we ought: but the Spirit itself maketh intercession for us with groanings which cannot be uttered. And he that searcheth the hearts knoweth what is the mind of the Spirit, because he maketh intercession for the saints according to the will of God. And we know that all things work together for good to them that love God, to them who are the called according to his purpose" (Romans 8:26–28).

This passage promises that God is not only on your side, but He is literally planning to make "all things work together for good." In other words, He will somehow bring good results out of even your bad decisions if you will surrender to His will. He will take your past, forgive it, and then turn it around for good in His eternal plan. What a promise!

It doesn't mean the effects are gone. It doesn't mean we can just sin willfully and claim Romans 8:28. It just means that God's grace and wisdom will somehow bring good from bad when we determine to love God and live according to His purposes.

This means that we are all "without excuse." Having a past of bad decisions doesn't excuse you from living in God's will right now. God's grace levels the playing field and gives everybody the same second chance for the future.

So beware of the battle scars of the mistake zone. Perhaps you're coming toward the end of your own mistake zone, and you didn't fare so well. The proper response would be to get on your knees before God, confess whatever sin is remaining, and then forget the things that are behind and start pressing forward. You may forever bear the scars and wounds of the mistake zone, but that's no reason to keep from experiencing God's best from this day forward.

A window of reversal

Before you put this chapter behind you, there's one more thing you need to know about bad decisions.

Sometimes—not all the time—but sometimes, a bad decision can be quickly reversed with relatively little damage being done to your life. This isn't the case with all major decisions, but it is with many of them. I would call it a "window of reversal." It's really a wonderful evidence of God's amazing grace and patience with us, and you need to be aware of it.

It's almost like God leaves the window of decision open for a few moments after you've made a bad decision. It's like He's giving you a chance to jump back through the window and still do things His way. The length of time that this "window" is open often varies greatly from decision to decision. Usually the circumstances vary widely so it's somewhat unpredictable, but I've seen that window open many times in the lives of young adults.

Now, there are many decisions that cannot be undone. In these cases, the damage is done the moment your decision is final. There's no preventing the pain at this point. You are now a slave of the consequences whether you like it or not.

For instance, if you decide to have immoral relationships, you are risking your very life—a decision that cannot be undone with effects that cannot be reversed. If you get married, that decision cannot be reversed or retreated from. There are many such "leaps" that cannot be undone.

Yet, there are some decisions where the window stays open and the damage hasn't been done.

I know young adults who determined to go against God's will in their college decision. In this case, up until the class registration deadline, their decision is "reversible"! In other words, there's a "sliver" of time when they can choose to come back to God's will and follow His leading with minimal spiritual effects.

Recently a young man in my youth group was being pressured by his unsaved father to go and live with him in a foreign country. Early in the summer he had made the decision to move away from all the good spiritual influences in his life so he could be with his dad.

Having a past of bad decisions doesn't excuse you from living in God's will right now.

While I fully understood his desire to spend time with his dad, I strongly urged him to reconsider his decision—so did every other spiritual influence in his life. We viewed this decision as a potential "death knell" for his spiritual health in God's will. I told him face-to-face that he was choosing between two distinct life directions—almost as if there were two scripts for his life, and he had to choose one. I knew that this decision was the watershed moment of his teen years.

Well, the window was open, but he didn't see it. His first words to me were "I've already made my decision and told my dad."

"Who cares," I said, "reverse it! There's still time! Did your dad consult you when he left you years ago?"

"No."

"Then why would you feel any obligation to his feelings in this matter? This is about doing what God wants you to do, regardless of the feelings of others."

Long story short, it took the better part of two months for this young man to see that his decision could be reversed. He was worried about hurting his dad, etc. He was completely missing the incredible long-term implications of following through with this decision.

My counsel to him was that this was literally an "emergency" and in an emergency, you do whatever it takes to save a life! In an emergency you're not worried about hurting feelings, losing money on plane tickets, or losing your security deposit! If the window is open and you realize you've gone wrong, you jump back through immediately regardless of the temporal costs! No temporary loss can compare to the long-term spiritual loss that results from such decisions.

Good news. He reversed his decision. We were at teen camp, and he approached me to say that he was staying in the USA with his mom and step-dad—and with the Lord! This meant he was staying in church and staying in God's will! He did it! He jumped back through! Wow, was I relieved—and he was too. He knew he was doing right, and I knew that God was going to bless him for it.

Sadly, most people never get back through the window. Most people are too far away from God in the process of a bad decision to even see the "window of reversal" much less to jump back through it. It's a grueling thing to see someone make a bad decision, to see that he could reverse it, and then to see him follow his own path any way. It's literally heartbreaking for parents, pastors, friends, and family.

Everyone can see the problematic results looming on the horizon—everyone except for the "decider"! Yet, they are all powerless. Parents and pastors can't force someone back through the window. Most often they try to persuade, they pray, and then they just hope for the best. They are powerless to do anything else. It's the most helpless feeling that anyone in authority can ever experience.

Here's my question. Are there godly authorities in your life that are peering through the window at you? Are they standing there praying, begging, pleading, hoping that you will turn back before it's too late? Have you made a decision that is still reversible?

If you have, I would beg you to stop in your tracks. Take off the dirty lenses that are blinding you to the dangers ahead. See the situation through the eyes of God and turn back quickly before the window closes and the long-term effects of your decision become irreversible! Make your heart right with God and come back to Him quickly while there is still time to minimize the damage that you have done to your future.

Swallow your pride! It's not worth the price you are going to pay. See the danger ahead before it's too late to turn back. God's grace is open to you; His arms are waiting to welcome you back; and a host of godly counselors will probably weep tears of joy at your return.

Heather's did! Heather is a sweet Christian girl who grew up in our youth group, started Bible college, and began setting a strong course for God's blessings. Somewhere along the path, for a number of reasons, she began to question her decisions, entertain other possibilities, and drift from her established course. She didn't fall into some dark sin or delve into deep defiance against God. She simply began to drift off course due to some internal and external pressures.

Everyone could see it, except her. Her parents, her friends, her sister, and her spiritual influences all began to counsel her to return to her God-given course. My wife and I both became very worried that Heather would make some very bad decisions that would influence her away from every good thing in her future. We had seen it so many times, and we prayed so desperately that Heather would avoid the same mistakes.

At the same time, we talked very candidly with her. At one point, on the phone, I remember strongly saying, "Heather, to make this decision, you will have to directly defy everything that God has done in your life up until now." That was a strong statement, but I meant it. It was true, and I was trying earnestly to help her see the reality of what was going on. In her mind it wasn't nearly that "critical."

Well, to make a long story short, Heather did make some initially bad decisions—relatively minor ones—but decisions that could have led her down a wrong path. We all felt helpless. We couldn't force her to do what was right. She obviously wasn't doing the best thing. All we could do was pray.

A few days later, after I feared the worst—that she would drop out of college and pursue a career that was tugging at her—she approached me in the hallway of our church. She was wearing a big smile and was carrying registration papers for college.

"I'm here!" she said. It was obvious that she had given in to the Lord. She was once again wearing the countenance of a surrendered person—a countenance of peace and joy from deep within. That troubled, confused face was gone, and a few days later, she made a follow-up decision to live in the dorms at Bible college—another decision we had prayed for and encouraged her to make.

Seven years later, Heather's decision to "reverse" her bad decision has changed the entire course of her future. Today she is married to a youth pastor and is serving the Lord faithfully. And God recently blessed her and her husband with a little girl! Good things always happen when bad decisions are reversed!

> *For all of our bad decisions, God has an eternal "window of repentance" that is always open thanks to the Cross of Calvary and the blood of Jesus Christ.*

If you're facing this same sort of scenario, I hope you too will learn the lessons that Heather did. You'll never regret reversing a bad decision while there is still time!

God's eternal "window of repentance"

There's an even more important Bible principle that you need to know about. It's called the "mercy" or the "forbearance" or the "longsuffering" of God. He says in Romans 2:4, "Or despisest thou the riches of his goodness and forbearance and longsuffering; not knowing that the goodness of God leadeth thee to repentance?"

For all of our bad decisions, God has an eternal "window of repentance" that is always open thanks to the Cross of Calvary and the blood of Jesus Christ. Though there may be some lingering effects and scars of your bad decisions, you can always return to God in repentance. No matter where your bad decisions take you, your Heavenly Father is always pursuing, always waiting, and ever watching for your return. He stands with open arms to forgive you, to welcome you, and to restore you into His perfect plan for the rest of your life.

You cannot get so far from Him that He will not welcome you back. You cannot sin so much that He will not forgive and cleanse you. You cannot be separated from His love and grace, no matter what you've done or become. There is no power on earth that can change His feelings for you. Because of the Cross, you can step through the window of repentance at any time!

There's no doubt about it—bad decisions happen in everyone's life. We all have our "pet chicken" stories! We're all human, and we all fail. So, regardless of where you are on the "road map" of God's will, choose to be a "come-back-kid"! Follow the example of the Apostle Paul in "forgetting those things which are behind." Regardless of the mistakes you've made, God's perfect will is waiting for you—starting today!

Am I the only one craving KFC right about now?

"And the word of the LORD came
unto Jonah the second time..."
—Jonah 3:1

"He saith to him again the second time,
Simon, son of Jonas, lovest thou me?"
—John 21:16

seventeen

Hey, Dad, What's Tomorrow?
Understanding God's Call on Every Believer

The summer before my fourth grade year was unforgettable. Other than the normal routines of bike jumps and bubble gum, it was my first summer to attend church camp. Our church attended a camp in the mountains of North Carolina, and this particular junior camp was a life-changing experience for me. It was far more than games and fun—it was transforming.

I don't remember the night or the preacher, but I do remember the decision. I do remember having the strong desire to pray at the altar and completely surrender my life to do whatever God wanted me to do. So I did! I remember the prayer. I remember the spot where I prayed. Most of all, I remember giving God my life. I really had no idea what that meant. I only knew that I wanted to serve Him, and I hoped He would let me.

Was I called into ministry? Looking back I have no doubt that I was—that I am. Did I know it then? No. In fact, until I was about twenty-five, if you had asked me, I would have just told you I volunteered to go into ministry. I wouldn't have said that God called me.

I had always envisioned that being called into ministry involved some kind of spiritual lightning strike or some kind of strong emotional experience. I never had that. Therefore, I didn't think I was called. Yet, honestly, that didn't really matter to me. Some deeper truths had gripped my heart. Eternal values had compelled me to "volunteer" to spend my life serving God's eternal cause.

I often meet young adults wrestling with this and similar questions. Am I called into ministry? How will I know? What if I am and don't know it? What if I'm not and I try to go into ministry? On and on these questions could go, and the longer you consider them, the more circular the process becomes.

As we come to the end of our "talks" together, I want to finish up with some thoughts about your life's calling—another way of referring to destiny. Stay with me for a few more pages; we're almost there!

First things first

Whether you realize it or not—you *are* called. True, you may not be called into full-time Christian ministry, but you are still called. You are called to God. If you have trusted Jesus Christ as your Saviour, then you have been bought by His blood, redeemed by His grace, and enlisted into His cause. You are called to Him, to His purposes, and to His control—regardless of what you do for a living.

I meet a lot of young Christians who seem to draw a line of separation between those who serve in ministry and those who don't—as if there is a lesser commitment required "if I'm not called into the ministry." This is just not the case. God has placed the same call upon the life of every one of His children, regardless of where their "paycheck" comes from. Here's how God says it:

"Who hath saved us, and **called us with an holy calling**, not according to our works, but according to his own purpose and grace, which was given us in Christ Jesus before the world began," (2 Timothy 1:9).

"But as he which **hath called you** is holy, so be ye holy in all manner of conversation;" (1 Peter 1:15).

"But ye are a chosen generation, a royal priesthood, an holy nation, a peculiar people; that ye should shew forth the praises of him **who hath called you** out of darkness into his marvelous light:" (1 Peter 2:9).

"For even hereunto **were ye called**: because Christ also suffered for us, leaving us an example, that ye should follow his steps:" (1 Peter 2:21).

"Among whom are **ye also the called of Jesus Christ**: To all that be in Rome, beloved of God, **called to be saints**: Grace to you and peace from God our Father, and the Lord Jesus Christ" (Romans 1:6–7).

"And we know that all things work together for good to them that love God, to them who are the **called according to his purpose**" (Romans 8:28).

"Moreover whom he did predestinate, **them he also called**: and whom he called, them he also justified: and whom he justified, them he also glorified" (Romans 8:30).

"God is faithful, by whom **ye were called** unto the fellowship of his Son Jesus Christ our Lord" (1 Corinthians 1:9).

"But as God hath distributed to every man, as the **Lord hath called every one**, so let him walk…" (1 Corinthians 7:17).

"I therefore, the prisoner of the Lord, beseech you that ye walk worthy of the vocation **wherewith ye are called**," (Ephesians 4:1).

"That ye would walk worthy of God, **who hath called you** unto his kingdom and glory" (1 Thessalonians 2:12).

"Fight the good fight of faith, lay hold on eternal life, **whereunto thou art also called**, and hast professed a good profession before many witnesses" (1 Timothy 6:12).

There's something very important to know about most of the above verses. The Holy Spirit wrote them to regular Christians. These verses were written to normal lay people like the ushers in your church or the teachers in your Sunday school. Every one of these verses makes it clear that with our salvation came the call of God upon each of our lives.

So, if you asked me, "Am I called to serve God with my life?" The biblical answer is absolutely YES! Without hesitation, you need to recognize that God wants you to serve Him with your whole heart and soul for the rest of your life. Aside from the question of whether you should enter full-time ministry, you should first commit yourself to the clear call that God has placed on the life of every believer.

In answer to this call, you should commit yourself to a lifetime of faithful service to Jesus Christ. There should be a foundational commitment in your life that no matter where you go or what you do, God will be the "center" of your life! Everything should flow from Him and ultimately be turned back towards Him for His glory. Seems extreme? Not at all! In light of the Cross of Jesus Christ, it's just our reasonable service (Romans 12:1–2).

The question of church attendance, tithing, ministry service, sharing the gospel with others, and personally walking with God should never come up in your heart. These are the non-negotiables! These are the things that *must be*, regardless of where life takes you. Regardless of the career you choose or the opportunities you seek, these foundational commitments should remain steadfast and unmovable.

How will I know if God is calling me into ministry?

Understanding God's call to full-time ministry is actually pretty simple if you've followed the principles that are outlined in the previous chapters. Simply put, as you yield your life completely to God, He will make it abundantly clear what you should do and when.

It's really not a formula or a predictable experience. God's "call into ministry" happens differently for various people. For me, it was more of a strong desire that I believed was my own. For others, it's more of a momentous occasion when God strongly urges them. For yet others, it's a gradual transformation of desires from within.

For example, over the years I've known many young people who didn't feel "called" into ministry, but they did feel called to God. Over time, the Lord worked new desires into their lives that gradually began to compel them into full-time ministry. Sometimes this process happens over months or even years.

The point is don't try to conjure up some momentous "call" and don't think that because lightning hasn't struck your heart, you're off the hook. It's not a hook to begin with.

Sometimes it's the decision of a moment; other times it's a process of growth; and often times, God doesn't lead His children into full-time ministry at all. Often times, He calls His children to be His strategic ambassadors to the business world, the medical world, the legal world, the construction world and on and on it goes. Often times He chooses to provide His children with abundant financial resources through a secular career so that the cause of Christ can be funded and furthered. Whatever the case, God will place you exactly where He wants you, and in that place, you will be fulfilling the divine call of God upon your life!

Carlos was a senior in our youth ministry. He had great plans to be a doctor, and I was truly supportive of those plans. I was sure he was going to be a great doctor, and yet I suspected that perhaps God had other plans. Sometimes adults can just sense that God is going to call someone into ministry. In Carlos' case, I really believed it was only a matter of time.

On occasion we would go out soulwinning or visiting together, and we would talk about the future. Every now and then I would jokingly say, "Carlos, has God called you into the ministry yet?"

He would laugh and say, "No, not yet."

I was only half joking. There was a part of me that was hoping he would one day say yes. I really believed that he had great potential for God.

One day, I put my hand on his shoulder and asked one more time, "Carlos, has God called yet?"

"No, not yet."

"Well," I continued, "He called me and said He's trying to get through, but your line is busy!" With that, we both laughed. This time I really was joking.

To my delight and surprise, some weeks later, Carlos approached me in the hallway and said, "God got through! I surrendered my life to full-time ministry!"

Give ministry the same fair consideration and prayer that you would any other direction.

That was like Christmas Day for me! I'll never forget it. Today, many years later, Carlos is the Spanish pastor at our church, serving the Lord every week and bringing Spanish-speaking people to Jesus Christ. God has given him a growing family, a growing ministry, and a bright future—all because he surrendered when God called.

There's no place like God's will.

There truly is no place like the will of God! There's no place like being right with God, serving Him with your life, and following Him step by step. And if God would allow you to serve Him in ministry, there's no place like serving God full-time either!

I believe in the minds of some young adults, and even some older Christians, ministry gets a bad rap. Some people believe that if you surrender to ministry that means you're destined to live in poverty and suffer rejection your whole life. Some people believe that ministry requires less education or preparation than other careers. Some believe that a life in ministry is a "free-loading" lifestyle that lives off of the generosity of others. Others feel that ministry is limiting to your "true career potential." Blah, Blah, Blah. To all of these beliefs I would simply say, "Not true, not true, not true!" Every one of these assumptions is founded upon humanistic, secular thinking—which has no place in the heart of the Christian.

This book has not been written to coax you in one direction over another; it has been written to bring you in line with God's will and purpose for your individual life. Yet, with any hint of the mindsets mentioned above, you're not playing on a level field. In other words, if you have deliberate, unfounded reservations against ministry or against any specific future, you're not being fair with God.

So rather than try to coax you into ministry, I would simply say to you, "Level the playing field." Give ministry the same fair consideration and prayer that you would any other direction. Give God a chance to touch your heart in that area. What are you afraid of?

Having spent the bulk of my time in or around ministry since I was eight years old, I can honestly say that serving God with your life is one of the happiest and greatest investments you could make. It's awesome and the blessings are new every day!

Let God be God in your life.

So, whether lightning strikes or not, just remember that you *are called*. You are called to be a faithful ambassador for the King of Kings. Answer that call, and at all costs, live out God's call upon your life one day at a time and don't let the potential of a "ministry call" spook you out. And, whatever you do, don't conjure one up. Just be content to be "called to God" and let God work out the details from there. Everything else will fall right into place.

One night when Lance was about four, after I prayed at his bedside and tucked him in, he asked me a profound question.

In all sincerity and childish honesty, he simply said, "Dad, what's tomorrow?"

I paused.

Now, I knew what he meant, but the question struck me. What's tomorrow? It was as though in that moment, the Lord pricked me with Lance's childish trust and transparency. In Lance's four-year-old way of seeing the world, Dad was in complete control of tomorrow. Everything that came into his world, every opportunity he would experience (by his own way of thinking) was somehow a product of Dad's control.

I could have answered him honestly. "Son, I have no earthly idea what tomorrow holds. It could be anything from a day at play to a nuclear holocaust—or somewhere in between. How in the world am I supposed to know?" I could have been forthright in admitting that, actually, I had no control over tomorrow. I could have simply said, "Son, it doesn't look good. Let's just pray for the best." But, honestly, that's not what he was asking, and it's obviously not what he needed.

Being overwhelmed at his obvious dependence upon me, I knelt back down by his bed and softly said, "Well, Buddy, you'll probably wake up in the morning and play some. Mom will fix you something to eat. I'll be at work, and when I get home we'll play some more. I'm sure it will be a great day."

"Okay," he said, and then quietly closed his eyes. That was enough. Just knowing that I had a good day planned for him was enough to help him sleep peacefully all night long.

As you pillow your head tonight, can you rest in knowing that your life is safe and secure within the Almighty hands of God? Are you fully surrendered to His will and resting upon His promises? Can you say, "God, what's tomorrow?" and be okay with any answer? If you can, then you get to be a "kid" the rest of your life! And you've got the best Dad that any kid ever had, because He really is in total control of tomorrow!

"For ye have not received the spirit of bondage again to fear; but ye have received the Spirit of adoption, whereby we cry, **Abba**, Father" (Romans 8:15).

That word *Abba*—that's a great word.
It just means "Dad."

"…as the Lord hath called every one, so let him walk."
—1 Corinthians 7:17

conclusion

Conclusion
You're Gonna Love Him!
A Few Final Thoughts

In the 1940's a few crazy men and their deadly regimes were threatening the free world. In other words, life as you know it was under attack, long before you were even a dream. Where you live, who your parents are, how you go to school, church, etc.—all of this and much more could have easily been lost. Since you and I have grown up in a free society, we have very little comprehension of the price paid to keep it free. We've known relatively few "threats" to our freedom in the past fifty years.

Yet, these threats were only too real to your great-grandparents and their generation. All of their plans for a free life in America were suddenly put on hold—December 7, 1941—when Pearl Harbor was attacked. Suddenly America was thrust into a conflict that would require the lives of thousands of young men and women.

During this crisis, known as World War II, the entire country was called to battle. An entire generation of Americans was called to put their futures on the line in order to preserve peace and freedom for generations yet to come—you and me, and our kids. This war affected every single person in the country. Many were called into the bloody fields of battle. Many others were called into factories to create ammunition, battle ships, planes, and supplies for a massive war effort. By the millions, Americans stepped up to the call, placed everything near and dear on the line, and willingly did whatever was required to save America and the free world! Thousands of men were brutally slaughtered in the front lines of battle. Thousands of mothers and wives gave their sons and husbands for the cause of freedom.

Some have dared to call this generation of Americans the greatest generation that any society has ever produced. Their courage, their commitment, their sacrifice, and their spirit were immeasurable. Think of it this way—everything good and wholesome about your lifestyle as an American came to you as a direct result of the price paid by this generation. Sort of puts a new perspective on your great-grandfather's military service, doesn't it?

My point is this, the choices made by a generation of people more than half a century ago have directly and pointedly impacted your life in personal and intimate ways—probably more than you could ever count or comprehend. Most of these people never knew you, and you never knew them. Yet, their decisions radically influenced your life today. That's big stuff!

Make no mistake about it, young adult. Your decisions today bear the same kind of consequences for someone else. Your decisions right now will radically impact the lives of your immediate family, your soon-to-come family, your grandkids, their kids, and beyond! It's literally immeasurable! It's not only about you and what you want right now. It's about generations that you will influence, and it's about answering to God for that influence.

If I could show you a videotape of your life lived out in God's will and another videotape of your life lived out in your own will— it would be an easy decision. You would choose God's will every time, without hesitation! You would be consumed with seizing the moment and following God immediately. It would instantly become that urgent to you. It is my prayer and hope that this book has helped to develop that kind of urgency within you.

Many young adults default into life by doing whatever feels right for the moment. This "default" approach to life creates a future of uncertainty and instability—like a ship without a sail. This approach leads to a life with no driving purpose, no clear vision, and no foundational guidelines or landmarks.

If you will truly follow the principles we've covered, you will arrive at every major decision in a very Christ-centered, scriptural way that will give you a deep spiritual security in knowing you are following God and in knowing that He will never lead you astray!

If it hasn't occurred to you yet, life is relatively unpredictable! You never know what's around the next bend. You never know what you might face in the next moment. Tomorrow might bring bad news as easily as it might bring good news. It's completely out of our hands. (Kind of nerve racking, isn't it?)

Yet, when you completely surrender to God's purposes and you know you are following Him, then you know that every circumstance of life fits within His eternal plan for you. Whether tomorrow brings blessings or trials, you can rest in knowing that you are living out God's perfect will, and He is working all things together for your good.

When you're following God, you know that every step in life has eternal significance. You know that you are a part of a wonderful plan that's far bigger and more awesome than you can comprehend. This is bigger than politics, prestige, or power. It's truly the most fulfilling way to live life.

The sacred delight of God's love

On another recent trip to Disneyland, while my wife and boys visited Tom Sawyer's Island, I found a comfortable bench, sat down with my mom, and let Haylee chase birds and look at flowers for a few moments. We found a nice circular park area with relatively few people and just relaxed while Haylee played.

Some distance away, a tall, elderly gentleman, dressed in a ragtime costume, was playing a baritone saxophone. He was wandering from person to person, entertaining park guests, but Haylee hadn't seen or heard him. In fact, in her short two years of life, she had never even heard a saxophone. Little did we know what was about to happen.

As the man drifted our direction, cute, little Haylee happened to catch his eye. Her back was turned toward him as she watched birds and pointed out various colored flowers. In complete silence this tall stranger gently stepped up behind Haylee and lifted his saxophone to his lips. I sat and waited with anticipation at what might happen next. He sort of winked at me with a smile, and he stood still for a second. Haylee was completely oblivious to his presence. She was in her own little world—which was about to be delightfully shattered.

Then, in an instant, the warmest, deepest, richest melody you could imagine began to flow from the bell of that saxophone— which was mere inches from Haylee's ears. By this time, passers-by had stopped to watch with anticipation.

As suddenly as the melody began, Haylee spun around in the most fabulous "little-girl style" that I have ever seen! Her head shot straight up to this towering figure above her—her already big eyes widened like half dollars, and her jaw dropped lifelessly in stunned amazement. There she stood, frozen in time, for all of fifteen seconds or more. She was captured—spellbound—at this enrapturing experience. It was absolutely the cutest moment I have ever had with one of my children. I felt like I was looking at a postcard or a Norman Rockwell painting.

After the initial shock, Haylee looked over at me and smiled with overwhelming delight. Strangers stopped in their tracks just to watch her childlike joy. Even the sax player was amazed. He could barely continue playing.

As the song finally came to an end, Haylee reached up to this loving stranger who had so suddenly entered her life. She gently grabbed his hand, smiled at him, and said, "I yuv you!"

"I love you too, Sweetheart." He patted her head, laughed our direction for a few seconds, and began to walk away.

At that point Haylee came running over to me, pointing to the tall stranger, and said, "I yuv him!" Then, to all of our surprise, she began to run after him. About a half a block away, she caught up to him, grabbed his hand, and said again, "I YUV YOU!"

Two more times, after I went to retrieve her, Haylee went running after this total stranger who had invaded her world with such delight. She was willing, in an instant, to leave her whole life behind and follow this man all over the park. She was willing to blindly trust this one who had singled her out of thousands to dazzle her heart.

You know, the best thing that could happen in your life would be for your loving Heavenly Father to delightfully shatter your world with the incredible delight of His presence, His love, and His plan. In that moment, whatever has your attention would instantly fade in comparison to the captivating wonder of His greatness.

I truly wish you would stand at His feet—eyes wide, jaw dropped—and stare in wonder at His overwhelming goodness. I wish you would sense His incomparable care and His undeniable infatuation with you. I wish you would see that you have "caught His eye"—that you have "captivated His attention." I wish you would spin around and be delightfully surprised by His wonder and majesty.

In that moment, you would most certainly reach out to Him in total trust and surrender. You would be absolutely taken hostage by His kindness and grace. You would reach up in childlike innocence and say, "I yuv you!" One true glimpse would cause you to quickly leave your petty plans behind to follow this "tall, gentle, Father" anywhere He would lead you. Your whole world would melt into His perfect love and grace, and your whole future would take on a sacred delight unlike anything you've ever experienced.

Here is God's promise to you from Genesis 15:1:

"…Fear not, Abram: I am thy shield, and thy exceeding great reward."

So, go forward! Discover your destiny. Live the dream. Fall in love with your great God and let Him unfold His masterful plan one wonderful day at a time! It's a great journey. You're going to love it.

Most of all, you're going to love HIM!

"Eye hath not seen, nor ear heard,
neither have entered into the heart of man,
the things which God hath prepared
for them that love him."
—I Corinthians 2:9

The Destiny Journey Summary
Reviewing What We've Learned

PART ONE—The Right Foundation for Right Decisions

1—Start the journey from a point of need.

2—Understand the mistake zone of life.

3—Understand that God made you with an eternal purpose.

4—Recognize that your gifts and abilities were given by God for His eternal purposes.

PART TWO—The Right Tools for Right Decisions

Tool 1—You must have a serious mind.

Tool 2—You must have a pure heart.

Tool 3—You must have a courageous spirit.

Tool 4—You must have God's wisdom.

Tool 5—You must have a heart of faith.

PART THREE—The Right Steps to Right Decisions

Step 1—Refuse to trust yourself.

Step 2—Seek and surrender to God's perfect will.

Step 3—Pray about your decision.

Step 4—Seek godly counsel.

Step 5—Expect testing and refuse to turn back.

Final Thought 1—Don't let past decisions derail future blessings.
Final Thought 2—You're called by God!

About the Author

Cary Schmidt serves as an associate pastor at Lancaster Baptist Church and an instructor at West Coast Baptist College. He leads the student ministries, music ministry, and the media and publications ministries of the church. His other books include *Life Quest; Hook, Line and Sinker; Music Matters; and Done.*

Visit us online

strivingtogether.com

dailyintheword.org

wcbc.edu

lancasterbaptist.org